Benedict XVI: Rethinking Africa

Other Books of Interest from St. Augustine's Press

Maurice Ashley Agbaw-Ebai, *Light of Reason, Light of Faith:*
Joseph Ratzinger and the German Enlightenment

Maurice Ashley Agbaw-Ebai, *The Essential Supernatural:*
A Dialogical Study in Kierkegaard and Blondel

Maurice Ashley Agbaw-Ebai and Matthew Levering, Editors,
Africae Munus: Ten Years Later

Maurice Ashley Agbaw-Ebai and Kizito Forbi S.J., Editors,
An African Perspective on the Thought of Benedict XVI

George Gänswein, *Who Believes Is Not Alone:*
My Life Beside Benedict XVI

Roberto Regoli, *Beyond the Crises: The Pontificate of Benedict XVI*

John Tanyi Nquah Lebui, *The Cross and the Flag:*
Papal Diplomacy and John Paul II's
Struggle Against the Tyranny of the Possible

Peter Kreeft, *Ha!: A Christian Philosopher of Humor*

Peter Kreeft, *If Einstein Had Been a Surfer*

Peter Kreeft, *A Socratic Introduction to Plato's Republic*

Peter Kreeft, *The Philosophy of Jesus*

Peter Kreeft, *Socratic Logic (3rd Edition)*

Jean-Luc Marion, *Descartes's Grey Ontology:*
Cartesian Science and Aristotelian Thought in the Regulae

Josef Pieper, *In Tune with the World*

Michael Davis, *Electras*

Roger Scruton, *An Intelligent Person's Guide to Modern Culture*

Roger Scruton, *The Meaning of Conservatism: Revised 3rd Edition*

Roger Scruton, *The Politics of Culture and Other Essays*

Roger Scruton, *On Hunting*

D. C. Schindler, *God and the City*

Benedict XVI: Rethinking Africa

Tasks for Today

EDITED BY

MAURICE ASHLEY AGBAW-EBAI

AND KIZITO FORBI S.J.

ST. AUGUSTINE'S PRESS

South Bend, Indiana

Manufactured in the United States of America.

1 2 3 4 5 6 29 28 27 26 25 24

Library of Congress Control Number: 2024936713

Paperback ISBN: 978-1-58731-084-3
Hardback ISBN: 978-1-58731-085-0
Ebook ISBN: 978-1-58731-086-7

∞ The paper used in this publication meets the minimum requirements of the American National Standard for Information Sciences – Permanence of Paper for Printed Materials, ANSI Z39.48-1984.

St. Augustine's Press
www.staugustine.net

In Memoriam

Bernadin Cardinal Gantin (May 8, 1922 – May 13, 2008)
An illustrious Son of the Church in Africa

Table of Contents

Critical Responses

Preface by Fernando Cardinal Filoni
Benedict XVI Rethinking Africa: Tasks for Today

Rethinking Africa. A continent so rich in spiritual, human, environmental, and cultural resources, and yet, in many ways, facing profound socio-economic and political challenges. Benedict XVI was fascinated by its human warmth. And he gave witness to this on the occasion of his Christmas meeting with the Roman Curia on 21 December 2009. In truth, Africa had also fascinated Paul VI and John Paul II who visited it. Two Synods then outlined its features. But it is not enough. Africa in the last few years seems to have let itself go to the new colonial powers that are occupying and plundering it. The evils (corruption, the emigration of so many forces that could have helped but prefer Paris, London, USA; the desire to emulate political and social realities different from oneself; indifference and passivity towards their own people who suffer or die on the trafficking routes of many, humiliated young men and women) seem never-ending.

In the final stages of his life, Benedict XVI wrote some beautiful reflections, in which he exposes his thoughts and in which, among other things, he deals with: (1) the dignity of the person, (2) the courage of truth, and (3) the role of evangelization in the context of today's society. He wrote a small book with a captivating and significant title: *"L'elogio della coscienza. La verità interroga il cuore,"* [The praise of conscience. The truth questions the heart]; I find it very interesting to quote it here, as I have been asked to present this publication: *"Benedict XVI Rethinking Africa. Tasks for Today."* The good reader will appreciate its value. However, having spent several years dealing with the African continent as Prefect of the Congregation (now Dicastery) for the Evangelization of Peoples, allow me to provide some considerations on this Continent, beloved since I was young, for the missionary ecclesial commitment which I longed for, and for the Episcopal pastoral service, linked to the responsibility that was entrusted to me by Benedict XVI, who explicitly wanted to tie me to the missionary work in the world. It was a responsibility that I loved with deep dedication.

Rethinking Africa has a broad meaning. I believe that every political and religious leader has the duty to reflect and involve himself without delegating to others or shaking off his responsibilities. I was negatively impressed by a very high and veteran political leader of an African country to whom I asked for greater commitment against the atrocities among Africans, who were eliminating each other with guerrillas who devastated the central Region. He diplomatically exonerated himself. Benedict XVI instead speaks of a *conscience* that we can never escape and that must be defended against the threats of a subjectivity that does not take into consideration its own foundation, that is our relationship with the *Law of God*, while on the contrary, adapting itself to pressures that conform socially and politically to circumstances. Indeed, *conscience* —according to Benedict XVI—must seek and question the heart and mind in order to find value, dignity and strength; those in authority have supreme responsibility for it. Today, almost everywhere, various pressures and the preference for an ethical, but also social and political relativism, prevail without perceiving the need to open up to the truth. Rethinking Africa in the depths of its ancient and rich anthropological culture that knew how to relate —not always easily, however —with the environment, ethnic groups, etc., historically devastated by the phenomena of slavery and of predatory colonialism, and today, by tendencies to grab a fast and often ephemeral progress.

Rethinking Africa, after the missionary evangelization that came from other continents in the past centuries, which can now become the master of the proclamation of Christ, faithful to the millennial tradition of the Church, but also taking care, in its own methods, to show what the "Kingdom of God" means to his sons and daughters. The vocational crisis currently affecting Western Christianity, once rich in extraordinary generosity, leads back to the full assumption of the responsibilities of the young local Churches towards evangelization itself, which indeed began with the Second Vatican Council. Today in Africa 90% of Ecclesiastical Catholic Circumscriptions are in African hands, not to mention parishes and other institutions. Two Synods have taken stock of the situation. But it is not enough, because today's phenomena almost daily surpass all imagination; from forced migration to insane guerrillas and the poverty induced by those who take goods, but do not invest locally in order to produce work, to harmful violence for ideologized religious reasons that leave immense suffering and pain.

Rethinking an Africa that can bring and share the richness of its own healthy values in the world and an indigenous Church that, in the African context, would like to be like the *sacrament*, that is, the sign and the instrument in the midst of this human race, which does not exclude God, and is aimed at creating harmony, solidarity, and credible and effective communion (see LG 4.)

Rethinking a *Christian* Africa with a role to play, assumed, above all, by its children. This means abandoning a victim mentality and sometimes still charged with begging; a mentality always fighting for the conquest of power and prestigious positions. Therefore, it must give evidence of a truly transparent and beautiful capacity, an extraordinary service in pastoral activities, open first of all to the African continent itself, as conceived by Benedict XVI and before him by John Paul II.

Rethinking an Africa at an ecclesial level that needs, therefore, to find its place in the universal Church; it happened to notice sometimes non-fraternal and prejudiced judgments (few indeed) towards the Church in Africa, considered not inclined to understand the socio-anthropological and moral processes manifestly flaunted in some Western countries. Africa is not traditionalist. It has traditions that during its evangelization it has been able to enhance in relation to Christ and the faith of the Church. A vision deeply anchored to the *Mystery* of Jesus, who is not only the one who guides the Church, but who *innervates* and *vivifies* it, and it is organically connected to Him, according to the perspective of the Letters to the Colossians and the Ephesians, vividly emphasized by Benedict XVI. (See "Paul. His Letters and teaching," LEV/San Paolo 2009.)

Rethinking Africa, means that Christ and Africa are tied by mutual fidelity and the Church has the task of defending this immeasurable gift, not only for the sake of this continent, but for the whole world too. It is up to Africa to become aware of this. This volume intends to contribute to it. And it is also my wish.

Fernando Cardinal Filoni
Prefect Emeritus
Congregation for the Evangelization of Peoples

Rome, 22 November 2023

Introduction

On November 19th, 2011, in the Republic of Benin in West Africa, Pope Benedict XVI published the Post-Synodal Apostolic Exhortation, *Africae Munus: On the Church in Africa in Service to Reconciliation, Justice, and Peace.* This Exhortation has two parts. Part One, "Behold I Make All Things New," includes many elements of Ecclesia in Africa, the document that followed the First Synodal Assembly for the Church in Africa. In the first part, Benedict XVI acknowledges a new dawn of Christian maturity on the African continent. Part Two focuses on the constituent members of the Church — clergy, consecrated persons, men and women missionaries, lay pastoral leaders, the elderly, youth and children—and challenges Church leadership to recognize and embrace their gifts, so as to give an appropriate and holistic response to the pastoral needs of the time, and to lead by example rather than just teaching.

Africae Munus challenges the Church's commitment to service, reconciliation, justice, and peace.[1] The burden of creating a just social order falls especially on those persons in the economic and political sphere who are builders of society.[2] The role of the Church is to serve as the watchdog in this process and lead all members of God's family to live in harmony. *Africae Munus* is a shot in the arm for the Church in Africa and a challenge to Church leadership. An interesting observation is the Pope's reference to Africa as a "spiritual 'lung' for a humanity that appears to be in a crisis of faith and hope."[3] Africans remain resilient despite the collective trauma they have been subjected to in the past two centuries due to their deep spiritual roots, a deep sense of hope, and connectedness to nature.

The challenge for African bishops and pastoral leaders is how to *"dialogue with the various constituencies within the church and*

1

society,"[4] to embrace the contributions of all members of the family in justice and peace so that the Church can transform theology into pastoral care.[5] Within this context, *Africae Munus* calls on the universal Church to recognize and celebrate Africa's rightful place within the Church and the world.[6]

In addressing the role of women in society, the Pope notes the violence that is often perpetuated against women, points to the "much too slow" understanding and "evolution of thinking" with regards to the rights and dignity of women,[7] and urges the Church to embrace their voices and talents. In doing so, the Church contributes to the *"recognition and liberation of women, following the example of Christ's own esteem for them,"* so that in turn women can continue to contribute to *"the humanization of society."*[8] The question is how to attend to internal structures and attitudes that preclude participation of women in the apostolates?

Africae Munus is a strong encouragement to the Church in Africa and a challenge to her leadership. As did his predecessors, especially Paul VI, the Pope challenges the Church in Africa to embrace elements within its culture that serve as the cornerstone for the Gospel. Doing so will advance its maturity and enrich the universal Church.

The present Conference proposes to make an evaluation of the Post-Synodal Exhortation of Pope Benedict XVI, *Africae Munus* on the engagement of Africa, ten years after its promulgation in 2011. This assessment, which brings into discussion different disciplines of the human and social sciences, will be carried out in the light of the challenges facing Africa and which challenge the Church as a major actor on the African scene, in considering its historical, social, and cultural dynamics.

Promulgated on November 19th, 2011, and in the aftermath of the fiftieth anniversary of the independence of 17 African countries celebrated in 2010 and in the midst of the *"Arab Spring"* storm, *Africae Munus* was intended to be a reference in the impetus for new dynamism in Africa. Pope Benedict XVI entrusted to episcopal conferences the task of working on this text in order to bring out its concrete applications. A very strong invitation is made to work in the regions. Africa is divided into nine regions. *This is the opening of a construction site*. In a way, the Second Synod had assessed the 15 years of the previous synod, *Ecclesia in Africa*. With *Africae Munus*, Benedict XVI gives the Church in general and to bishops in particular a road map whose backdrop is really to be agents of reconciliation, finding the practical modalities to do so.

Ten years later how have the Churches of Africa appropriated this Post-Synodal Exhortation? What remains of the relevance of this document given Africa's current challenges with regard to reconciliation, justice, and peace? What is the place of the Church in the face of questions of the existence, survival, and even the future of Africa, which are expressed in socio-political, economic, cultural, and ethical challenges? These important questions invite a fresh reading of the Post-Synodal Apostolic Exhortation, *Africae Munus*, given the opportunity for evaluation offered by the tenth anniversary of its promulgation. It is to respond to this that the Benedict XVI Institute for Africa (BIA) and the Catholic University of Cameroon (CATUC) organized an international conference held from February 15th to 17th, 2021, on the premises of CATUC in the Bamenda, North West Region, CAMEROON. Our immense gratitude goes to Virginia M. Greeley for her masterful editing of this work, and to St. Augustine's Press, South Bend, Indiana, for accepting to publish this text.

Maurice Agbaw-Ebai and Kizito Forbi, S.J.

Note

The 23rd of February is celebrated every year as the memorial of St. Polycarp, the martyr and Bishop of Ecclesial unity. In the afternoon of that day, as if in a prolongation of the liturgical celebration of that morning, some 170 persons from all walks of life united at the St. Joseph Metropolitan Cathedral Hall, Big Mankon, under the auspices of the **Catholic University of Cameroon, Bamenda** to join the scholars invited by the **Benedict Institute for Africa** and the **Centre for Interdisciplinary Research in Philosophy and**

Education to reflect on the person, thought, and work of Pope Benedict XVI in relation to the Church in Africa.

This International Conference on Joseph Ratzinger/Benedict XVI was the second organized by the **Benedict XVI Institute for Africa** on Cameroonian soil. The first took place at the Catholic University of Central Africa, Yaoundé, from 27th to 29th November 2019, to mark the 10th anniversary of Pope Benedict XVI's visit to Cameroon. Experts in four ecclesiastical disciplines, namely Theology, Philosophy, Canon Law, and Social Teaching of the Church, took turns to give the audience at the Franz Kamphaus University Amphitheatre a review of the reception and implication of the thought of Pope Benedict XVI to the Church in Africa 10 years after his first visit. Two years later, the Benedict XVI Institute for Africa launched an invitation to yet another intellectual banquet. This time the reflection targeted the Post Synodal apostolic Exhortation, *Africae Munus,* signed by the emeritus pontiff at Ouidah in Benin on the 19th November 2011.

This International Conference, *"Africae Munus* – Ten Years Later, In Service of Reconciliation, Justice, and Peace," which featured the work contained in this volume, took place on Wednesday, 23 February, and came to a close on Friday, 25 February 2022. As the participants continued the spirit of camaraderie one could sense the beginning of the fulfillment of the dream of Pope Benedict XVI who had said in Yaoundé:

> This century will perhaps permit, by God's grace, the rebirth, on your continent, albeit certainly under a different and new form, of the prestigious School of Alexandria. Why could we not hope that Africans today and the universal Church might thereby be furnished with great theologians and spiritual masters capable of contributing to the sanctification of those who dwell in this continent and throughout the Church?[9]

Perhaps that dream is already coming true. If it does, it will prove that Benedict XVI was right on yet another observation he made about the Church in Africa: *"a precious treasure is to be found in the soul of Africa, where I perceive a spiritual 'lung' for a humanity that appears to be in a crisis of faith and hope. However, if it is to stand erect with dignity, Africa needs to hear the voice of Christ who today proclaims the love of neighbor, love even of one's enemies, to the point of laying down one's life: the voice of Christ who prays today for the unity and communion of all people in God."*[10] Ecclesia in Africa, the time is now!

Rev. Herbert Niba
John Paul II Institute of Theology, Buea
Secretary of the Conference

Keynote Lecture:
The Theology of Law of
Joseph Ratzinger/Benedict XVI:
Pastoral Perspectives for the Church in Africa
in the Light of *Africae Munus*, Ten Years Later
Most Rev. Andrew F. Nkea, J.C.D., D.D.
Metropolitan Archbishop of Bamenda, Cameroon

Introduction

Joseph Ratzinger/Benedict XVI's reputation as a theologian needs no introduction. Often referred to as the "Mozart of Theology," Ratzinger quickly established a solid credential of a rigorous theologian unafraid to engage the prevailing currents of thought of the twentieth and twenty-first centuries. In doing so, Ratzinger sought all along to remain in the bosom of the Church. In other words, his theological opus is rooted in the thought of the Fathers and the Scripture. He is a perfect example of a thinker rooted in the living tradition of the Church—tradition, which G. K. Chesterton once called the democracy of the dead. To Ratzinger, therefore, it was never a question of seeking to establish a theological novelty, but rather of delving with creative enthusiasm into the Church's tradition for resources that could help the men and women of today enter into a living relationship with Jesus Christ, the Incarnate Son of God. As he himself maintains,

> I have never tried to create a system of my own, an individual theology. What is specific, if you want to call it that, is that I simply want to think in communion

with the faith of the Church, and that means above all to think in communion with the great thinkers of the faith. The aim is not an isolated theology that I draw out of myself but one that opens as widely as possible into the common intellectual pathway of the faith.[1]

For Ratzinger, therefore, the methodology is one of an immersion into and an updating of the insights of the great theologians and spiritual masters of the Church, making them contemporaries of today's Church. In other words, Ratzinger follows the path that runs from an examination of the present circumstances and challenges to the faith, considered from the perspective of what the Fathers, Doctors, and Saints of the Church might have to say to the question under consideration, with a view of giving meaning to the present and the future. As with his engagements with other aspects of theology, this is the approach that Ratzinger adopts in his treatment of law and the just ordering of the social order. In other words, the Church's engagement with the social order is rooted in the hermeneutics of faith. And this is what constitutes its uniqueness and particularity for Benedict XVI.

Benedict's Legal or Juridical Considerations for a Just Social Order

The question, "What constitutes a just social order or society?," cannot be answered without a consideration of the juridical or legal nature of society. Therefore, in responding to the call of Benedict XVI in *Africae Munus* to build a just social order by forming upright consciences receptive to the demands of justice, it is important to examine the nature of law and how it ought to be applied in society. This consideration opens before us the wide doors into the gold mine of Benedict XVI's great contribution to the juridical sphere.[2]

The Juridical Building Blocks of a Just Social Order

The task entrusted by Benedict XVI to the Church in Africa is to ensure that justice and peace and reconciliation reign on the continent. In other words, establishing a just social order. The question to be asked is, "What are the requirements or raw materials necessary to construct this edifice of social justice?" The foundation of a just social order requires that society understands what is right and wrong. Without knowledge of what is right and wrong, there can be no justice. *From this assertion, one can infer that at the basis of a just society is the respect of rights*, what the jurists refer to as *ius*. This word has no exact equivalence in the English language. But very often it is translated to mean one of the following: Justice, right, jurisprudence, jurist, jurisdiction, law. The Roman jurists in defining *ius* always linked it to the idea of justice. Celsius defined it as *"ars boni et aequi,"* that is, the art of goodness and fairness.[3] The jurist Paulus defines it as *"id quod semper aequum ac bonum est,"* that is, what always is fair and good.[4] It is for this reason that Aquinas considered *ius* as the object of justice (*utrum ius sit obiectum iustitiae*).[5] In the words of Bernard Murphy, *ius* for Aquinas is that which is ethically just.[6] This means therefore that *ius* precedes justice, for justice presupposes the existence of what one is owed by right. Hervada puts it differently, "justice follows the law. It does not precede it, but it is posterior to it in the sense that it operates in relation to existing law (*derecho* or right)."[7] Therefore, for a just social order to exist, society must have *ius*. These laws or rights are at the foundation of the building of a just social edifice. But one may ask the question, "What is the nature of this law or *ius* that must be there as foundational?" What type of law should serve as the *ratio* for justice in society? This is a question which Benedict XVI took very seriously in his encounters and dialogues. His speech to the Bundestag was a reflection on the foundation of law. In the field of law, his pertinent question has been this: "How do we recognize what is right?"

Benedict XVI realizes that the answer to what is right has become more complex and harder as a result of the positivist hijack of the understanding of the nature of law, leading to a chasm between ethics and law, between the "is" and the "ought." In his words, a positivist conception of nature yields only functional answers.[8] This means that those answers can change with time. How

8

can that which is transitory be the foundation of law? Benedict XVI does not simply reject positivism. He sees the value in it, but he decries its exclusiveness which prevents society from looking beyond itself. He compares this positivistic self-obsession to a concrete bunker with no windows, in which the human being provides the lighting and atmospheric conditions without reference to God.[9] Such a society will eventually suffocate from lack of juridical fresh air. What then does Benedict XVI propose as a solution to this crisis of law in society?

To better understand Benedict XVI's response or proposal, it is important to take a step back and reflect on Thomas Aquinas' treatment of the four aspects of Law in his Treatise on Law. This would provide a tapestry on which to paint Benedict XVI's legal contribution, a proposal which is implied in *Africae Munus'* call for a just social order.

The Four Aspects of Law

Key to understanding the different aspects of law is the distinction between *lex* and *ius* made by jurists beginning with the Romans to modern times. In a nutshell, *ius* was employed to refer to law in general while *lex* had a narrower signification.[10] In the Digest, Celsius' definition of *ius* is employed, "The art of the good and the fair."[11] In the Institutes of Gaius, *lex* is what the "*populus* orders and establishes."[12] *Lex*, therefore, is the law which man posits, while *ius* refers to law in general or right. Aquinas added significantly to the understanding of *lex* and *ius* especially in his presentation of *lex* as statutory. That is a law which is promulgated by an authority or law as found in a code, a definition which Thomas Hobbes later endorsed when he wrote that it is *lex* that "determineth and bindeth" either to do or to forbear.[13] His understanding of *ius* is restrictive for he applies it only to what is just. So that *ius* becomes what one is owed in justice or what one owes.[14] In other words, right or *derecho*, or *droit*, *recht*. The anticipates of Aquinas on this were the Roman jurists (especially Ulpian) who made a distinction between *ius naturale*, that is, that which nature has taught all animals and the *ius gentium*, that which natural reason has established among all peoples.[15] What this means in relation to the four aspects of law is that each stresses either the positive or statutory aspect of law, *lex*, or the normative aspect or source of law, *ius*, or both. Thus, one finds these different meanings of law in the varieties of law which Aquinas developed, and which Benedict XVI presupposes to be at the basis of a just social order. These include the *lex aeterna, lex naturalis, lex humana*, and *lex divina*.[16] These four hierarchical varieties of law have a relationship.

The *Lex aeterna* or eternal law emanates from him who governs the whole universe by divine reason. And the divine reason's conception of things is eternal. Therefore, such law is not subject to time. It is eternal.[17] Consequently, it is the ultimate source and foundation of all law. As a result, anything that does order human society draws its authority from eternal law. For this *ratio divina* moves all things to their proper end. Any human law that contradicts eternal law is not a true law because it goes contrary to the *ratio divina*.[18]

The *Lex naturalis* becomes the human participation in the *summa ratio* which is the *lex aeterna*. Natural law becomes the basis of moral law for it is the eternal law written in the heart of man and woman. It is thus accessible by reason. This is very much in tandem with the Roman jurist conception of the *ius gentium*—what natural reason has truly established among all peoples.[19] Natural law, therefore, is not posited by human legislators, and it is not also contingent on time, circumstance, and place but universal and accessible to all human beings through the use of reason.

Lex divina on the other hand, is divine positive law which is not accessible by reason. It is law that is ordered to eternal destiny of man and woman. Given the uncertainty of human judgement regarding contingent and particular things so much so that one can easily err, divine law directs man and woman to secure knowledge of what is to be done and avoided. It is the concretization of eternal law into particular precepts. An example would be the Ten Commandments.

Lex humana or human law translates natural law and, in some cases, divine law into concrete norms governing particular peoples in different circumstances. This is possible because law is a dictate of practical reason. Thus, we can distinguish two types of human law. The *ius ecular* and the *ius sacrum*. The former being the positive laws which regulate secular governments and whose foundation is the natural law. The latter being the merely ecclesiastical laws[20] or the positive laws of the Church whose foundation is divine positive law as well as natural law. It is contingent and it is posited by human legislators and thus subject to change. Because it is human law it must not contradict eternal and natural law which is the basis and foundation of law.

The interaction of these four types of law plays a very pivotal role in Benedict XVI's juridical appreciation of what constitutes the basis of a just social order as alluded to in *Africae Munus*. Returning to the question, "who determines what is right?" it becomes clear that the answer has to consider the understanding of the various types of law and the hierarchy of values inherent in them. This becomes Benedict's key concern when he interacts with secular society and politics.

Natural Law as Central to Benedict's Vision of a Just Social Order

Benedict XVI's appreciation of natural law and its centrality in the juridical structure is captured by his allocution to the Roman Rota at the start of the judicial year 2012. He said: "True law is inseparable from justice. The principle is obviously valid also for canon law, in the sense that it cannot be shuttered within a merely human system of norms, but must be connected to a just order of the Church, in which a higher law is in effect… Human law is held in value inasmuch as it is an expression of justice, above all for how much it declares as Divine law."[21] This take on the nature of Canon Law, which addresses the Church *ad intra*, paints a picture of his legal conception of the nature of human law in relation to natural and divine law. Canon law is human law, it is ecclesiastical law promulgated by humans, but it must have recourse to higher law, which is divine natural law. Without natural and divine law, human law is impoverished.[22] This is also true of human law in society. In his Address to the Bundestag he reminded them that the Church has never proposed a juridical system based on Revelation; instead, she has always pointed to nature and reason (Natural law) as the true sources of law.[23]

This concern with the centrality of natural law in the positing of human law is further strengthened by Benedict XVI's observation of the rapidly positivistic outlook of society which considers nature as purely functional. This to him has a catastrophic impact on the nature of law, for law ceases to be grounded on the truth of natural law. Positivism, as he puts it, is at the root of the unbridgeable gulf that now exists between the "is" and the "ought" since the two are now situated on completely different planes.[24] This is catastrophic precisely because it extends to the field of reason. Positivism in this regard holds that anything that is not verifiable or falsifiable according to the scientific method is extraneous to reason and as such should be placed on the shelter of myths. This understanding, as Benedict XVI points out, means that ethics and religion are excluded from the dialogue table of law since they are extraneous to reason. In other words, natural law is excluded from the considerations of human law. And if that is the case, then law becomes handicapped, for it loses its external light.[25] That is what happens when human law loses sight of the natural law. It becomes deflated and majority rule becomes sufficient. The danger becomes immediately clear, for how can majority rule become the criterion when fundamental issues such as human dignity are at stake. What the majority decides today to be human dignity, can be decided by the majority of tomorrow to be something else, as has happened so often in the history of national parliaments the world over.

Having denounced the negative influence of positivism on law, Benedict proposes an answer to the question, "How do we know what is right so that we can form a just social order?" This answer has at its core a return to the natural law, a theme that St.

John Paul II also emphasized when he spoke to the Italian Catholic Judges reminding them that the foundation of natural law is rooted in all human persons. Thus, every juridical order that is true and sound must be at the service of the human person.[26] Benedict XVI's answer is similar to this. He notes that the culture of Europe (including the legal culture as well) arose from the encounter between Jerusalem (Monotheism), Athens (Reason), and Rome (Law). To lose sight of the conviction that the creator God knowable by reason is what gave rise to the idea of human dignity and equality before the law, is tantamount to a legal implosion of society. If society fails to recognize that there are objective norms governing right action and accessible to reason,[27] then the laws which arise from such a society would be a caricature and destruction of justice and eventually produce, in the words of Benedict XVI, a highly organized band of robbers capable of threatening the whole world and driving it to the edge of an abyss.[28] Therefore, every true positive law must have natural law as its solid foundation.

And to Benedict XVI, the recognition of the natural law provides a caveat for an opening to the supernatural, especially when one thinks of the intertwining relationship between natural and supernatural laws. One could readily summarize Benedict XVI's address at the Bundestag as follows: "All worldly power, even democratically legitimate power, to avoid being misused, has to recognize that it is always subject to a higher truth beyond all human manipulation."[29] In effect —and as already been pointed out—building a just social order cannot be limited to majority consensus, but must be rooted in the truths of reason as contained and revealed in natural law. In this light, Christianity does not propose any political system. Christianity is a not a theocracy. Thanks to reason and the natural law, it points to the objective discernment in conscience and in reason, of the social order from the subjective commitment of everyone that is involved in the legislative process, as an arm of government. Hence, natural law constitutes an indispensable feature of the establishment of a just social order, from a Ratzingerian perspective.

A consequence of the neglect of natural law in the formulation of human law is the complete absence of the notion of charity and forgiveness. A theme which Benedict hearkens to in his allocution to the Roman Rota, wherein he reminds them of the principle found in the Encyclical *Caritas in Veritate*, n.6, that "charity goes beyond justice." He explains further that every authentic work of charity includes an indispensable reference to justice. Hence, justice and charity are inseparable for Benedict XVI. However, charity without justice, he notes, is not charity but a counterfeit, because charity itself requires that objectivity which is typical of justice and which must not be confused with inhuman coldness. Therefore, a culture without truth, that is a culture not rooted in natural law, falls prey to contingent subjective emotions and opinions which end up destroying or distorting charity to the point where it comes to mean the opposite.[30] Such creates no space for forgiveness or reconciliation. But for justice and peace to be complete, there also has to be forgiveness or reconciliation which heals and rebuilds troubled human relations from their foundations. For a society that is only just is an intolerable society; for if a person is only given what is just there would be no friendship, no solidarity, nothing that allows for the normal and adequate development of social life.[31]

Conclusion

In conclusion, *Africae Munus'* call for the establishment of a just social order becomes Benedict XVI's invitation to Africa to delve deeper into the core of the authentic expression of law rooted in nature. Once Africa does that, it will come face to face with the authentic expression of justice which arises from the recognition of the fundamental equality of human beings rooted in natural law. It is this vision of justice that would enable African jurists and legislators to posit human laws that are not positivistic but laws that are rooted in reason and charity. In that way, Africa can build a just social order that is capable of reconciliation and peace.

Problematization of the African Reality

Africae Munus raises many issues of concern to the continent of Africa. For instance, the challenge of enculturation by syncretic movements that capitalize on the social and economic needs of the people to offer *"a religious veneer to a variety of heterodox, non-Christian beliefs."*[32] According to Benedict XVI, the syncretic movements can present an opportunity to enculturate the faith in Africa, by drawing our attention to certain peculiar features of the African culture. The Exhortation also raises the issue of memorized and lived catechesis, and an effective commitment to living the Gospel. The responsibility of politicians and good governance as essential for a better future of Africa is another issue that has to be confronted, as per *Africae Munus*. By quoting Genesis 2–3, the Pope wants to provide a theological contribution to the contemporary ecological problems with particular reference to the African continent. The problem of immigration is also raised with acuity. These and several other problems or issues span *Africae Munus*. This section aims at isolating some of the problems to see if they have been solved and how; if they still exist as they were and why; if they have intensified and why. In the face of the many challenges that Africa seeks to address in order to become more and more a land of promise, the Church, like Israel, can easily fall prey to discouragement; yet our forebears in the faith have shown us the correct attitude to adopt. Moses, the Lord's servant, *"by faith … persevered as though he saw him who is invisible"* (Hb 11:27). Bringing the problems to light will expose the quality of perseverance exhibited by Africans.

Christians in the City:
The Political Commitment According to
Africae Munus
By Jean-Paul Tagheu, O.P.

Introduction

The first Post-synodal Exhortation, *Ecclesia in Africa*,[1] appears to be the African reception and interpretation of the conciliar Pastoral Constitution of the Church in the Modern World, *Lumen Gentium*. As for the second Post-synodal Exhortation, *Africae Munus*,[2] it appears to be the African reception and interpretation of *Gaudium et Spes* and of *Ad Gentes* (The Church's Missionary Activity in the World). With regard to this, one cannot understand *Ecclesia in Africa*, *Africae Munus*, or any other synod in contemporary times without reference to Vatican II Documents, which are the common foundations of the theological reflections of the Church since 1965.[3] Thus, the Second Vatican Council is the main inspirational source for the special assemblies for Africa of the synod of Bishops.[4]

The Church is "the family of God,"[5] in which we are brothers and sisters from the same God, our Father. In the first African Synod of bishops, the Church, the family of God was called to evangelize the whole of Africa in her mission towards the year 2000. Emphasis was then put on the enculturation of the Gospel, so that the salvific message of Christ may reach the whole of Africa in its cultural and socio-political diversities. But, since the sixties, the family of God which is in Africa faces different issues regarding politics, economy, justice, and peace.[6]

Therefore, if the first Synodal Assembly for Africa were more theological, because of the emphasis put on enculturation, the aim of the second synod was to call for "transforming theology into pastoral care, namely into a very concrete pastoral ministry...."[7] The theme of reconciliation, justice, and peace was applied to commit the Church to that concrete pastoral care and ministry. This theme takes us more on the terrain of Christian social responsibility and that of action and witness.

Our purpose, in this reflection, is to recall these issues in the line of Christian political commitment in the society. Our postulate or premise lies in this consideration: the civilities of/for the Kingdom of God are not fundamentally incompatible with those of the city of men and women. In other words, we are Christians in a city. Our incarnation in a socio-political environment engages us in socio-political affairs, directly or indirectly, actively or passively. The cause of the nation does not exclude the cause of God. The concern for God does not discount that of the nation. If, from Christian perspective, God is the accomplishment of all being, the life of the city and in the city is one of the means to reach that accomplishment in the divine.

The problematic is then obvious: Can we reconcile Christian life and political life in the society? How can someone be a Christian in a socio-political context like that of *Africae Munus*? To what extent can a Christian be involved in political affairs? What is the call for Christian political commitment in *Africae Munus*?

To address these questions, we will discuss in the first part the compatibility between the earthly city and the divine city. Christians, in the earthly city, are also citizens. That is why dialogue between secularism and religion is as important as the distinction, without separation, between the socio-political order and the Church's order. In the second part, we will address the call for political commitment regarding reconciliation, justice, and peace in *Africae Munus*. The Church's life of reconciliation, justice, and peace engages her in socio-political affairs, and sets for her some paths of implementation of her mission in the society. In the third part, we will discuss the issues and significance of Christian theology of *polis* as the means to inform and to form Christians' consciousness, to awaken in them their socio-political responsibilities and commitments.

17

Caesar and God, Citizens and Christians

The goal of this part is to find out if there is a discontinuity or a continuity between citizenship and "Christianship," between religion and the secular, given that the Church order and the political order are different.

City of Men and City of God: Discontinuity or Continuity

"One is not born a Christian," Tertullian says, "one becomes a Christian."[8] But, somehow, one is born a citizen, because of the natal soil that determines us. Each person is born in a socio-political soil as its son or daughter. That is why Aristotle defines a person as a "*zon politikon*," that is, a political animal. Each citizen is then political, not necessarily in the sense of a politician doing politics, but in that of being an active or a passive member of the society he or she belongs to. In this regard, the human being is connatural to the city. Just as citizens are in the city as their political habitation, the city also is in the citizens through laws, customs, cultures, and other policies that regulate life in the city. Out of the city, we are either angels or dead persons, but not human beings. Inside the society or city, we are political members, passively or actively involved in political affairs.

Augustine of Hippo speaks of two cities: the city of man and the city of God. He presents them as being opposed due to their different principles and aims.[9] But fundamentally speaking, the way to the Kingdom of God and its civilities are not incompatible with those of the political reign. From the Christian perspective, if God is the accomplishment of all being, life in the city on earth can be a prolegomenon for the heavenly life. For this reason, the way to heaven passes through the earth within a socio-political arena of human life. The gateway of the earthly kingdom can then open to that of the divine's, in the sense of perfection and fulfilment by the latter.

To love a city means to serve it properly. To serve it properly makes us its citizens. Christians are citizens in this world and at the same time citizens of the coming world. It is with good citizens that we can make good Christians. It is with good Christians that we can make good citizens too. A bad Christian produces a bad citizen and *vice versa*. In this regard, there can be continuity between the virtues and values of the society and those of the Kingdom of God. However, the values and civilities of Christians do not lie only in the constitution or the laws of the state they belong to. They also lie in the Gospel, which for them ranks itself superior to any other laws pertaining to Christians in the city.

Religion and Secularity

With the advent of post-modernity, there is a radical secularization that seems to oppose religion and separate it from socio-political affairs. Doing so, it forgets about what Edgar Morin called *"homo complexus,"*[10] that signifies complex human or human being with multiple dimensions. As noted by Claude Rivière:

> Modernity is totally intelligible only if one examines religion as one of its constituents, and only if we take into account the recomposition of the Church's role in the face of politics and economy. Thus [come] the current relations, problems between religion and democracy, the context's influence on the political commitment of such religion, taking into account the historical evolvement of secularism's principle.[11]

Along the same line of thinking, Benedict XVI speaks of a sane secularity or "laicity" against what we may call the secularity of exclusion, a merely horizontal secularity. For him, sane secularity is an open secularity. It is open to the transcendent. It is a vertical secularity inasmuch as it can dialogue with religion. Only in this secularity's openness could religion be part of the modern *polis*, without confusion or deceitfulness. According to Benedict XVI:

> No society can sanely develop itself without a reciprocal affirmation between politics and religion, by avoiding

the constant temptation of mixing or opposition…
Both—politics and religion—are called, even in the
necessary distinction, to co-operate harmoniously for
the common good. Such a sane secularity guarantees
that politics should operate without instrumentaliz-
ing religion and guarantees religion to freely live
without being burdened by politics dictated by interest and sometimes not in conformity with, or even
contrary to, belief. This is why sane secularity (unity-
distinction) is necessary and even indispensable to
both.[12]

For this to be effective, there should be a clear distinction
without separation between the Church's order and the socio-political order.

The Church Order and the Socio-Political Order

We surely know this famous quote of Bishop Dom Helder Cam-
era, martyred under the military and dictatorial regime in Brazil.
He said: "When I give food to the poor, they call me a saint. When
I ask why they are poor, they call me a communist."[13] In some
francophone countries of sub-Saharan Africa, if you question in
that way the state of the poor and the poorest, they shall call you
a terrorist, an insurrectionist, or an opponent of the regime.

The call on Christians, by *Africae Munus*, to be in the service
of reconciliation, justice, and peace, is a call for political commitment. As noted by Benedict XVI:

The task we have to set for ourselves is not an easy one,
situated as it is somewhere between immediate engagement in politics—which lies outside the Church's direct
competence—and the potential for withdrawal or evasion present in a theological and spiritual speculation
which could serve as an escape from concrete historical
responsibility.[14]

The appeal in *Africae Munus* is a paradoxical appeal given the very nature, mission, and finality of the Church, which is of spiritual and transcendental order. In fact, according to the *Gaudium et Spes*, "The Church, by reason of her role and competence, is not identified in any way with the political community nor bound to any political system. She is at once a sign and a safeguard of the transcendent character of the human person."[15]

Therefore, distinction, wisdom, and borders' definition are at stake here between the Church and the political community, so as not to merge them up in their missions and complementary tasks in the society.[16] As the Second Vatican Council states, "The Church and the political community in their own fields are autonomous and independent from each other. Yet both, under different titles, are devoted to the personal and social vocation of the same men and women."[17] In the political society the tasks which Christians, enlightened by the Gospel, carry out in conscience and due to their responsibility as citizens are different from those of their pastors and ministers.[18] On this note Benedict XVI made it clear in *Africae Munus* when he addresses bishops and priests to focus on their first duty:

> Your first duty is to bring the good news of salvation to all, and to offer the faithful a catechesis which leads them to a deeper knowledge of Jesus Christ. See to it that laypeople acquire a genuine awareness of their ecclesial mission and encourage them to engage in it with responsibility, always seeking the common good. The permanent formation programmes offered to laypeople, and above all to political or economic leaders, must insist on conversion as a necessary condition for the transformation of the world. It is fitting that they should begin with prayer and continue with a catechesis that will lead to concrete action.[19]

In other words, though we may all be citizens, the political commitment in the society depends on the state of life; on the charism and vocation of everyone. The political duty of a priest differs from that of a lay faithful fully engaged in the world and society.

The Call for Political Commitment in Africae Munus

The purpose of this part is to address some areas of social-political commitment for Christians, in *Africae Munus*.

Christian Commitment within a Tragic History

God speaks to humankind through its history. For Jean-Marc Ela, we have to take seriously the historicity of African societies with their pains and joys, contingencies and predicaments, because "it is at the heart of that historicity that Revelation reaches us."[20] Revelation is at the improvement of the historicity of African societies, which we need to re-appropriate and to reinterpret in the light of the Gospel. Ela says:

> Rethinking faith, by taking into account the burden of our history is a grave affair [...] In keeping the eyes fixed on the links existing between the African person and the Passion of that Palestinian Jew, that one executed by hanging Him on the wood (Acts 5: 20), we must take the risk to understand the mystery of God in assuming the questions raised to Africa's Churches by some men and women who are asking themselves how is God their concern, in the dramatic situations in which they are living today.[21]

The Church in Africa lives in the context of neo-colonization, with the old sequels of slave trade and of colonization, which were very violent and oppressive. After the years of independence and even after the fallacious wind of democracy (so-called western wind of the nineties), Africa went through many civil wars, genocide, social dislocation, political instability, economic crises, devaluation of currency (such as the *Franc cfa*), etc. "Africa's memory," Benedict XVI says, "is painfully scarred as a result of fratricidal conflicts between ethnic groups, the slave trade and colonization. Today too, the continent has to cope with rivalries and with new forms of enslavement and colonization. The first Special Assembly likened it to the victim of robbers left to die by the roadside" (cf. Lk 10: 25–37).[22]

In the sub-Saharan Africa, mainly in francophone countries, an epidemic of coup-d'états is going on under the motive of bad political and economic governance of state's affairs.[23] Thus, we are Christians in a continent with a tragic history. The call for political commitment sounds within a dramatic context of wars, terrorism, social injustices, corruption, poverty, and misery. These plagues were already a concern in *Ecclesia in Africa*:

> The Synod Fathers were unanimous in acknowledging that the greatest challenge of bringing about justice and peace in Africa consists in a good administration of public affairs in the two interrelated areas of politics and the economy. Certain problems have their roots outside the Continent and therefore are not entirely under the control of those in power or of national leaders. But the Synodal Assembly acknowledged that many of the Continent's problems are the result of a manner of governing often stained by corruption. A serious reawakening of conscience linked to a firm determination of will is necessary in order to put into effect solutions which can no longer be put off.[24]

In *Africae Munus*, the call for commitment to reconciliation, justice, and peace aims at addressing these socio-political scourges, which undermine and slow down an African commencement in terms of emergence and progress.

Commitment to Reconciliation and Peace

In *Africae Munus*, the Church bears the mission of reconciliation in view of peace. The Church is reconciled by God, and she also reconciles in God and for God.[25] She is reconciled in order to be the reconciler. A reconciled Church is the Church who recognizes in herself, the wounds of division and hatred, and seeks for healing in the mercy of God. Hence, according to Benedict XVI, the Church "too needs the Lord's healing, so that she can credibly bear witness that the sacrament of Reconciliation binds up and heals wounded hearts."[26] Reconciliation in the line of the Gospel and of the Church is not a political reconciliation between the nations, based sometimes on the economic interest, and without justice. Reconciliation is to bring humankind to the mercy of God; it is to become friends of and friendly with God through the divine mercy brought by Jesus. By reconciling ourselves with God, we reconcile also with the Church, with the society to which we belong, and with our neighbor.

Thus, there are two dimensions of reconciliation, the vertical and the horizontal. Reconciliation means communion between God and humanity and communion among humans themselves.[27] That is why reconciliation involves, as a duty, every person in the society. "Indeed," states Benedict XVI, "only authentic reconciliation can achieve lasting peace in society. This is a task incumbent on government authorities and traditional chiefs, but also on ordinary citizens."[28] The only true reconciliation, and its power to purify the citizens' hearts, comes from God. The new evangelization presupposes that the Christians reconcile with God and with one another; it overcomes every kind of barrier— barrier of language, gender, culture, tribe, and race.[29] But reconciliation cannot go and be sustained without justice.

Commitment to Justice and Love

The call on the Church, in *Africae Munus*, is about justice. A justified Church which justifies the society is, without doubt, a Church building a just social order.[30] It is a Church living in accordance with Christ's justice. It is a Church preaching what she lives and living what she preaches all the same.

Justice is not to be taken merely in its juridical sense, where the tribunal declares someone culpable or non-culpable, condemns or releases him/her. Justice in the sense of the Church goes beyond doing right and avoiding unrighteousness. Justice, according to the Bible, is to conform our will to the will of God (Mt 1:19). In this way, a just nation is a nation which, by respecting human rights and liberties, lives according to the will of God. In other words, true justice for God goes beyond punishing the unjust and sinner. It extends to forgiveness. True justice is the justice of love "which, (for Benedict XVI), gives itself to the utmost, to taking upon itself the 'curse' laid upon persons, that they may receive in exchange the 'blessing' which is God's gift (Gal 3: 13–14)."[31]

As it is limited and imperfect, human justice is accomplished in divine justice. That is why we need God's forgiveness and friendship to be really justified in God and by God. The task of the Church, as *mater et magister* is to be a witness to this. Making a just nation, a just continent means, for the Church, to educate people in the consciousness and practice of justice, in the consciousness of their civic responsibility in the city.

Jesus is our Justice (cf. 1 Co 1: 30; 2 Co 5: 21; Jr 23: 6; 33: 16). The new and just society that we need for Africa is a society animated by Christ's love; a society where all are able to participate actively with their talents in social and economic life.[32] In Christ Jesus, the man of Beatitudes and the Beatitude itself, God's Justice is already manifest in the Paschal mystery with a preferential option towards the poor, the hungry, the sick due to AIDS, malaria, cancer, tuberculosis, Covid-19, etc.[33] The Church's mission of Justice is *ad intra* and *ad extra*, that is, from within the Church and from without her. The efficacy of her service of justice towards the continent is from within; it is in herself, as being the justified Church of the Righteous One, Jesus, that the Church can eagerly justify evangelically.

The justified Church, then, will show or preach her justification in Christ her Spouse, as paradigm of justice and justification through Christ, in the society to which she belongs. For this reason, the ecclesiastical *Justice and Peace Commission* has to help the people, the Christians and the non-Christians, to pardon and to reconcile themselves, so that, even after the secular processes and judgements, the protagonists of the court do not become enemies after all. Rather, they will be able to acknowledge the sentence of the court, and to live and work together in peace and for peace.

In all ways, as mentioned before, justice in the Christian sense is beyond the legal or juridical justice. In Jesus it is a justice of love; it is a restorative justice which, in the thought of Benedict XVI, promotes "the return of victims and offenders to the community" and to God, beyond a punitive or an exclusive justice.[34] *That is why the love of justice has to be linked with the justice of love.* Love does not undermine or diminish the imperative of justice, and *vice versa.* "Justice is never disembodied. It needs to be anchored in consistent human decisions. A charity which fails to respect justice and the rights of all is false. I therefore encourage Christians to become exemplary in the area of justice and charity (*Mt* 5:19–20)."[35]

In sum, reconciliation, justice, and peace are three related elements of the Christian political commitment in society. Reconciliation leads to peace through justice, truth, and love. Benedict XVI clearly states:

> Human peace obtained without justice is illusory and ephemeral. Human justice which is not the fruit of reconciliation in the "truth of love" (*Eph* 4:15) remains incomplete; it is not authentic justice. Love of truth – "the whole truth," to which the Spirit alone can lead us (cf. *Jn* 16:13) – is what marks out the path that all human justice must follow if it is to succeed in restoring the bonds of fraternity within the "human family, a community of peace," reconciled with God through Christ.[36]

Paths towards Christian Political Commitment

These commitments are not stated in the air. They are some concrete indications, in which they can be implemented and rooted.

In fact, in the second chapter of the first part of *Africae Munus*, Benedict XVI listed paths toward reconciliation, justice, and peace. He proposes four paths:

a) *Care for the human person.*[37] The achievement in this path supposes an authentic Christian *metanoia*, for only converted Christians can really impact their society in terms of justice, reconciliation, and peace. The care for the human person goes with the sacrament of penance and reconciliation and with a spirituality of communion at the vertical level with God and at the horizontal dimension with the Church and other persons. Caring for human persons also takes into consideration the enculturation of Gospel and the evangelization of culture, accomplished in the gift of the Eucharist and the word of God. If, per essence, human beings are political subjects, then to care for them, to watch over them, is part of the political enterprise. In this sense, politicizing means caring in a large semantic proportion of the word caring.

b) *Living in harmony.*[38] This path towards the Church's commitment embraces human families with all its members: men and women, young and old. Harmony of and in the city depends on the harmony of the political subjects who are members of the society. Without harmony, there will be no reconciliation, no justice, and no peace. Tranquility and harmony among citizens are the fruits of justice, reconciliation, and peace; just as bustle and disharmony constitute a lack of or claim for reconciliation, justice, and peace.

c) *African vision of life.*[39] The third path towards reconciliation, justice, and peace considers the protection of human life. This path advocates moreover for ecology, for the need for good governance of African states, and for the issues of migrants, displaced persons, and refugees. It recalls the question of globalization and international aid. Globalization and international aid must not become another way of recolonizing poor countries, as Tibor Mende, the Hungarian journalist used to say.[40] For *Africae Munus*, no society can survive if it does not value human life and show attention and respect for creation and the ecosystem. No society can survive if it does not create conditions for good governance, so as to avoid war, injustices, corruption, and their consequences in terms of migration, refugees, and displaced persons. As such, defending human life against these predicaments is part of the political game. For if we define politics as management of the city, any political ruler needs to have living and happy subjects under his/her ruling: s/he cannot rule over dead persons. The life and the welfare of the citizens depend on the life and the welfare of the country they live in. In this regard, to stand for life against murders, poverty, misery, injustice, and corruption constitutes an act of political commitment in the society pertaining to all the societal members. Human life is political.

d) *Dialogue and communion.* Dialogue and intercommunion among the believers are other names for being committed to reconciliation, justice, and peace in a society like ours.[41] Due to religious fanaticism and terrorism, religions today are part of the crises and violence in the world. However, the religious element can be a part of the solutions and remedies to heal the world. It could be so if believers take into consideration interculturality, living in dialogue, and communion;[42] if they truly understand their mission and responsibility through Christian political teaching.

For a Christian Theology of the *Polis*

What does "Christian theology of *polis*" mean to Christian political commitment?

The Good News of Politics

Politics, in the sense of organization, management, and functioning of the city is experiencing today a great unease. From unfulfilled promises to abuses, political leaders inflict burdens on their people. They oppress and exploit them. They steal the common good. With this, there is an urgent need to regain the true sense and finality of politics and the political affairs. For politics is too serious a matter of the life of a nation, and that of the world, to be left to politicians alone.[43] According to the French Bishops' Permanent Council, "our society, and more broadly all life in common, cannot do without politics."[44]

For the common good, politics as organization are practical strategies undertaken in the exercise of power, which comes from the people through electoral games. But political affairs (*le politique*) is that great personal pronoun "We" that integrates all citizens' existences and goes beyond all particularities. It searches for common good and general interest. For the French Bishops' Council, political affairs (*le politique* or *la chose politique*) precede politics (understood as art of managing or governing public affairs). The former founds and defines the latter.[45] There is politics (*la politique*) only if there is political affairs (*le politique*) beforehand.

In this sense, the Church cannot be truly at the service of reconciliation, justice, and peace in view of the integral human development if she does not also develop a good Christian theology of the *polis* and that of economy, just as she does with moral and social theology. Under the concept of theology of the *polis*, or of the economy, let us understand a theological reflection on politics and economy. To the concept of "political theology," François Daguet proposes four senses.[46] Among others, we retain this one especially:

> The term "political theology" refers to the consideration of the communitarian aspects of human life by Christian theology. We are here in a strict perspective of theology. Since nothing that falls within the scope of the created order escapes the field of theology, it is natural that the communitarian dimension of man and the existence of human communities be taken into account.

Moreover, the communitarian character of God's plan alone justifies the elaboration of a political theology, that is to say [theology] of the common.[47]

Christian revelation is not, as such, a discourse on politics and on economics. Nor is it a discourse on political and economic systems. However, as being the enlightening Word of God, revelation can shed light on politics and economics, insofar as all that is created or belongs to the order of the created things cannot escape the prism of God and his creative Word. This is very good news on politics. The spiritual, when it is well received from God and lived in society by the beneficiary, has always a positive and transformative impact on the temporal. Benedict XVI underlined it in this way:

> A just social order is part of the competence of the political sphere...The model *par excellence* underlying the Church's thinking and reasoning, which she proposes to all, is Christ. According to her social teaching, "the Church does not have technical solutions to offer and does not claim 'to interfere in any way in the politics of states.' She does, however, have a mission of truth to accomplish... [One] that the Church can never renounce. Her social doctrine is a particular dimension of this proclamation: it is a service to the truth which sets us free.[48]

According to Emmanuel Mounier, it is true that "Christianity is often lagging behind in political and social matters," in the matters of some awaiting answers and solutions of faith inherent to the rapid and growing changes in the world.[49] Certainly, this slowness can be justified by the Church's prudence and discernment in order to bring a necessary and just wisdom. It can be justified too by her unfortunate and dramatic experiences of the past, where the Church was too glued to politics more than to Christ, her Spouse, and to His message of grace.[50]

The Need for a New Generation
of African Leaders and Managers

However, the presence of the Church and her awareness of being a living community in the *polis*, in the society, require her to be more of the leaven of transformation. In other words, as Vincent Cosmao indicated, "If the Church has a role to play in the transformation of the world, the political effects of the preaching of the Gospel must be taken into account."[51] The Gospel itself and its preaching have messages and effects that are political and temporal, underlying those spiritual and eternal truths that they proclaim. Therefore, a theology at the service of justice, reconciliation, and peace gives us to think of a political, economic, legal, and social theology—with all the precautions it entails so as to avoid political drift, and the drift of socialism and economics. This is because the terms *justice, reconciliation,* and *peace* are not only of religious or theological order. They are also political and social.

As stated in the *Lineamenta* of the Second Synod for Africa, the good management of the public affairs, both in the political and economic fields, constitute major problems now in Africa. African nations suffer partly from these two areas (political and economic). They are the greatest challenges for the realization of justice and peace.[52] Thus, for Benedict XVI, "one of the tasks of the Church in Africa consists in forming upright consciences receptive to the demands of justice, so as to produce men and women willing and able to build this just social order by their responsible conduct."[53] In this regard, there is an urgent need for new African leaders and managers with a strong consciousness of the common good, of justice, truth, love, and sharing; an urgent need for good governance and with the determination to implement them. In fact, from the *Lineamenta* in preparation for the Second Synod:

(...) Africa's immense resources are in contrast to the state of misery of the poor in Africa (...) Hence the urgency of studying the ways, and the means to promote the rise [of students, businessmen, managers...], of honest politicians determined to protect the common heritage against all forms of waste and diversion."[54]

These ways and means consist in the formation and transformation (or conversion) of consciences, of mentalities, and ways of life. For, if the city makes everyone because it is prior to us in space and time, the human being makes the city by his/her commitment to its betterment. The Church of truth and love, of reconciliation, justice, and peace will always make truthful and loving memberships; righteous, peaceful, and reconciling participants. Because of the commitment to truth and love, to justice, reconciliation, and peace, a social and political Christian should be separated from partisan politics, from being an accomplice to bad governance, to injustice, fraud, corruption, tribalism, misery, and poverty.

Conclusion

The social and the Church orders are different, in terms of their modes of operation and their final goal about human beings. But they are not strictly incompatible. They are two ways to serve human beings in their temporal and spiritual, earthly and transcendental dimensions. As such, being a Christian in the city is one of the means to live a Christian life without confusion or betrayal, despite prosecutions and temptations. In that, *Africae Munus'* call on the Church to serve reconciliation, justice, and peace is still relevant and actual. Reconciliation, justice, and peace are both political and spiritual virtues. They can constitute a common ground of interaction between religion and politics, secularity and spirituality, earthly and heavenly citizenship.

Looking at the world's happenings and predicaments, *Africae Munus* was a prophetic magisterial and ecclesiastical document, especially in the African context. It came as a support or approval of some concerns raised beforehand, in the twentieth century, by African theologians and other thinkers on social justice, freedom, and integral human development. All over Africa today, groans and claims are raised for justice and peace, for a new social order. Armed conflicts, secession threats, terrorism, popular revolutions, epidemic of coup d'états (in the Sahel), injustices, poverty, and misery constitute some challenges of the time in Africa. They are echoing trepidations addressed in *Africae Munus*, ten years ago, for the Church in Africa and in the whole world.

"To have hope for the future," says Bernard P. Prusak, "is to recognize the need for the world to be *otherwise*. It is to recognize the need for action to recreate the values and structures whereby humans have shaped a world filled with injustice, poverty, hunger, hatred, violence, and suffering."[55] For this reason, we need a new generation of African leaders and managers with converted consciousnesses, with converted lives and ways of life, who, at the center of their political actions, place above all the common good of their nations and the service of their citizens. Truth and love meet together, justice, reconciliation, and peace embrace together (cf. Ps 85(84), 10), when indeed we consider human beings and God as our ultimate concern in whatever we do.

The Task of the Church in the Process of Peace and Reconciliation: Perspectives from *Africae Munus*

By Valentine Banfegha Ngalim, Ph.D.

Introduction

A thought-provoking assertion in *Africae Munus*, (AM), revealing a dialectic in the intersection between church and state, religion and politics, states that:

> The task we have set for ourselves is not an easy one, situated as it is, somewhere between immediate engagement in politics—which lies out of the Church's direct competence—and the potential for withdrawal or evasion, present in a theological and spiritual speculation, which could serve as an escape from concrete historical responsibility.[1]

Highlighting the above, one finds a critical situation faced by Church ministers with regard to their engagement in political matters. The debate on the Church's involvement in public life is not new. This controversy dates back to the medieval period as expressed in the thoughts of Augustine of Hippo and Thomas Aquinas. Canon Law and the doctrine of the Church define the boundaries within which the Church or religious persons have to interfere in politics. Despite these directives, there is no satisfactory solution to conflicting opinions, tensions, and controversies surrounding the role of religion in politics or the Church's interference in political issues. The teachings of Pope Benedict XVI, as expressed above, indicate that this is not an easy task. From a quick observation one wonders why there is continuous ambivalence/ambiguity in understanding the intersection between Church and State. This paper sets out to analyze the assertion above and determine the extent to which religion/the Church can interfere in political matters. Our findings are meant to clarify and define the boundaries between the two institutions in order to ease the process of justice, peace, and reconciliation in the light of the socio-political crisis in Cameroon.

Background and Problem

As initially indicated, questions surrounding the intersection between religion and politics, Church and State are not new. Saint Augustine of Hippo and Saint Thomas Aquinas had already reflected on these issues during the medieval period. In *Civitas Dei*, Augustine makes a distinction between two cities. These include the temporal city of Babylon and the eternal city of Jerusalem. Babylon promises all the glories of Eden, without the presence of God. Jerusalem is a city that comes down from heaven. It represents God's grace, contrary to the self-made monstrosity of Babylon. In this distinction he explains that the eternal city reflects the dwelling place of the infinite and eternal God the creator, and the temporal city reflects the finite and limited dwellings of mortals whose vocation is the return to God the creator. Rome, the new Babylon, represents all that is worldly, and Jerusalem (the city of heaven) represents Christian community. In our world, there is a mixture of two cities, but the temporal city, *civitas terrena* will eventually perish giving way to the eternal city. Envy, power, and greed, characterize the earthly city. For Augustine, the two cities coexist as a *"corpus permixtum"* [mixed body].[2] This sub-section examines two perspectives in order to provide a foundation for the dialectics of religion and politics. First, we consider politics as subordinate to religion with justifications of the Eternal law of Augustine and the Divine law of Aquinas. Second, the social contract theories of Hobbes and

Locke serve as antitheses to the subordination of politics to religion/State to the Church.

State as Subordinate to the Church

The State is an earthly institution concerned with the well-being of mortals in the temporal city, which is subordinate to the eternal and everlasting city of God. Within this framework of thought, Augustine referred to the Eternal law of God, which puts in place the natural law that constitutes the basis for the positive laws governing affairs in the life of the city. Augustine traced political life in the moral law that governs persons or individuals in society. He argued that there is a single source of truth, and this truth is not subject to changes of human life. All persons recognize this truth and know it as natural law or natural justice. For Augustine, the natural law is our intellectual sharing in God's truth, which is the eternal law. The notion of the eternal law was anticipated by the Stoics in the concession of the principle of reason that governs nature. It is reason that rules and controls everything. Though the Stoics conceived the principle of reason as an impersonal force of rational principles in the universe, Augustine interpreted the eternal law as the reason and will of a personal God. He writes that the eternal law is the divine reason who is in control of the natural order of things in the universe.[3]

With the equation of the eternal law and God's reason that commands order in the universe, the eternal principles therefore represent the natural law. This reinforces the fact that the laws of the state are temporal laws that must be subordinate to the natural law, which in turn is derived from the eternal law. The main point of Augustine is that the political state is not autonomous. The state is expected to follow the values of justice. Justice is conceived as a standard that precedes the state and is eternal. This is a novel meaning of justice, which distinguishes Augustine from other thinkers. Justice has to be discovered in human nature and one's relation to God. Augustine therefore makes the laws of the state subordinate to the natural law. Positive laws must be in harmony with natural laws and justice. The absence of this standard nullifies the character of laws and the existence of a state. Considering this argument, it has to be retained that justice is not limited to relations between people. The primary relationship in justice is between a person and God. Augustine also rejects the separation of collective justice from individual justice. This Augustinian thesis could be traced in Plato's correlation between justice in the individual soul and justice in the State.[4]

Moreover, Augustine observes that to serve God is to love God. This love of God is manifested in the love we have for others in society. Augustine bases the concept of justice on love. Love which emanates from God should diffuse to the whole society. He, therefore, places God's law in a superior position to political institutions. However, he accords to the state the right to use coercive force. In this context, the origin of the state is traced in the sinful condition of human nature. It is a necessary agency to control human behavior on earth. Augustine recognizes the importance of the state on earth. This state cannot manifest the full power of love, but her actions can limit the expression of evil in human society. On this count, he makes a distinction between two types of love. The first is the love of God, and second, the love of self and the world. These two conceptions account for the origin of two cities. The former refers to the city of God and the latter to the city of the world. Wherever those who love God are, this will be the city of God. Where there are those who love the world, this will be the city of the world. Augustine retains the fact that human beings can only attain happiness when love of God reigns in the state.[5]

Beside the Eternal law of Augustine, another important thinker is Aquinas who argued that the state is a natural institution. This means she has been derived from the intrinsic nature of human beings. This view, traced back to the Aristotelian conception of the state, holds that people are by nature (political) social animals. Aquinas' conception of the state becomes distinct from that of Aristotle because of their different views on human nature. Aristotle supposed that the state could provide for all the needs of the human being. This is because he limited all the needs to human and natural needs. Aquinas on the contrary widens these needs and includes the supernatural realm as part of human needs. For Aquinas, the state is not equipped to direct us to this end. It is the role of the Church. However, instead of separating the two realms of human concern, Aquinas made a synthesis by tracing the origin of the state to God's creation.

For Aquinas, the State is willed by God and possesses God-given functions which address the solid components of human nature. Aquinas did not agree with Augustine that the State is a product of people's sinfulness. In the state of innocence, people would have to live as a society. There is a need for someone to control and establish the common good. The function of the State is to secure the common good by keeping peace, organizing the activities of the citizens, providing the resources to sustain life and preventing obstacles to good life where possible. The function to preserve a good life is our ultimate end and this accounts for the State's relation to the Church. In this context, Aquinas makes the State subordinate to the Church. For Aquinas, there is no contradiction in according the State a sphere where she has her legitimate function and at the same time is subordinate to the Church. Within her own sphere, the State is autonomous, but the State cannot serve as an obstacle for persons to attain their supernatural end. She cannot hinder or frustrate the spiritual life of her citizens. The Church does not challenge the State's autonomy, but she reminds the State that she is not absolutely autonomous. This is precisely because the State ensures the natural end of its citizens, but our spiritual end cannot be achieved within the competence of the State. Therefore, the State has to be subordinate to the Church only to ensure that her ultimate spiritual needs have to be taken into account.[6]

Again, Aquinas argues that the State is the source of human law. Each government has the task of enacting statutes to ensure a harmonious functioning of the society. Aquinas thought that law-making cannot be arbitrary but must be founded on the natural law which involves human participation in (divine law)

God's eternal law. Human-made laws must consist of particular values derived from the natural law.[7] Any human law that violates the natural law loses its character as law and loses its binding force in the conscience of humanity.[8] The law maker has the authority to legislate from God and he is responsible to God. If the sovereign decrees an unjust law by violating God's divine law, Aquinas observes that such a law should not be obeyed. This is justified on the grounds that the raison d'être of the State is to ensure the common good. The political sovereign has the authority from God. Authority must not be used as an end in itself or for selfish interests. The common good must not be interpreted in such a way as to lose sight of individual rights within the collective whole. For Aquinas, the common good has no meaning except it ensures the good of individuals. The good of any part is taken in comparison with the whole.

Church as Subordinate to and Distinct from the State

The thesis of subordinating the State to the Church as seen with medieval thinkers Augustine and Aquinas was contradicted by modern thinkers. This move was championed by Thomas Hobbes. This distinction and separation betrayed the tendencies of post-modernity. It was not only limited to politics, but it extended to the republican tendencies of separating religion from science and technology. For Thomas Hobbes, the Leviathan, the body politic epitomized sovereignty. Consequently, religion, which was considered as one of the institutions of the State, was subordinate to the State and controlled by the State. As opposed to medieval thoughts of Augustine and Aquinas, the State of Hobbes was autonomous and in control of all aspects including religion/church. This separation was later perpetuated by John Locke who made a distinction between the Church and the State. Locke's thesis hinged on religious tolerance, whereby plurality in religious worship was emphasized. In these perspectives of social contract thinkers, religion and politics, the Church and the State, are placed as autonomous institutions. However, politics is more binding and autonomous since all the activities of the Church are subordinate to the laws of the State.[9] This provides a secular perception of religion as the Church is presented as a human institution.

Despite efforts to separate the Church from the State, controversies, tensions, ambiguities, abuses of power in both realms, and misrepresentations persist on the intersection between religion and politics. This is precisely because one wonders whether Church ministers could make moral pronouncements and at the same time avoid interference in politics. In such contexts, Church ministers are advised to stay away from politics by most politicians, especially when the discourses in Church obstruct their interests. Most often, politicians advise Church ministers to simply preach the good news, stay away from politics and leave politics with its idiosyncrasies to politicians. At the same time, it is not uncommon to find an abuse of power by some Church ministers. Some may propound what they consider to be the truth with uncharitable language, which at times degenerates into hate speech and the compromise of the gospel of love, the basis of peace and reconciliation. If one were to simply sample the socio-political crisis in Cameroon, one would discern these tendencies in order to interpret conflicting roles, abuses of power, and misrepresentation of the role of the Church in political matters. Owing to all these, what is the extent to which religion/Church is allowed to interfere in political matters given the contention in *Africae Munus*, #37 that "the Church wishes to be a sign and safeguard of the human person's transcendence. She must also enable people to seek the supreme truth regarding their deepest identity and their questions, so that just solutions can be found to their problems?"[10] Who determines the extent and what are the critical issues to be addressed by religion in society? Though religion and politics are autonomous institutions, they have a common objective, which is the well-being of human beings. For this precise reason, any arbitrary separation is artificial and unacceptable. The gospel of love, which enhances the salvation of humans, lies within the subject matter of both religion and politics/Church and State.

Conceptual Framework

The Church refers to the body of Christ under the auspices of the Pope, the representative of Saint Peter. It is within this body that each and every Christian is a living stone. Thus, the Church is an institution or formal organization with a particular objective. In popular minds the Church is associated with buildings and missions. *Ekklesia* is the Greek word that provides the meaning of the Church. *Ek* is "out of" and *"kaleo"* to call, to invite. This refers to a group of people who are called. Religion refers to the expression of beliefs, feelings, rituals and practices that portray one's relationship to the supernatural creator, God.[11] These concepts will be used interchangeably in this essay. In all, the practice of religion is the duty of the Church.

Politics derives its meaning from the Greek word *"polis,"* meaning city. Socrates and Plato talked about Greek city-states, referring to *polis* in the *Republic*.[12] Aristotle traces the origin of the State within the framework of the family where every individual is a political animal. In this context, politics serves the purpose of ensuring the well-being of the people. Justice is one of the principal virtues of governance in the *Republic* of Plato and it is within that framework that happiness, *"eudaimonia,"* could be attained. Aristotle also identifies *"eudaimonia"* as the primary goal of every political action. Owing to these ancient perspectives, the meaning of politics is far from the mundane understanding of it as deception. The primary objective of politics is to ensure the well-being of the people in the life of the city.[13] This is only possible through the practice of virtues like wisdom, courage, temperance, and justice.

Peace is more than armistice, more than the cessation of violence. Peace is unity and harmony. In a peaceful world, people are all pleased to cooperate with one another. When we have attained true peace, there will be no person who has any purpose that any other person seeks to thwart. In a peaceful world, everyone will feel the truth of justice and happiness. In this case, peace refers to a state of harmony that leads to communal living with

41

the assurance of the well-being of all. It is a product of justice. Karl Peschke defines peace beyond the absence of war, terror, and violence. He emphasizes the assurance of opportunities for self-realization, transcending conditions that limit human potential.[14] Peace amongst humans presupposes peace with God and His will. Prerequisites for peace are solidarity and the promotion of justice, sensitivity to others, freedom from prejudice, tolerance, ability to compromise and readiness for reconciliation.

The egalitarian says that justice is equality. There is a conceptual difficulty in specifying how beings as different from each other as humans are could ever be equal unless we create a society where all humans are clones of one another. (This should be technologically feasible within a few decades if it is not already.) But I do not think that egalitarians want a society of clones. Ackerman has offered a suggestion for determining whether any persons among a genetically diverse group are genetically disadvantaged. Ackerman also asserts that every person has a right to be genetically undominated.[15] John Rawls has proposed that the talents that individuals possess be regarded as a common pool and that those who have more than an average share have an obligation to compensate those who have less than an average share.[16] Ronald Dworkin has made the contractarian suggestion that people can justly be required to pay an income tax that represents the insurance against being untalented that they would have desired to purchase before they knew what talents they would have.[17] Ackerman suggests that each person who is genetically dominated is owed compensation by those who dominate him.[18] All of these suggestions should be rejected. Talents are not a common pool from which some persons have taken more than their share.

Another perspective considers justice as retributive. This refers to prosecution or criminal accountability. All these are extremes. Sustainable peace addresses the root causes. This is because most conflicts are outcomes of flagrant injustices and human rights abuses committed by elites and institutions. Where there is lack of harmony between the bodies involved, there is lack of justice. Consider the system theory. *Africae Munus*, # 41 defines justice as charity when it states that "solidarity is the guarantee of justice and peace and hence of unity, so that the abundance of some compensates for the want of others. Charity which ensures a bond with God goes beyond distributive justice. (...) anything that takes man away from God cannot be justice."[19]

Religion as Politics

In this sub-section, I contend that the task of the Church in establishing justice, peace and reconciliation in the society obliges her to be involved in political matters. The point one needs to explain is the extent to which religion, which is within the competence of the Church, has to intersect with politics. Following the assertion from *Africae Munus*, this task of the Church is not an easy one. It is not easy because of the challenges involved in defining the boundaries within which the Church has to be engaged in politics in order to distinguish it from what the Church is not expected to do. It will be very simplistic to think that religion could possibly be separated from politics. This is because if the Church in its religious preoccupations has to render discourses on moral education, raising questions of justice, condemning evil practices like embezzlement, electoral manipulation and fraud, oppression and exploitation in repressive regimes, then the Church has to be necessarily involved in politics.[20] It is the Church's duty to ensure the well-being of the citizens in the State, primarily because these citizens constitute the body of Christ, as members of the Church.[21]

Considering politics in the real sense of the term as initially explained, the practice of politics within this understanding is justifiable. From the foregoing understanding of politics, what has religion got to offer to ensure the establishment of justice, peace, and reconciliation in times of crises in the state? Should the Church simply stay away from all political discourses and preoccupy herself with preaching the good news for the salvation of souls? Should the preaching of the good news not have a bearing on the practical experiences of the people? Is heavenly salvation possible without an appropriate healthy, happy, and good life on earth? These questions are not meant to be answered, but simply to provoke thought and to present the Church/religion as an institution capable of providing practical solutions to the daily problems of the citizens as well as Christians in the *Polis*. *Africae Munus*, #19 states that "Unless the power of reconciliation is created in people's hearts, political commitment to peace lacks its inner premise."[22] Again, this text reads that "it is only through the grace of God, that reconciliation is guaranteed."[23] On the basis of this thesis, one is advocating for an "ecclesiastical politicking" to ensure peace and reconciliation in times of divisive politics and the oppression of the masses.[24]

In order to buttress the above argument, it is imperative to refer to the impact of events and ideas from the 20th to the 21st centuries.[25] During this period, we experienced a paradigm shift to post-modernity. This period experienced an unjustifiable trust in science and the growth of the tendency to exclude religion, the divine, the Church from the affairs of the world as well as science. The increase in the experiences of repressive regimes, militarization, fake news, deception in politics, the growing divide between the rich and the poor, destruction of rainforest, global warming, massive violation of human rights, and lack of educational facilities provide the justification for religion to get involved in politics. These experiences are obstacles to the well-being of persons in the *polis*. These are acts of injustice betraying the absence of peace in the world.[26] Given the Church's mission to promote peace, religion is perceived as an invaluable means for the achievement of this goal. "Peace I leave with you, my peace I give you" says the Lord, and he adds "not as the world gives do I give to you" (Jn14:27). This commission to the Church justifies its engagement in politics, though not always an easy task.

The invaluable role of peace for the well-being of the citizens in the *polis* justifies the Church's involvement in several political debates in the world today. Considering the present situation in the post-modern world, human survival and the survival of the planet is dependent on peace.[27] This peace can only be achieved between persons, families, tribes, cultures, nations as well as churches. Referencing Küng, this peace is only possible within dialogue. Religion/Church is an archetype of dialogue. Consequently, dialogue is not possible without the capital role played by religion.[28] The process of justice, peace, and reconciliation has to be fostered within the framework of the Church's meaning of peace. "(...) Not as the world gives, do I give you" (Jn14:27). The socio-political crises in Cameroon betray a crisis of care, a crisis of love, and a crisis of forgiveness. Martin Buber offers a therapy to these crises in his celebrated text *Ich und Du*. He asserts that *"Alles wirklich Leben ist Begegnung."*[29] In his thesis, encounter is at the basis of all relationships. The relationship we have with the other has to reflect our dialogue with God. From this understanding, religion appears as a very strong agent of peace in political practice. *Africae Munus*, #42 reiterates the justice of love.[30] Jesus' visit to the house of Zacchaeus (LK 19:1–10), portrays a wider perspective of justice. It is therefore important for one to investigate the insights of religion that serve as the tradition for global ethics of justice, peace, and reconciliation in the world and in Cameroon in particular.[31] How could religion serve as a prophylactic to future political crises in Cameroon and the world at large?

The practice of politics in the past has revealed unjust experiences of torture, assassinations, and violation of human rights by repressive regimes. What is discernable is that post-modern times with the banishment of religion lack a sense of how to guide changes that occur with devastating effects.[32] The misuse of scientific research and abuses of power justify most of the political interventions of the Church in the world. Silence is the weapon of the oppressor, and the Church has to understand that silence in the face of injustice is complicity with injustice.[33] Moral questions regarding life and the suffering masses require rigorous interventions from religious bodies. In this light *Africae Munus*, #38 contends that "grave injustices abound in the world especially in Africa."[34] This is because there is much that religion can contribute to the process of peace and reconciliation. First, the teachings of religion provide a consistent concern for human well-being viz.

human dignity, freedom, and respect for rights. Also, religion provides norms for basic human behavior. Take, for example, the Decalogue with all prohibitions against killing, stealing, and immorality.[35]

Religion is politics because it provides the bedrock for peace. Peace does not mean tranquility. In *The Republic*, peace entails harmony in all parts of the whole, where each and every part has to play its own function.[36] The practice of democracy entails morality, whose foundation is religion. Dewey argues that democracy is primarily moral rather than political.[37] Within democracy, there must be transparency, checks and balances, so that the massive interests of some individuals and groups are put under control. Scandals of corruption, embezzlement, and human rights violations compromise the process of peace. The Church cannot search for peace in the face of such malpractices in the *polis*. The search for peace without justice is baseless. And true justice necessarily leads to peace. In the midst of political matters, the silence of the Church to address issues that are related to the well-being of her Christians who are the citizen of the State is complicity to injustice.[38] This phenomenon becomes glaring when an individual plunders the whole nation of her resources leaving the poor masses to languish in abject poverty. At times these are members of the Church brandishing their ill-gotten wealth to enjoy a high profile and a blessed status in the Church. Most often, they are referred to as blessed, lucky, and persons who have experienced a breakthrough.[39] While this reality is common with politicians, they expect Church ministers to preach the beatitudes and shelve moral questions addressing issues of justice. Reading *Africae Munus*, #38 corroborates this argument "(...) the plundering of the goods of the earth by a minority to the detriment of entire peoples is unacceptable, because it is immoral. Justice obliges us to render to each his due, *ius suum unique trubuere*."[40] The search for peace cannot be attained by simply reciting the beatitudes to Christians. Hard facts and questions on morality have to be handled in order to ensure democratic values of life.

Again, religion is the foundation of education to good citizen-ship. Good citizenship entails proper respect for the rights and du-ties one is expected to observe. There can be no peace without good citizenship. *Africae Munus*, #34 states that "The Church is involved in civic formation of citizens and assisting in electoral process in a number of countries."[41] The education of the citizens is also the mis-sion of the Church, and this is only possible with the Church's en-gagement in politics. Citizenship education also entails participation in free and fair elections, respect for the rights of others, and the per-formance of one's duties in the State. Religion gives grounds for all these and testifies to all persons that every authority comes from God. The laws of the state are not arbitrary, but they owe their ori-gins in the natural law—which is derived from Eternal and Divine law.[42] At the same time the Church's teachings on the well-being of persons in the *polis* provide grounds for protest and resistance to unjust living conditions.[43] Justice and Peace Commissions within the heart of the Church ensure that there is concern for human well-being, dignity, freedom, and respect for human rights even within Church institutions. Religion serves as the base for the principles of basic human behavior, promoting the golden rule, offering genuine inspiration and motivation for living a moral life with samples of heroic virtues, and providing justification for suffering with the joy-ful hope of salvation.[44]

Church as Distinct from the State and Politics

This sub-section offers grounds for the Church to keep away from politics. The interference of religion or the Church on some polit-ical issues raised here is unacceptable and against the autonomy of the State. The thesis to be developed here is that the State is secular, and it is unacceptable for the Church to interfere in certain political matters. *Africae Munus* asserts that politics "(…) lies out-side of the church's direct competence- (…)."[45] Here, we are re-sponding to the initial question which sought to limit the power of religion in politics. There are several arguments to be advanced here and these include: keeping away from partisan politics, holding office of responsibility in civic life without prior permission of the local ordinary, perpetuating electoral fraud through uncritical political discourses, abuse of the pulpit with sentimental politics and hate speech, and hasty expressions of motions of support.

First, the Church has to stay away from partisan politics. Partisan politics here refers to militant participation in a particular political party. Christians come to Church with diverse political opinions, and it could be very scandalous for them to follow religious teachings that show sympathy to some political ideologies to the relative neglect of the others. There are several ways through which Church ministers could fall prey to this prohibition of the canon law. A Church minister whose sermons highlight the ideals of one political party at the dawn of elections to the relative neglect of the other is guilty of partisan politics. Canon law advocates neutrality on the part of Church ministers. Consequently, sermons have to serve as pedagogic pieces to enlighten Christians on right choices without necessarily expressing one's sympathy for a particular political opinion. In this context, religion is a strong pedagogic means for good political choices without degenerating into partisan politics.

Second, Church ministers are not allowed to accept appointments in public life without the prior permission of their local ordinary. This perspective is also expressed in the spirit of Canon law 285 paras. 3–4 and it is argued that such permissions could only be granted in a case of extreme necessity.[46] This comes with the permission of the Bishop, and one will not celebrate the Sacraments in public. For a Church minister who receives this appointment, he will be excluded from the exercise of religious duties. This is the context in which we argue for the distinction between the State and Church. When Joseph Owusu Agyemang—a Catholic priest from Southern Ghana—was sworn in as judge of High Court of justice, questions related to this law were raised. Also, Archbishop Ahouna of Bouake, appointed President of the National Commission for Reconciliation and Compensation of Victims (CONARCIV) in 2015, raised further questions because this was a structure to compensate victims of the 2010–2011 post-election violence.[47] Here, the Church is clear that a priest is not allowed to run for political office and thus the intersection is not possible, and both bodies operate as autonomous.

Third, Church ministers should be weary of being accomplices to electoral fraud. Here, sermons with political pronouncements on the day of elections are unacceptable. Church ministers are also advised not to tell the people of God who to vote for. They are not supposed to actively campaign, endorse, or publicly support particular candidates or parties. This attitude could breed hatred and violence, thus compromising transparent elections. This point is also discernable in a context where Church ministers use parish cars to escape with filled ballot boxes for egoistic interests. This direct participation in the political process is out of the direct competence of the Church. This attitude could compromise the moral authority that a Church minister enjoys within the community. "The role of the Church is not political in nature. Her task is to open the world to the religious sense of proclaiming Christ."[48]

Fourth, sentimental political pronouncements and hate speech from the pulpit are unacceptable. The Church is critical, and her ministers have to exercise sensitivity and a good sense of judgment within the political drama of a country. This is far from saying that they have to be silent in the face of injustice. The point is that truth is patient and gentle and it has to be expressed in the language of love, "*Veritas in caritate.*" Verbal violence begets more violence, and this contradicts the very essence of God. God is rational and every discourse arising from His house has to promote peace and reconciliation. The word of God cannot be a source of violence. If God is order, then everything divine has to participate in the order set in place by God. Absolute reason cannot beget violence and disorder. This violates the principle of non-contradiction. Thus, religion provides the basis for peace and reconciliation without the abuse of the practice of politics.

Lastly, hasty expression of motions of support on behalf of the Church has been very controversial even amongst Church ministers. It is not the place of the Church to express popular will on political matters especially within doubtful electoral proceedings. At times one wonders whether this is necessary or whether someone is speaking on behalf of others. This is not an attitude that promotes peace and unity, but it is very divisive in its nature. Church ministers have to be neutral in making such pronouncements because this political experience is out of the direct competence of the Church. Religion, which is a unifying instrument, could be an agent of division if its members abuse its autonomy and dabble in issues that are not meant to ensure the well-being and happiness of the people of God. Hasty declarations from ministers of the Church on electoral matters could be guilty of *argumentum ad verecundiam* (misplaced authority).

Religion in Dialogue with Politics

In this sub-section, I argue that religion and politics are two sides of the same coin. The controversy that arises from the intersection between religion and politics is because of the abuses experienced and the misrepresentation of the role of religion for egoistic interest. A keen study of the objective of religion betrays the practice of social life, which necessarily involves questions surrounding justice, peace, happiness, reconciliation, and respect of the rights of all.

Considering the argument that every authority comes from God, one is justifiably correct to assert that all the laws of the State are subordinate to the laws of God. Aquinas argues that if the laws of the State contradict the natural law, which is derived from divine law, they should only be obeyed for the sake of peace.[49] This is a rationalist approach to the respect of the law. Commands and actions here are not respected because they have been commanded, but rather because they concur to the dictates of reason. God is absolute reason, and no rational instruction escapes the will of God. On the grounds of this argument, no representative of religion has the right to stir up prejudice, hatred, and enmity towards any groups of persons, or even incite legitimate wars.[50]

Consequently, the state is meant to foster the well-being of her citizens through political organization. The politics that compromises the happiness of its citizens compromises its primary objective. This will probably be politics for the interest of the stronger party perpetrated by repressive regimes and massive violations of human rights. This despotism is far from what is truly willed within the realm of political life. Politics in the true sense has to foster critical initiatives that protect life, ensure the well-being of al,l and deliver persons from all forms of oppression. An intersection between religion and politics ought to commit to a culture of non-violence and respect for life, promote a culture of solidarity and a just economic order, and lastly a culture of tolerance and a life of truthfulness. "No woman or man, no State or Church or religious community has the right to speak lies to other human beings."[51] This assertion is true for journalists, media workers, artists, writers, and scientists in their exercise of academic freedom. In addition, this is a prohibition to leaders of countries, politicians, and political parties to whom we entrust our freedom. *Africae Munus*, #130 reinforces this argument by stating that "The church for her part is committed to promoting within her own ranks and within society a culture that respects the rule of law."[52]

Conclusion

Owing to the preceding arguments on the role of religion in public life, one can discern the dialectic that characterizes the whole debate. However, it has to be retained that to a large extent, the practice of religion entails major political preoccupations. The role of the Church has to be balanced by her servants' engagement in the public sphere. What remains very critical is that the Church has to learn how to phrase her religious presuppositions in secular reasoning and language. This is the only way she will capture the increasing secular worldview. The salvation of souls is the primary objective of the Church.[53] It has to be noted that this salvation begins on earth, for a miserable life and poor living conditions could compromise this mission. *Africae Munus*, #127 observes that the "Church in Africa must help to build up society in cooperation with government authorities and public and private institutions that are engaged in building up the common good."[54] Through a systematic, sustained, and collaborative approach involving ecclesiastical bodies, organizations and government, the happiness of Christians who are citizens of the State will be achieved. A haphazard confrontational approach has no practical bearing to the well-being of the people of God.[55] Peace and reconciliation cannot be attained without God.[56]

Africae Munus on Catholic Education as a Precious Resource for the Transmission of African Values: Creating the Bonds of Peace and Harmony in the Society

By Nelson Shang, Ph.D.

Introduction

Ours is a globalized, post-modern world characterized by secularism, moral relativism, materialism, atheism, and hedonism. Catholic schools have a mandate, informed by Gospel values, to maintain a distinctive Catholic ethos and identity. How do Catholic schools balance the demands to achieve quality in secular terms while, at the same time, upholding Catholic educational principles? This is a fundamental problem facing Catholic education today worldwide. The Church in Africa is not immune to this challenge.

Pope Benedict XVI's Exhortation, *Africae Munus*, which is divided in two parts, treats his views on education in part two titled: "To each is given the manifestation of the spirit for the common good" (*1 Cor* 12:7). Looking at the situation of the African continent "marked by contrasts," the Pope urges that the Church should act, "on the one hand, under the guidance of the Holy Spirit, and on the other, as a single body." By exhorting each member of the Church family to be "the salt of the earth" and "the light of the world" (*Mt* 5:13–14), Pope Benedict XVI insists strongly that each Catholic Christian should act, through the Spirit, for the common good. This, he says, is because "one can never be a Christian alone." This brings to mind the admonition of the *Catechism of the Catholic Church* that although faith is personal, it has a communal dimension.[1] This corroborates Pope Benedict XVI's argument that "the gifts given by the Lord" to each and every one of us "must all contribute to harmony, communion, and peace in the Church herself and in society."[2] It is important to keep these values in mind because I will revert to them later in my presentation. The Pope ends the introduction to this part by exhorting the African Church "to show *solidarity* and *creativity* in relieving those who bear heavy burdens, thus opening them to the fullness of life in Christ (cf. *Mt* 11:28)."[3] Solidarity and creativity, to me, are fundamental virtues that Catholic education should inspire and instill in the mind of the each and every child.

The Exhortation treats education in chapter two of part two titled "Major Areas of the Apostolate." The Pope is categorical that the:

> Lord has entrusted us with a specific mission, and he has not left us without the means of accomplishing it. Not only has he granted each of us personal gifts for the building up of his Body which is the Church, but he has also granted the whole ecclesial community particular gifts which enable it to carry out its mission. His supreme gift is the Holy Spirit. Through the Spirit we form one Body and "only in the power of the Holy Spirit can we discover what is right and then do it."[4] Certain means are needed if we are to act, yet these remain insufficient unless God himself disposes us to cooperate in his work of reconciliation through "our ability to think, to speak, to listen and to act."[5] Thanks to the Holy Spirit, we become truly "the salt of the earth" and "the light of the world" (*Mt* 5:13–14).[6]

From the above, it is clear that the call and identity of the Church is to be at the service of humanity. This brings to mind the central message of Pope Francis' papacy—that the Church should be service-oriented. In his Apostolic Exhortation, *Evangelii Gaudium*,

Pope Francis argues that "an evangelizing community should get involved by word and deed in people's daily lives; it should bridge distances, it is willing to abase itself if necessary, and it embraces human life, touching the suffering flesh of Christ in others."[7] One major channel through which this is most clearly manifested in the education of the young.

Catholic Schools: A Precious Resource for Continent

Pope Benedict XVI very clearly states that "Catholic schools are a precious resource for learning from childhood how to create bonds of peace and harmony in society, since they train children in the African values that are taken up by those of the Gospel." As such, Bishops and institutes of consecrated persons should "enable children of the proper age to receive schooling."[8] This, to the Pope, is not just "a matter of justice for each child" but equally forceful is the fact that "the future of Africa depends on it."[9] The Second Vatican Council had earlier argued in this same light that "all men and women of every race, condition and age, since they enjoy the dignity of a human being, have an inalienable right to an education that is in keeping with their ultimate goal."[10] In this section of this lecture, I will focus my analysis on two key points: Education as a matter of justice for each child, and education as the transmission of African cultural values.

Education as a Matter of Justice for Each Child

Pope Benedict XVI's insistence that education is a matter of justice for each child is based on the conviction that every child has a right to education and that it is the duty and obligation of the parents/guardians, the state, and ultimately the church to provide such education. Article 26 of the United Nations Universal Declaration on Human Rights 1948 clearly states:

Everyone has the right to education. Education shall be free, at least in the elementary and fundamental stages.

Elementary education shall be compulsory. Technical and professional education shall be made generally available and higher education shall be equally accessible to all on the basis of merit.[11]

In the same vein, Article 28 of the United Nations Convention on the Rights of the Child states:

Every child has the right to an education. Primary education should be free. Secondary and higher education should be available to every child. Children should be encouraged to go to school to the highest level possible. Discipline in schools should respect children's rights and never use violence.[12]

What this means is that our society (the Church included) has a moral obligation to provide adequate educational opportunities to every child so as to instill in them necessary skills needed to live decent lives and to eventually contribute their own share as adults to the society. Alfred North Whitehead argued rightly that "in the conditions of modern life the rule is absolute; the race that does not value trained intelligence is doomed."[13] Jean Jacques Rousseau, on his part, makes a succinct analogy: "just as plants are shaped by cultivation, so too is man shaped by education."[14] Immanuel Kant opines that "the purpose of education is to enable humanity to develop and to improve, for man can only become man by education."[15]

Thus, as a right and as a matter of justice, education is not only beneficial for the child; it is equally beneficial to the society as a whole. Education is, thus, in:

Society's best interest as it is a social waste if some children do not receive a good education. It means that human talents that could contribute to society are not nurtured. All students have talents that grow through formal learning. By failing to develop those talents, society loses opportunities for enrichment and progress. Further social waste is gained by the long-term social and financial costs of poor education. Inadequate education leads to large public and social costs in the form of lower income and poor economic growth, reduced tax revenues, and higher costs of health care, social security, and increased crime.[16]

It is thus doubtful whether any child can be expected to succeed these days, and indeed if the human society can succeed, if proper educational opportunities are not provided. That's why the Pope encourages "bishops and institutes of consecrated persons to enable children of the proper age to receive schooling" and through these schools, children would be trained "in the African values that are taken up by those of the Gospel."[17]

Education as the Transmission of African Cultural Values

Drawing inspiration from Alfred North Whitehead who argues that "education is the art of the utilization of knowledge,"[18] I treat education in the traditional African set-up as a process of the transmission and renewal of cultural values. What this means is that adult members of the society carefully guide the development of the young, initiating them into the culture of the society.[19] As such, education, as Carter Good says, is "the art of making available to each generation the organized knowledge of the past."[20] Peter Snelson sees education as "a condition of human survival ... the means whereby one generation transmits the wisdom, knowledge and experience which prepares the next generation for life's duties and pleasures."[21] It is in this line of thinking that Michael B. Adeyemi and Augustus A. Adeyinka argue thus:

> For infants and young children, education often takes the form of indoctrination, that is, the process of compelling the child to 'eat' or 'play' or do his/her homework at particular times of the day. In the training or

upbringing of children, a measure of freedom is allowed so that they can have the opportunity of learning at their own rate and behaving in their own particular ways, provided their learning processes and general behavior do not present a wide departure from the accepted social standards and conventions of their society. Freedom is therefore a relative term and the extent of freedom a person enjoys depends largely on the culture of the society to which he or she belongs and the values which that society upholds. Hence, what society "A" values as freedom may be condemned as an act of indiscipline by society "B."[22]

As such, education involves a process whereby a generation inherits the culture of the society from the older generation (transmission) and then modifies (renewal) the culture they inherited and adapts it to their own existential situatedness: the political, social and economic situations of their time. Finally, they pass on the modified culture to the generation following them. Adeyemi and Adeyinka, however, observe that:

As the society becomes more highly urbanized and detribalized, particularly in an age of science and technology, the process of education becomes more complex. Education could be seen as the process of interaction between the guardians and the seekers of knowledge. It could be seen as a dialogue between the men and women with ideas and skills and the adolescents and young adults seeking to acquire and develop those ideas and skills, knowledge that they need to earn a living in an age of computers, science, and technology. Education today is more than what the schools, colleges, or universities alone can give. Industry, the mass media, the internet and related sources of learning in society are intended to complement institutionalized education; and, as we now live in a new century, the 21st century, no person would be deemed to have been truly educated if he or she is not computer-literate. Further, he or she should be able to tap into information through the electronic media, to complement whatever information has been obtained in the formal classroom situation.[23]

What are some of those cultural values that Pope Benedict XVI insists that Catholic education should focus on in order to achieve peace and harmony on the African continent? Sense of hospitality, sense of the sacred, sense of the sanctity of life, Ubuntu-communalism, respect for elders, etc.

Education and Truth

Turning his attention to Catholic universities and academic institutions, Pope Benedict XVI confers a twofold responsibility: "it falls to you, on the one hand, to shape the minds and hearts of the younger generation in the light of the Gospel and, on the other, to help African societies better to understand the challenges confronting them today by providing Africa, through your research and analyses, with the light she needs."[24] He further admonishes Christians and African youths in particular, to "study the educational sciences with a view to passing down knowledge full of truth: not mere know-how but genuine knowledge of life, inspired by a Christian consciousness shaped by the Church's social doctrine."[25] In this section, I will highlight three points: passing down knowledge full of truth, not mere know-how, and genuine knowledge full of truth.

Education as "Passing Down Knowledge Full of Truth"

The admonition to pass down knowledge full of truth is particularly important because it is the mission of every educational institution to be involved in a disinterested search for truth/knowledge and to disseminate that knowledge to whoever is interested. In a world marked by relativism, Pope Benedict XVI's call for us to pass "down knowledge full of truth" is all the more relevant especially as one recalls, with dismay, that in 2016 the *Oxford Dictionary* declared the word *Post-Truth* as the word of the year while in 2017 the Trump Administration promoted the word *Alternative Facts*, thus fanning into flames the already existing debates surrounding the nature of truth. This gave more impetus to adherents of *social constructionism* (lik, Bruno Latour, Edith Butler, Peter L. Berger, and Thomas Luckmann, etc.) who argue that truth, knowledge, gender, and reality as a whole, are socially constructed, they are not a given. As such, truth is no longer seen as a conformity between the thing and the intellect—*adequatio rei et intellectus*[26]—but as constructed by science, society, etc.

These modern-day theories of Relativism, Post-truth, Alternative facts, and Social Constructionism are a manifest attack on the very backbone of metaphysics, the concept of *essence*—the nature of things, as well as a conceptual distortion of the fundamental nature of reality and the appropriate function of the human intellect. The definition of truth by St. Thomas Aquinas as the conformity between the thing and the intellect aptly expresses the fundamental nature of truth. According to Alejandro Llano, this definition expresses the nature of truth formally, in that the very essence of truth consists in the conformity or identification of the thing and the intellect.[27] In his 1979 address to the Pontifical Academy of Sciences on the commemoration of the centenary birth of Albert Einstein, Pope John Paul II argued, and rightly so, that:

> The search for truth is the task of basic science. (…) Pure science is a good, which every people must be able to cultivate in full freedom from all forms of intellectual slavery or intellectual colonialism. Basic research must be free with regard to the political and economic authorities, which must cooperate in its development, without harnessing it to serve their own purposes. Like any other truth, scientific truth is, in fact, answerable only to itself and to the supreme truth, God, the creator

of man and of all things. Science can be seen as revealing the wisdom of God in the order of creation. Every scientific discovery about the universe, far from raising difficulties for religion should rather be a source of inspiration, a revelation of the scale and grandeur of the purposes of God. Science is a quest, a search for truth, and all truth is ultimately God's truth.[28]

It is this kind of knowledge full of truth that Benedict XVI is exhorting all African youths to pursue and pass on to future generations. That is why he urges teachers at Catholic universities and academic institutions to play an essential role in the "patient, rigorous and humble search for the light which comes from Truth. Only a truth capable of transcending human standards of measure, conditioned by their own limitations, brings peace to individuals and reconciliation to societies."[29] In his *Address to Catholic Educators*, Pope John Paul II said, inter alia:

> The Church looks upon you as co-workers with an important measure of shared responsibility (...) To you it is given to create the future and give it direction by offering to your students a set of values with which to assess their newly discovered knowledge (...). [The changing times] demand that educators be open to new cultural influences and interpret them for young pupils in the light of Christian faith. You are called to bring professional competence and a high standard of excellence to your teaching (...). But your responsibilities make demands on you that go far beyond the need for professional skills and competence (...). Through you, as through a clear window on a sunny day, students must come to see and know the richness and joy of a life lived in accordance with Christ's teaching, in response to his challenging demands. To teach means not only to impart what we know, but also to reveal who

we are by living what we believe. It is this latter lesson which tends to last the longest.[30]

Education is not the Transmission of "Mere Know-How"

This brings to mind the pertinent question of the ambiguous power of technology. Africa is a continent with a youthful population that is ambitious about the advancements of modern-day techno-science. Africa can no longer be left behind. Ours is an era that has turned to science-based technology as a source of fulfillment and hope. Technology has offered power, control, and to a certain extent, the capacity to overcome our helplessness and dependency. Why then does Pope Benedict XVI warn African youths to beware of simply amassing and transmitting mere know-how? I think it simply is because for all its benefits, technology has not brought the personal fulfillment or social well-being it promised. A nuclear holocaust would wipe out modern civilization and produce climate changes and famines that could conceivably jeopardize human life itself. Toxic chemicals, deforestation, soil erosion, and multiple pollutants are severely damaging the environment. Computers, automation, and artificial intelligence will have powerful impacts on work, social organization, and our image of ourselves. Genetic engineering offers the prospect of altering the structure and behavior of living forms, including those of human beings. Large-scale technologies contribute to the concentration of economic and political power, increasing the gaps between rich and poor within nations and the gaps between rich and poor nations.[31]

This ambiguous power of technology vividly creates in one's mind the consciousness that "ours is a planet in crisis." This is the central message of Pope Francis' Encyclical Letter, *Laudato Si* (On Care for our Environment) in which he presents what he calls, "several aspects of the present ecological crisis,"[32] such as pollution and climate change, the issue of water, the loss of biodiversity, the decline in the quality of human life, and the breakdown of society. He then articulates the "tremendous responsibility"[33] of humankind for creation, the intimate connection among all creatures and the fact that "the natural environment is a collective good, the patrimony of all humanity and the responsibility of everyone."[34]

Thus, while craving the technological developments on the continents, every educated African youth must keep in mind the *Ubuntu* spirit–communalistic conception of the person and of the African world-view. This means that there is a symbiotic relationship between us and the environment, thus necessitating a responsible use of nature on our part. Thus, our *Ubuntu* spirit enables us to realize that for us to properly care for the environment, we must develop a deep love for humanity. Pope Francis articulates this firmly when he says:

> A sense of deep communion with the rest of nature cannot be real if our hearts lack tenderness, compassion and concern for our fellow human beings.... Concern for the environment thus needs to be joined to a sincere love for our fellow human beings and an unwavering commitment to resolving the problems of society.[35]

He goes forward to state:

> Whether believers or not, we are agreed today that the earth is essentially a shared inheritance, whose fruits are meant to benefit everyone. For believers, this becomes a question of fidelity to the Creator since God created the world for everyone. Hence every ecological approach needs to incorporate a social perspective which takes into account the fundamental rights of the poor and the underprivileged. The principle of the subordination of private property to the universal destination of goods, and thus the right of everyone to their use, is a golden rule of social conduct.[36]

What this means is that in order to love our neighbor we must consider the impact of industrialization on communities, on the created world and on the dignity of the human person. Pollution and hazardous industrial conditions harm our neighbors, our environment, and ourselves. If man and woman have dominion over the earth, they have the responsibility to care for, protect, oversee, and preserve the environment so that every community would take from the bounty of the earth whatever it needs for subsistence. The natural environment is a collective good, the responsibility of everyone. Those who benefit the most from exploiting natural resources also have a social debt. We also have a duty to protect the earth and ensure its fruitfulness for future generations.

For the admonitions of Pope Francis to be successfully implemented, we must add to it what Pope John Paul II had earlier warned humanity in 1978 in his Encyclical Letter, *Redemptor Hominis*, about technology: "The man of today seems ever to be under threat from what he produces. This seems to make up the main chapter of the drama of present-day human existence."[37] Hence human beings seem to be a victim of their technological productions. Men and women must emerge victorious from the present environmental crisis which threatens to degenerate into a tragedy, and they must find again true kingship over the world and full dominion over the things they produce. For this to be a reality, Pope John Paul says that we must be conscious of three things: "the priority of ethics over technology, the primacy of the person over things, and the superiority of spirit over matter."[38]

Education as the Transmission of "Genuine Knowledge of Life"

For Catholic education to truly become a precious resource for learning from childhood how to create bonds of peace and harmony in society, as Pope Benedict XVI strongly admonishes, Catholic schools must become alive with knowledge, what Benedict XVI calls "Genuine knowledge of life." Education must take into consideration the cultural, historical, and current existential background of the learner so to avoid what Whitehead calls an education with "inert ideas" or "dead knowledge."[39] Whitehead emphasizes that in education, we must remember that a "pupil's mind is a growing organism (...) it is not a box to be ruthlessly packed with alien ideas."[40] For him, it is the purpose of education to stimulate and guide each student's self-development. The task of the educator is not simply to insert into his students' minds little chunks of knowledge. In this way education aims at producing not merely well-informed people but those who can be integrated in the society full of cultural values and true knowledge. This is because, for Whitehead, "education is the acquisition of the art of the utilization of knowledge." Thus,

> What we should aim at producing is men who possess both culture and expert knowledge in some special direction. Their expert knowledge will give them the ground to start from, and their culture will lead them as deep as philosophy and as high as art. We have to remember that the valuable intellectual development is self-development.[41]

Corroborating this point, Martha Roth opines: "The purpose of education is to stimulate and guide self-development" and as such it is vital that "teachers should be alive with thoughts."[42] Confirming this assertion G. Brooks and M. Grennon state:

> Education never starts with a tabula rasa situation. On the contrary, education always has to take into account the developmental stage and individually varying earlier educational processes of the single, unique pupil. It must never be forgotten that education is not a process of packing articles in a trunk. Such simile is entirely inapplicable. It is, of course, a process completely of its own. Education instead has to enhance learning processes that are active processes of integrating new ideas into the already existing, idiosyncratic system of concepts (ideas).[43]

From the above citation, it is evident that education is a process of acquiring knowledge and of assimilating new experiences and thereby a process of reciprocal accommodation of the new impressions and already acquired ideas that build up the existing cognitive system. In this light, Paul E. Johnson defines "knowledge" acquired through education as that inferred capability which makes possible the successful performance of a class of tasks that could not be performed before the learning was undertaken.[44]

The central problem of education, for Whitehead, consists in keeping knowledge alive, preventing it from becoming inert. This depends on four main factors: the genius of the teacher, the intellectual type of the pupils, their prospects in life, the opportunities offered by the immediate surroundings of the school. Teachers should be alive with thoughts. It is not enough to ask students to take knowledge and use it. Teachers should impart information in a way that encourages students to turn what could be (in other hands and circumstances) inert knowledge into active, vibrant, and engaged tools.[45] This awareness on the part of the teacher will facilitate "the evocation of curiosity, of judgment, of the power of mastering a complicated tangle of circumstances, the use of theory in giving foresight in special cases."[46] Without this awareness, the teacher can, without meaning to, pump into the student's mind a certain quantity of inert knowledge. This should be avoided as much as possible if Catholic schools are to live up to the challenge posed by Pope Benedict XVI on passing on genuine knowledge of life to students.

Catholic Education in Contemporary Africa Amidst the Rapid Spread of Secularism

Secularism advocates for the separation of religion from the public life of the state and relegates it to the private life of the individual. One manifestation of secularism is asserting the right to be free from religious rule and teachings or, in a state declared to be neutral on matters of belief, from the imposition by government of religion or religious practices upon its people.[47] Another manifestation of secularism is the view that public activities and decisions, particularly political ones, should be uninfluenced by religious beliefs and/or practices.[48] Secularism then is the doctrine according to which the world is self-explanatory, without any need or recourse to God, who thus becomes superfluous. Secularism can be seen as the situation in which the secular is observed to dominate or even replace the sacred. With secularism, religious faith, for one reason or another, is felt to be unnecessary. It is a state in which organized religion loses its hold both at the level of social institutions and at the level of human consciousness. As such, secularism is a datum of modern society. It is a world view which, in theory and/or practice, denies the immanence of God.[49] Ludwig Feuerbach clearly articulates this position of secularism thus:

> In place of the love of God, we ought to acknowledge the love of man as the only true religion. In place of belief in God, we ought to expand man's belief in himself, in his own strength; the belief that humanity's destiny is dependent not on a being higher than humanity itself, that man's only demon is man himself—the primitive man, superstitious, egoistic evil, but that similarly man's only God is man himself.[50]

This clearly expresses the dream of the Enlightenment with its motto: *sapere aude*—dare to think for yourself. Here there is the explicit rejection of God and anything religious is relegated to the realm of superstition. Yet this is foreign to the traditional African.

The African traditionalist is religious, and all his activities are guided by his religion. African traditional religion, as John Mbiti says, "permeates all the aspects of the departments of life (of an African); there is no formal distinction between the sacred and the secular, between the religious and non-religious, between the spiritual and the material areas of life."[51] Hence Mbiti is right when he says that Africans are deeply religious. Yet colonial rule—with the introduction of Western education and religion (Christianity)—ushered in a crisis of cultural identity and a crisis of religious identity made possible by secularism and secularization. As such, it is true that secularism and modernism have created a crisis of religious identity.[52]

"Africans are notoriously religious."[53] These opening words of John S. Mbiti's classic work *African Religions and Philosophy* are, in the words of S. Aylward and E. Onyancha, "just as notorious as the African religiosity they purport to describe."[54] These words have been universally quoted and they still correspond to most people's idea of the African reality. The picture is one of ancient religious traditions and rituals still vigorously flourishing, of a fanatical Islam dominating huge areas of the African continent, of Christians in their first fervor filling churches to overflowing, of new religious movements proliferating everywhere.[55]

However, it is undeniable that this influence of religion on public life has declined and that modern civilization, governed by economic values, is producing minds closed to transcendent values. This tragic trend which we characterize as secularism constitutes a very serious danger especially to the youths of today, many of whom—either consciously or unconsciously—are to their own peril swallowing up the secular culture in huge gulps.[56] Walter Rodney in his book *How Europe Underdeveloped Africa* opined that Africa's contact with Europe robbed her of great potentials both in human and material resources. This has caused the myriads of developmental challenges and loss of cultural values because colonialism impoverished Africa's cultural values. Frantz Fanon believed that "colonialism was a system of racial oppression, all more insidious, because of its impact as well as physical distortion of attitudes and behavior." More importantly, in pre-colonial Africa, cultural values revolved around the African ideology and concept of God, and this made most of the norms and laws acceptable to the people. In this regard, Benson Igboin explains:

> It is a fact that in African traditional belief, God is the explanation of all things. The world was created by

him. The Africans therefore believe that the environment is knitted to the presence of God. As Mbiti puts it, "God is the explanation of man's origin and sustenance; it is as if God exists for the sake of man."[57] God's agents are charged with the responsibility of maintaining law and order in the society. Thus, both physical and supernatural forces are always present in the administration of the society.[58]

Hence, although laws and norms differ from place to place depending on the people's culture or religion, the people held them important and attended to them in awe, until their contact with foreign cultures, which dispossessed them of their valued system.[59]

Secularism at the Educational level (Case Study: Cameroon)

From the very onset, education in Cameroon was in the hands of the missionaries, who reserved an important place to the study of religion and the cultivation of the fear of God. These missionaries were very conscious of the fact that the quality of the society depended heavily on the quality of education received and that religious principles constituted one of those pillars necessary to direct the operations of society. This was reiterated by the 1963 *West Cameroon Education Policy* in the following words:

> Government believes that education is an investment in human material which can reap rich dividends. No policy for education can be relevant unless it takes into account all the economic, social, political and spiritual factors of our time and circumstances.[60]

The same West Cameroon government recognized and appreciated the role played by religious institutions in education and appreciated the fundamental influence of sound religious training in the formation of character. This is the text in full:

In speaking of the basic aims of education, it should not be overlooked that, in West Cameroon, the educational system has been carried out, with the express wish of the West Cameroon Government, mainly by the religious Voluntary Agencies. The idea has always been to produce an educated person of sound moral and religious background, and government reiterates its wish for the continuation of this end. Government wishes this section in the 1955 policy on education to be repeated—"Government appreciates the fundamental influence of sound religious training in the formation of character, and it is our intention to see that religious instruction takes its rightful place in the curriculum of all schools." In defining the term "religious instruction" Government emphasizes that this does not necessarily mean Christianity. It firmly holds to the belief that education should be open to all, irrespective of race, class, greed, color, or religion (...) In view of the policy to give religious instruction in all schools, the teaching of religion is undertaken in all West Cameroon educational institutions. This is not the case in Government institutions in East Cameroon. Government recommends that when Federal Government educational institutions are introduced in West Cameroon, religious instruction should form a part of the curriculum.[61]

Then came the process of secularization of the schools by which the government decided to take away the control of most schools from the missions, beginning from 1972. In the process of this government takeover of schools, it threw away religious studies and whatever had to do with God. On account of this secular outlook, religious studies was scrapped from the program of studies and various attempts to reinsert it were vehemently rejected by the powers that be. The final report on the National Forum on Education held in Yaoundé in May 1997 reads thus:

The idea of religious education being introduced into Cameroon educational system raised a lot of dust and arguments came up again and again until the closing session. Advocates for this course argued very strongly that with the moral decadence gradually setting into our society, it was imperative to instill in our youths, through religious instruction, the fear of God and love of the good (...). But the chairperson as well as a good number of members of the committee evoked in very strong terms the secular nature of the state which should be applicable to schools.[62]

This attitude of secularizing education started in France in the 19th century. L. Rummel in his article *The Anti-Clerical Programme as a Disruptive Factor in the Solidarity of the Late French Republic* tells us that as far back as 1845, A. Munnier had argued that "since the state is laic, the instruction given in the name of the state ought to be laic."[63] The wind of secularism that has penetrated into the Cameroonian society in the area of education has been blowing from her former colonial master—France.

The effect of this secularization of education is that the dual purpose of education, corresponding to the double role which a person has to play in life, both as an individual and as a member of the society—the development of the whole personality of the individual and his sense of value—are here placed in jeopardy. As far back as 1973, W. Banboye laments in an article *Correct Perspective in Education* about the weakness in Cameroon's educational system:

Thus, the key to our educational system is knowledge and progress. But purposeful education must stretch out beyond the pursuit of mere knowledge and material progress. The sound development of moral character and ethical value does not, in my opinion, receive the due attention it should in our educational system.[64]

This plea of Banboye succinctly expresses the aspirations of any genuine intellectual. Education is not only the acquisition of knowledge. The formation of character is of prime importance and that is one of the primary objectives of religious studies. Proper education should train the head, the hands, and the heart, otherwise we end up producing learned monsters who would lead the human society to ruin.

Conclusion

The African continent is facing a myriad of problems, including high levels of poverty, starvation, wars, human rights abuses, and disregard for human dignity. The main argument in this paper is that a Catholic educational system based on African values, inspired by the spirit of social justice, can be a great means of creating bonds of peace and harmony in society. Such values would enable the continent to achieve reconciliation, justice, peace, and social transformation. The several wars on the continent underscore the need for reconciliation, justice, and peace. Therefore, *Africae Munus* is timely, responding to the needs of those African countries which are emerging from conflicts or still experiencing conflicts. Education, in this case, is seen as a means and process by which human beings ensure the transmission, from generation to generation and from society to society, of what are considered relevant ways and means of knowing and doing at the mental, societal, and material levels. Thus, education not only helps to create culture, or to preserve it, it also helps to change it.[65]

Yet, any meaningful educational system in Africa should aim at making Africans self-reliant. How can we explain the fact that in the 21st century a multitude of Africans are still very poor whereas the continent is very rich in natural and human resources? This to me is partly due to the fact that we still have a dependent mentality that our help must come from "above"—that is, from the West. Catholic education should have a distinctive mark of helping the young to eliminate four mentalities for Africans to become self-reliant: the Colonial mentality, the Tribal mentality, the mentality of Laziness, and the mentality of Sorcery / witchcraft.

Every society functions on the basis of the know-how of its inhabitants. Our knowledge has a variety of sources, values, and functions. But not all forms of knowledge are necessary for development. For instance, development will not be a reality if we possess and cherish knowledge that comes only through popular opinions and gossips, etc. In the same light knowledge that is esoteric and initiative cannot lead to development because it is discriminatory knowledge, the privilege of a few. We are meant to leave and share our existence with others and so esoteric knowledge doesn't help that much. Truth has the character of being universal. Also, we cannot develop if our knowledge is based only on our lived experience. This form of knowledge is very much subjective and relative. This leaves us with rational knowledge, knowledge that flows from the construction of human reason, particularly theoretical and practical reason. This is where modern science comes in. Yet, we must avoid a blind copying and pasting of techno-science from the West.

An Examination of *Africae Munus* in View of the *Tria Munera* of Canon 204 §1

By Rev. Denis Tameh, J.C.D.

Introduction

Africae Munus is a call from the depths of Benedict XVI's heart, for a restoration of a just social order in Africa, based on the foundations of peace, justice, and reconciliation. For that reason, this post-synodal exhortation opens with the Pope's address to the intended target audience. He addresses it to the bishops, clergy, consecrated persons, and lay faithful of the Church in Africa.[1] This means that the Pope envisions a *munus* that involves all of Christ's faithful. But if one were to take a step backwards and reflect, certain questions that are often glossed over start popping up. Who are the *christifideles*? What is the juridic reality that makes the *christifideles* valid recipients of the task of *Africae Munus*? What does the task required of Africa tell us about the nature of this papal magisterial teaching and what obligations does it impose on the faithful? And how can an effective expression of the *tria munera* help restore justice, peace and reconciliation in Africa?

The answers to these questions open before us a canonical vista or a canvas on which to paint the juridic condition of the *christifideles* in the Church as outlined by canon 204 §1, and thus provide a canonical background on which this document can be examined. This canon provides the fodder that *Africae Munus* assumes in obliging the faithful of the Church in Africa to engage in this task of establishing a just social order. This presentation will be divided into three main parts. The first part examines the canonical and ecclesiastical understanding of the *christifideles* as

74

spelled out in c 204 §1; the second part focuses on the juridic implications of the *christifideles* in the Church; and part three examines the implications of this canonical doctrine for the implementation and understanding of *Africae Munus*.

Who are the *Christifideles*?

This is one of the most misunderstood concepts in the Church. C. 204 §1 defines the *christifideles* or the Christian faithful as those who inasmuch as they have been incorporated in Christ through baptism, have been constituted the people of God and made sharers in their own way in Christ's priestly, prophetic, and royal function, the *tria munera*.[2] Therefore, baptism is what distinguishes the Christian faithful from every other person. This is a fundamental distinction which has loaded implications for the functioning of the Church of Christ. The canonist Robert Kaslyn notes the implications of this canon when he concludes that all the baptized constitute the *Christifideles*.[3]

The question which arises from that conclusion is, "who are all the baptized?" Herein emerges an ecclesiological implication of baptism that is not always taken note of. For the baptized involve not only those in full communion with the Catholic Church as stated in c. 205, that is, those who are joined with Christ in the visible structure of the Catholic Church by the bonds of the profession of the faith, the sacraments and ecclesiastical governance; but all those who though not in full communion with the Catholic Church have been baptized and incorporated into the Church of Christ. This would mean that by the word *christifideles*, are all those Christians, Catholic or not, whose baptism is considered valid. As stipulated in c. 869 §2, for such baptisms to be valid, the matter and form must be valid; that is, the use of water and the trinitarian formula; and the consideration of the intention of the baptized and the minister of baptism must be taken into account.[4] John Huels provides a list of those non-Catholic ecclesial communities whose baptisms are recognized as valid by the church.[5] Therefore, when the term *christifideles* is used in the Church as well as in Roman documents of which *Africae Munus* is one, it expresses the universality of the Church of Christ which also includes those who are not in full communion with the Catholic Church.

This means that the invitation given by *Africae Munus* for a Church that speaks and lives justice, peace, and reconciliation is one that is extended not only to Catholics in full communion, but also to our separated brothers and sisters who are incorporated into the Church of Christ by baptism. This reflects Vatican II teaching in *Lumen Gentium* n.15, which is the source of this canon. The distinction between incorporation and membership should always be borne in mind. Incorporation is more of a dynamic term reflecting the ongoing and hopefully deepening relationship between the individual and God and between the individual and the community of faith.[6] Membership involves the visible bonds which ties one to the Catholic Church.

Another important caveat that emerges from the understanding of the *christifideles* is the fundamental notion of the equality of all the baptized as stated in c. 208.[7] This equality arises from baptism and reflects an ecclesiology rooted in the teachings of Vatican II, especially *Lumen Gentium* n. 32. This fundamental equality of all the baptized does not mean an equality of functions. It is an ontological equality rooted in baptism which at the same time does not prevent the various members of the *christifideles* to engage in different functions. This marks a sharp change in the perception of the Church as it was before Vatican II and reflected in the 1917 Code. In the previous code, the Church was perceived as a society of unequals, depending upon whether one had received ordination or not.[8] Canon 107 introduced a subtle canonical distinction between clerics and laity, which reflected the ecclesiology of the age: "By divine institution, there are in the church clergy distinct from laity."[9] The Church was seen as a perfect society with her members divided into two groups: the clerics and the lay faithful, the active and the passive, the teachers and the taught, the pastors and the sheep, those in the hierarchy and those subordinate to them, those who could exercise the power of jurisdiction and those who could not. It was a church that emphasized more the juridical status of cleric and laity than the baptismal status of ontological personhood in the church.[10] As a result, there emerged a truncated view of the *christifideles*, which portrayed the non-ordained in a negative light. This was a mistake corrected by Vatican II, with a fundamental change in perception which reflected its *communio* ecclesiology. It placed participation in the Church not on the juridical distinctions of powers but at the fundamental level of baptism, so that the mission of teaching, governing, and sanctifying of the *christifideles* arises not from a mandate or concession of a competent ecclesiastical authority but from the ontological grounding of baptism.[11]

This participation is not univocal but differs according to each one's condition and function, as per c. 208.[12] What this helps to clarify and emphasize especially in the Church that is in Africa, is the wrong notion that the Church is the hierarchy, while the laity is the passive recipient. With such a prevailing notion, the fruits of *Africae Munus* will never be harvested because majority of the *christifideles* will see the *munus* at hand as the function of the clerics and religious. What *Africae Munus* does is to make practical the theological and canonical doctrine of fundamental equality and active participation in the *tria munera* by entrusting to each according to their functions the task of ensuring that justice, reconciliation, and peace reigns in Africa. That is the presumption behind part two of this document, which proposes what each member of the Church should do to fulfil the task at hand. Seven numbers are dedicated to the duties of the bishop, four to the priest, one to the missionaries, one to the permanent deacons, three to consecrated persons, three to seminarians, two to catechists and three to the lay faithful.[13] This task entrusted to the *christifideles* of Africa raises another important concern on the juridical nature of baptism that enables it to produce such obligations on believers.

The Juridic Effects of Baptism on the *Christifideles*

Baptism is rightly referred to as the portal of all the sacraments. And as a result, it has social or ecclesiastical, individual, and juridic effects. The ecclesiastical or social effect of baptism is the incorporation into the Church of Christ, the establishment of a communion of faith. (It should be noted that when the code and the documents of Vatican II talk of the Church of Christ, they refer not only to the Catholic Church but include all the ecclesial communities whose baptisms are valid).[14] Individually, it establishes a personal sacramental relationship of grace with Christ. However, the main concern here is the juridic effect of baptism. Canon 96 highlights the juridic effects of baptism when it states: "By baptism one is incorporated into the Church of Christ and is constituted a person in it with duties and rights which are proper to Christians in keeping with their condition, insofar as they are in ecclesiastical communion and unless a legitimately issued sanction stands their way." The first and most important juridic condition which arises from baptism is the constitution of the one who is baptized as a person in the Church. And as a person, he or she is invested with rights and obligations. This means, as Orsy notes, that the individual must move from any passive stance to a position of active responsibility.[15] And that is what *Africae Munus* is inviting the African Church to do in combatting the injustices that have ruined and made Africa to be compared to the man beaten and left on the road for death, waiting for a Samaritan to help him—an image which John Paul used in the apostolic exhortation, *Ecclesia in Africa*. However, the Samaritan this time won't come from outside; Africa should be her own Samaritan.

This is possible when the *christifideles* realize and live to the fullest the juridic effect of baptism which imposes obligations and rights on them. As mentioned earlier, one of the individual effects of baptism is a personal relationship with Christ. This also has juridical implications because this personal relationship results in the imposition of obligations of both a spiritual and juridic nature. One through baptism participates in the *tria munera* of Christ: the *munus sanctificandi,* the *munus docendi,* and the *munus regendi.* It is through these *munera* that the obligations of the *christifideles* are lived out. This explains why John Paul II in the apostolic constitution, promulgating the 1983 code, *Sacrae disciplinae leges,* explicitly links the participation of the faithful in the threefold functions of Jesus Christ—priest, prophet, and ruler with the obligations and rights of the faithful.[16] Thus a reading of canon 222 §2 which obliges the Christian faithful to promote social justice and assist the poor from their own resources, would serve as a clear indication of how baptism imposes obligations on the Christian faithful. And in this particular instance, it would serve as a very important canon on which to base the implementation of *Africae Munus* whose clarion call is the establishment of social justice.

Africae Munus a Juridical Obligation?

Because of the juridic reality of baptism which makes Christians persons with rights and obligations in the Church, the challenge given to the African Church becomes not only an apostolic exhortation, but an apostolic obligation rooted in the soil of the *lex ecclesiae.* The use of the Latin *obligatione* in c. 222 §2, suggests very firmly that what the Church is asking must be done.[17] As an obligation, *christifideles* through the *tria munera* which they share by virtue of baptism are called to be agents for the promotion of justice, peace, and reconciliation in the Church and society. One of the greatest temptations one may face is to look at this document as if it were addressed simply to society, *ad extra* and not the Church, *ad intra.* But "if the *munus* of the Church of Africa is to be authentic arbiters of reconciliation, justice, and peace, how can she accomplish this or how can she be the salt of justice and the light of justice if there is within the Church no justice at all? Therefore, the very first *munus* of the Church in my estimation is that she becomes that beacon of justice so that the light of justice from within her can illumine the continent of Africa. And the Church in Africa can become that light when she realizes the full implications of the juridic act of baptism which makes the baptized subjects of rights and obligations within the church."[18]

For the *christifideles* to implement the just social order called for by the exhortation, they first of all have to be just for one cannot give what one does not possess. It is in this light that one has to examine the *tria munera* in the light of justice within the Church. And to do this effectively within the Church, the canonical norms on obligations and rights have to be considered. Principles 6 and 7 of the Code Revision Process capture the importance of rights in the Church as a means of ensuring justice. Principle 6 states: "The use of power in the Church must not be arbitrary, because that is prohibited by natural law, by divine law and by ecclesiastical law. The rights of each one of Christ's faithful must be acknowledged and protected, both those which are contained in natural and divine positive law and those derived from those laws because of the social condition which the faithful acquire and possess in the Church."[19] Principle 7 stipulates that the principle must be proclaimed in canon law that juridical protection applies equally to superiors and to subjects so that any suspicion of arbitrariness in ecclesiastical administration will entirely disappear. This end can only be achieved by avenues of recourse wisely provided by the law which allows a person who thinks his or her rights were violated at a lower level to have them effectively restored at a higher level.[20] In the mind of the Church, justice must be felt at all levels and structures. Rights must be vindicated, and the Church has to be seen as the protector and guarantor of rights for her members.[21] When the *christifideles* exercise their shared mission, it has to be within the confines of justice which respects the rights of each and everyone.

The Munus Regendi
(Office of Governance in the Church)

Since this lecture is not dealing with the nature of authority in the Church, only the pertinent issues relating to justice, reconciliation, and peace with respect to governance will be examined. The power of governance in the Church as stipulated in c. 129 is exercised by those in sacred orders. They are the *habiles* of the power of jurisdiction. However, given the ambivalence of this canon, which also stipulates that the lay faithful can cooperate in the exercise of this same power, the juridical reality is different. For the power of governance is exercised in three ways in the Church: executive, legislative and judicial. The lay faithful hold offices in the Church which suggests that they too participate in the power of governance. (Finance officers c. 494; lay faithful in charge of a parish, c.517 §2, judge 1421 §2).

The *christifideles* sharing in the *munus regendi* of Christ have to ensure that justice is served. And that is the principle on which canon law is built. Effective governance in the Church must be rooted in justice. For one of the reasons for the existence of penalties in the code is the restoration of justice.[22] Because of this principle of justice in the code, it becomes clear why c. 221 is important. For it requires the protection and vindication of rights of all the *christifideles*. Therefore, the Christian faithful have rights to form associations of the faithful c. 215 in order to foster a more perfect life, promote public worship, Christian doctrine, exercise works of the apostolate and piety c. 298. They have a right not be dismissed from an association except for a just cause c. 308; they have a right to enjoy the presence of the pastor in the parish c. 529. Thus, a pastor who is never present in the parish acts unjustly and injures the faithful by depriving them of what is their right; or when the temporal goods of the Church are mismanaged c. 1284, the faithful are deprived of what is due to them. To be authentic messengers of the gospel of *Africae Munus*, the exercise of the *munus regendi* in the Church must be rooted in justice so that the Church preaches what she practices in governance.

Munus Sanctificandi

Book IV of the code deals with the sanctifying action of the Church. As outlined above, baptism guarantees a share in the sanctifying function of Christ. And the canonical expression of this sacramental reality is found in Book IV of the code. Concerning the principle of justice and rights in the code, two canons in book two lay a proper foundation. C. 213 states that the *christifideles* have the right to receive assistance from the sacred pastors out of the spiritual goods of the Church, especially the Word of God and the Sacraments. While canon 210 requires that *christifideles* direct their efforts to lead holy lives and to promote the growth of the Church and its continual sanctification. Thus, a deliberate failure on the part of the pastor to nourish the faithful with the Word and the Sacraments is an injustice and a violation of the rights of the faithful who are entitled by law to it. This implies, as Sarath Chandra points out, that the faithful have a right to the official liturgy of the Church, a right to proper liturgical observances and discipline (c. 846), a right to careful celebration of the sacramentals (c. 1167), a right to a properly celebrated funeral (c.1176), and an explicit right to the sacraments to any baptized person not prohibited by law (c. 912).[23] A failure to celebrate the Mass with dignity becomes an injustice to *christifideles*. The just spiritual order of the Church has to be maintained and taken into consideration as well.

The Munus Docendi

The teaching office of the Church which is given juridical expression in Book III of the code, offers *christifideles* another avenue to ensure that their mission in the Church is fulfilled. One of the fundamental rights in the Church is expressed in canon 211 and states that all Christian faithful have a duty and right to work so that the divine message of salvation reaches more and more people in every age and in every land. Canons 217, 218 corroborate this when they demand a right to a Christian education for all the faithful. Furthermore, the Christian faithful have a right to receive preaching from ordained ministers (c. 757, 762). A failure to prepare a homily becomes an injustice to the *christifideles* who by law are entitled to receive preaching from the minister. For the canon explicitly states that the faithful have the *omnino fas est* to require preaching. An expression which in law signifies an obligation.[24] Again, to intentionally teach false doctrine or a heresy is an injustice to the faithful who have the right to be taught the faith of the church. Furthermore, to send a bad priest to a parish (in cases of punitive transfers) is a form of injustice because the *christifideles* of the parish have a right to a good teacher of the faith according to c. 804.

What does examining the above *tria munera* mean to the nature of *Africae Munus*? A Church that lives out her baptismal mission becomes a Church that will effectively understand the mission of *Africae Munus*, which is a call to return to justice.

Conclusion

The task entrusted to the Church of Africa requires the active participation of all the Christian faithful. *Christifideles*, as demonstrated by this lecture, involve not only those in full communion with the Catholic Church but those also who by baptism have been incorporated into the Church of Christ in accordance with canon 96. By virtue of that baptism, *Christifideles* share in the *tria munera* of Christ. And it is through this *tria munera* that they effectively implement the vision of justice, peace, and reconciliation which Benedict XVI called for in *Africae Munus*. But for this to happen effectively, there has to be a critical self-examination on the part of the Church to see that she is, first of all a beacon of justice *ad intra*. And that is the blessing of *Africae Munus*, for it compels the Church to look within first before looking at justice *ad extra*. Only a just Church can effectively commit to a just social order. And a just Church is that in which the faithful live out the *tria munera* to its fullest. Only then can the Church have the moral grounds to challenge society to embrace the vision of justice, peace, and reconciliation which this document prescribes.

Ratzingerian Hermeneutics of Scripture and Eucharist Considering *Africae Munus* 39 – 41

By Maurice Agbaw-Ebai, S.T.D. Ph.D., Ed.C.

Introduction

In *Africae Munus* (AM) numbers 39–41, Benedict XVI presents the relationship between Eucharist and Scripture from the perspective of mutual enrichment. Benedict writes that "The Eucharist opens us to an understanding of Scripture, just as Scripture for its part illumines and explains the mystery of the Eucharist."[1] This lecture seeks, in its broader framework, to explore the Ratzingerian leitmotifs regarding Scripture and Eucharist in terms of the particularities that a Ratzingerian reading of the former and the latter can bring to the apprehension and engagement with the overarching theme of *Africae Munus*, namely, the Church in Africa in service to reconciliation, justice, and peace. The central nexus of this lecture is this: understanding the Ratzingerian idiosyncrasies in terms of Scripture and Eucharist can bring about a more profound and an enriching reading of *Africae Munus* and the subsequent call to action that Benedict XVI envisages for the Church in Africa. However, to understand Ratzinger context is crucial, which amounts to two essential factors—namely, Ratzinger's Theological Framework, on the one hand, and Ratzinger's Interlocutors, on the other hand.

Ratzinger's Theological Framework

There are two aspects that characterize understanding Ratzinger on Scripture and Eucharist, and the wider Ratzingerian corpus:

The *Ressourcement* Movement

The aftermath of the Second World War brought about a situation in Europe that posed a profound challenge to faith, particularly the Christian faith. Europe, an old Christian continent, found itself in the middle of another war. Largely Christian nations fought against each other. The old continent was devasted. A sense of hopelessness enveloped Europe. Following the devastation left by World War II, Ratzinger and his seminary confrères felt that the status quo especially regarding the faith and the place of the Church in a post-war Europe was not sufficient to meet the challenges of the hour. New questions had picked up greater intensity: Who is the human being? (Hobbesian? Marxist? Hegelian? Nietzschean?) What is the meaning of life? What does it mean to be a Christian? Who is God and what is the place of God in human affairs, if any? These questions, and more, led Ratzinger to view the mode of Neo-Thomism then dominant in European seminaries and theology faculties as insufficient to speak to the concerns of post-war Europeans, the conclusion that the scholastic medieval mode of theologizing was insufficient.

In effect, much more was needed than the clear-cut and ready-made answers that had come to define Neo-Thomism. Later on, as a young theologian following the conclusion of the Second Vatican Council, as they sought for answers to the challenging times, together with Congar, De Lubac, Balthasar and others, Ratzinger felt that turning to the sources of Christian thought could provide new opportunities for faith seeking understanding in the historical context of growing secularism, communal and personal alienation and loneliness, and a growing feeling of nothingness or emptiness, which the Church was not challenged to face and provide spiritual support. In effect, the spiritual energies that had to be unleashed from the Church to the world through evangelization, meant that the Church, by a process of ecclesiastical soul-searching, must draw from the storeroom of her riches. The thought or teachings of the Fathers, the Church's Doctors, and medieval thinkers proved indispensable in this effort. Hence, *ressourcement*, the return to the sources, became the theological methodology for Ratzinger and his cousinship of minds and hearts.

The establishment of the journal, *Communio*, was the decisive effort to standardized this hermeneutical framework of *ressourcement*, out of which the dominant ecclesial model of Vatican II, in the reading of Ratzinger and his theological like minds, was Church as communion. Ratzinger himself explains the contours of this movement, thus:

> The movement toward renewal, which has been observable in the field of Catholic theology since the end of World War I, understood itself basically as ressourcement, as a return to sources that were no longer to be seen through the eyes of Scholastic philosophy but were to be read in themselves, in their own original form and breadth. Granted, the sources that were to be discovered anew flowed first and above all in Holy Scripture; but the search for a new way in which theology could assimilate what was said in the Scriptures and realize it in the Church led of its own accord to the Fathers, to the era of the early Church, in which the waters of faith still flowed unpolluted and in all their freshness.[2]

The return to the sources of Christian faith in order to draw energy for the reform of the present as the defining principle of the *Ressourcement* movement, therefore, was, in a sense, a double dynamic reality, namely, the dynamism of the Fathers, on the one hand, and intrinsically related to that, the dynamism of Scripture, on the other hand. As Ratzinger puts it, thinkers like Hugo Rahner and De Lubac were close to the Scriptures because they were close to the Fathers.[3] To the Fathers, Scripture was not a scientific puzzle to be resolved. This is not to say that the Fathers did not foster a rigorous and scientific engagement with Scripture. One simply has to think of Origen, Jerome, Ambrose, Augustine—to cite but a few, to be struck by the scientific rigor with which the Fathers engaged Scripture. But the overarching trend which they sought to espouse was the living relationship between Scripture as the written Word of God, and Christian living. In effect, the Fathers did not approach Scripture as a complex text with an inaccessible message that could only be apprehended by subjecting Scripture to dictates of scientific positivism. On the contrary, to the Fathers, Scripture was precisely what the name entailed, that is, the Word of God, written, as Scripture itself states, for useful teaching, refutation, correction, and training in righteousness, so that the one who belongs to God be equipped for every good work (2 Tim. 3:16).

Thus, one clearly notices a very loving relationship between the Fathers and Scripture. Take Augustine of Hippo, for example. In the *Doctrina Christiana*, Augustine spells out the principles for the rightful interpretation of Scripture. One might classify that as the theoretical phase. But in *The Confessions*, we meet the flesh and blood Augustine on his knees in prayer, who speaks to God in praise, on the one hand, and, on the other hand, God, Almighty, speaking or responding to Augustine in the words of Scripture. Even the dramatic narrative of Augustine's conversion is rooted in Scripture.[4] Hence, *The Confessions* is not a monologue but a dialogue between Augustine and God, and Scripture plays a crucial role in this dialogue.

Benedict XVI characterizes this living sense of Scripture that one finds in the Fathers as one of approaching Scripture with a hermeneutic of faith, which he sees as a necessary complement to the gains of the historical-critical method. If the latter had to be useful to the study of Scripture, it could not assert itself as the only hermeneutical framework worthy of engaging Scripture from the world of the concerns of men and women today. Given the limits of the historical-critical method, as Ratzinger pointedly observes in the Foreword to Volume I of his trilogy on Jesus, it must be in the nature of the historical-critical method to point beyond itself, for we cannot bring the past into the present. As Ratzinger elsewhere explains:

The historico-critical method is essentially a tool, and its usefulness depends on the way in which it is used, i.e., on the hermeneutical and philosophical presuppositions one adopts in applying it. In fact, there is no such thing as a pure historical method; it is always carried on in a hermeneutical or philosophical context, even when people are not aware of it or expressly deny it. The difficulties which faith continually experiences today in the face of critical exegesis do not stem from the historical or critical factors as such but from the latent philosophy which is at work. The argument, therefore, must relate to this underlying philosophy; it must not attempt to bring historical thought as such under suspicion.[5]

In effect, the historical-critical method is a neutral instrument. Rather, it is guided by a certain philosophical presupposition that is typical of the scientific positivism that marked the Enlightenment movement, whose dominant trend was the correction of religious dogmas by reason. For this to happen, the Jesus of history had to be placed against the Christ of faith, casting a dubium about the historical accuracy that hitherto defined the figure of the Jesus of history who is likewise the Christ of faith.

One can thus understand Ratzinger's insistence that the historical-critical method open itself to other complementary methods, and to Ratzinger, the hermeneutic of faith, for example, could be a necessary enrichment to the historical-critical method. And the Fathers demonstrate this unity of living faith and the Scriptures, even for us today—a quality that marks Ratzinger's theology as well, according to his own estimation.[6] In effect, to engage Benedict XVI's treatment of Scripture in AM is to allow oneself to be drawn into the wide ocean of Christian sources as captured in the twin realities of the Fathers and their faith-hermeneutic engagement with Scripture. And what we say about Ratzinger, the Fathers, and Scripture, we can likewise say about the Eucharist, for both Scripture and the Fathers remain as the authentic guarantors of what St. Paul aptly described as that which he had received from the Lord which he was now transmitting to the Church in Corinth (1 Cor. 11:23–26). This apostolic teaching, testified to by Scripture and guarded and transmitted in the living tradition of the Church, has never escaped the attention and devotion of the Fathers. One readily thinks of Justin the Martyr, Cyprian, Ignatius of Antioch, Augustine, Ambrose, etc., and their rich catecheses on the Eucharist. In a word, to understand Ratzinger on Scripture and Eucharist is to read him from the womb of the *Ressourcement* movement.

Ratzingerian Interlocutors

In addition, a more profound comprehension of Ratzinger demands an intellectual attentiveness to his interlocutors. In other words, who is Ratzinger talking with? His theology must always be read from a contextual perspective, even if he is always open to the universal. In this light, one must ask the question: Why is Ratzinger saying what he is saying about the Scriptures and the Eucharist? Why the insistence on the hermeneutics of faith as a legitimate method for the interpretation of Scripture? Why the insistence on the Eucharist as a sacrament of communion? Why is the theology of the cross fundamental to understanding Eucharistic theology? And many more. From this perspective, it is obvious to see the necessity of understanding Kant, Hegel, Leibniz, Hume, Luther and others, as necessary interlocutors who provide a comprehensive and meaningful framework for understanding Ratzinger on Scripture and Eucharist.

Ratzinger on the Eucharist

Following the *Ressourcement* framework, Ratzinger's encounter with Augustine led him to develop a Eucharistic ecclesiology. As Pope, he penned *Sacramentum Caritatis*, which emphasized the intrinsic link between the Eucharist and the Church: the Eucharist builds up the Church and the Church makes the Eucharist.[7] In *Deus Caritas Est*, Benedict XVI taught that agape is another name for Eucharist and that in the Eucharist, "God's own agape comes to us bodily, in order to continue his work in us and through us

(...) A Eucharist that does not pass over into the concrete practice of love is intrinsically fragmented."[8] In AM 39–40, in talking about Scripture and the Eucharist, Benedict XVI underscores the intrinsic interconnectedness between Eucharist, communion, and cultures: "Men and women," Benedict XVI writes, "in the variety of their origins, cultures, languages and religions, are capable of living together in harmony."[9] God has pitched His tent amongst us and daily gives himself to us in the Eucharist.[10] The Eucharist has the force to bring together the scattered children of God and maintain communion between them (AM, 41). The Eucharist, flowing from its *communio* dimension, has great potential for social transformation and action.[11]

In Africa, for example, the challenge for Eucharistic theology, at least according to the mind of Benedict XVI, is the promotion of justice, peace, and reconciliation in a continent that has seen and continues to see tribal and national conflicts. What does it mean to celebrate the Eucharist in the context of the Rwandan genocide, the onslaught of the Boko Haram militant Islam in Nigeria, Cameroon, Chad, and the Central African Republic? What hope does the celebration of the Eucharist bring to the many women who are daily raped in the North Kivu region of the Democratic Republic of Congo? What does the Eucharist mean for Christians in Somalia? To live out the theology of Eucharistic *Caritas* in these contexts poses huge challenges for theological reflections and pastoral practice. Given these Benedictine insights and propositions in AM, what might constitute the Ratzingerian acumens that might further develop or flesh out AM?

Eucharistomen

To Ratzinger, understanding the meaning and nature of the Eucharist is derivable from the very terminology of the word. In his ex tempore remarks marking the 65th anniversary of his priestly ordination, Ratzinger pointed out *Eucharistomen*, thanksgiving, is the defining quality of understanding the Eucharist. Thanksgiving is both vertical and horizontal, both anabatic and katabatic. In the

Eucharist, therefore, we stand before God in thanksgiving in a Christological sense that is profoundly cosmic and also personal. This Christological personalism is on full display at the words of consecration: "**He took bread, and gave thanks.**" It is Christological in that only by entering the word uttered by Christ, can these words be true and fruitful. We are not to invent any word but must allow ourselves to be drawn into the words spoken by the Word of God. Any other word would amount to a false simulation, an empty chatter that is meaningless. It is personal because the word uttered is not extrinsic, not superficial, but takes the core of my being and transforms it into the image and likeness of God as revealed in Jesus Christ. It is personal because my "I" matters, for only if my "I" is truly something and someone can it be capable of being taking over by the "I" of God. And the response to this wonderful exchange between my subjective "I" and the "I" of God is thanksgiving, gratitude, *Eucharistomen*. I am grateful for the new that has come about in me and for me. Gratitude marks the life of the Christian, who is the priest of all creation. Gratitude to God for the gift of the new creation that I become because I am taken into the redemptive work of Christ (2 Cor. 5:17). In the final analysis, the Eucharist points to our dependency on God, so much so that we recognize that God is everything, and we are nothing, for cut off from God we can do nothing.

Transubstantiation of Substance and the Human Being

St. Augustine made this observation in the *Confessions*: "Eat the bread of the strong, and yet you will not change me into yourself; rather, I will transform you into me."[12] When we eat ordinary food, we assimilate the nutrients and, in a sense, the food is converted into us and disappears into our biological reality. But the reverse happens with the Eucharist: We disappear into Christ, who transforms the reality of our being into a new reality in his being. Ratzinger explains Augustine: "Normal food is less strong than man, it serves him and is taken into man's body to be assimilated and to build it up. But this special food, the Eucharist, is above man and stronger than man. Consequently, the whole process involved is reversed: the man who eats this bread is assimilated *by* it, taken into it; he is fused into this bread and becomes bread, like Christ himself."[13] This, in a sense, is the essence of Eucharistic fruitfulness, namely, that I become a new creature in Christ, something different, growing up into adulthood in Christ (Col. 2:7). The difficulty with this resides at the level of consciousness: How conscious are we that we are becoming something new and different at every Eucharistic celebration? And the question of consciousness points to the question of fruitfulness, for if I am unconscious of the working of sacramental grace in me, it would likely be the case that the fruitfulness that should come from celebrating the Eucharist might remain a distant reality.

Owing to this spiritual transformation by Christ of the recipient of the Eucharist, the communicant is joined to other communicants, even if one does not readily like the other: "When I am united with Christ, I am also united with my neighbor, (…), in the everyday experiences of being with others and standing by others."[14] This gives the Eucharist a social dimension, for by becoming one with the other, I get involved in their life situations, in their *Weltanschauung*, thereby validating my love for Jesus Christ. Ratzinger writes:

> Though many, we are one body, for we are one bread. The result of this insight is quite clear: Eucharist is never merely an event *à deux*, a dialogue between Christ and me. The goal of eucharistic communion is a total recasting of a person's life, breaking up a man's whole "I" and creating a new "We." Communion with Christ is of necessity a communication with all those who are his: it means that I myself become part of this new "bread" which he creates by transubstantiating all earthly reality.[15]

Herein is articulated the socio-anthropological consequence of the Eucharist, namely, the transubstantiation of the world. Just as there is a transubstantiation of the bread and wine into the body and blood of Christ, so it is as well with the recipient of the Eucharist. He or she becomes transubstantiated into Christ, putting on Christ (Rom 13:14). Eventually, this personal Christification—"I live no longer I, but Christ lives in me" (Gal 2:20), results in a Christification of the world. It is very telling that the great socially committed saints such as Martin de Porres, Teresa of Calcutta, John of God, were great Eucharistic saints as well. It is therefore not the case that a focus on the Eucharist detracts from attentiveness to the neighbor. The dialectical materialism of Marx misses the essential connection between Eucharist and social action or advocacy for the poor, that Benedict XVI so fittingly captured in *Deus Caritas Est*—a message that continues to be more than timely for the Church in Africa today.

In the mystery of the Bread and Wine, we encounter the true presence of the Incarnate Son of God. There is a Transubstantiation of the Substances, as dogmatically explained by the Council of Trent and reaffirmed down the ages by Popes, Doctors, and Saints. But there is a second Transubstantiation, namely, of the person: As I draw life from the Father, so whoever eats of my flesh draws life from me (John 6:57). The transubstantiated substances bring about transubstantiated persons. On thinks here of the result of the four loves of Bernard of Clairvaux: of the self; of God and of the self; of God; and of the self for the sake of God, in which self-knowledge and self-consciousness is transformed so much so that a new person emerges. Eventually, the transubstantiation of the self brings about the transubstantiation of the world in which we live, from a valley of dry bones to a garden of faith, hope, and love. Here again, we find the connection between Eucharist and social transformation and advocacy.

Beauty and the Eucharistic Mystery

From his Bavarian background, Ratzinger encountered and was thrilled by liturgical beauty, of the change of seasons, of the solemnities and feasts of the faith, of the gothic architecture that marked Bavarian churches. Theological studies will then become for Ratzinger, an opportunity to make the beauty of God more accessible and encountered by the contemporary world, especially through the art, music, and architecture of the Church. In a sense, the question of beauty, art, and music points to something deeper, namely, the search for God—the *Quaerere Deum*, which was the overarching desire or goal of St. Benedict and the monastic tradition that he molded. The external beauty that the Christian meets in the liturgy and the Church's works of art are pointers to the beauty of encountering God, and the work of the theologian is to make this beauty of art and music a step towards encountering the beauty of God. Ratzinger gives an apologetic status to the value of beauty to the theological enterprise and the life of the Church:

> I have often said that I am convinced that the true apologetics for the Christian message, the most persuasive proof of its truth, offsetting everything that may appear negative, are the saints, on the one hand, and the beauty that the faith has generated, on the other. For faith to grow today, we must lead ourselves and the persons we meet to encounter the saints and to come in contact with the beautiful.[16]

To Ratzinger, the theologian can never avoid the question of beauty of art, music, and the liturgy, for those are the primary areas of engagement between God and the believer. He emphatically remarked:

> The complete absence of images is incompatible with faith in the Incarnation of God. God has acted in history and entered into our sensible world, so that it may become transparent to him. Images of beauty, in which the mystery of the invisible God becomes visible, are an essential part of Christian worship. Iconoclasm is not a Christian option.[17]

94

This implies that physicality is a fundamental part of encountering the spiritual beauty of God. From the visible, the believer moves to the invisible and is caught up into an ecstasy of joy and delight. One discerns here a relationship between sacramental realism that is encountered in our bodylines as humans, and Christian spirituality. As Ratzinger maintains:

> The body is not something external to the spirit, it is the latter's self-expression, its "image." The constituents of biological life are also constitutive of the human person. The person exercises personhood in the body, and the body is thus the mode of expression; the invisible presence of the spirit can be discerned in it. Since the body is the visible form of the person, and the person is the image of God, it follows that the body, in its whole context of relationships, is the place where the divine is portrayed, uttered and rendered accessible to our gaze.[18]

And in another text, Ratzinger further explains Christian sacramental spirituality thus: Man needs to see, he needs this kind of silent beholding which becomes a touching, if he is to become aware of the mysteries of God. "He must set his foot on the 'ladder' of the body in order to climb it and so find the path along which faith invites him."[19] In effect, Christian spirituality is sacramental, to the extent that the artifacts of nature or creation can open us up to God. The challenge is to allow the beauty of nature to lead us to the God of beauty, for only in encountering the God of beauty can we get to the core of the beauty of nature. To end at the level of physical beauty would amount to a superficial experience of beauty. As Ratzinger again explains:

> The things of earth are not final and decisive. We hardly dare to say it any more, because people accuse us Christians of not having bothered about earthly matters, of having failed to build the new city in the world because

we could always take refuge in the other world. But it is not true. The man who clasps the earth fast, who regards the earth as the only possible heaven, actually makes a hell of it, for he is trying to make it into something it cannot be. In trying to make it ultimate, he is setting himself against himself, against truth and against his fellowmen. No; it is only when we realize that we are wanderers that we become free from ultimate covetousness, free for one another. Only then can we be entrusted with the responsibility of fashioning the earth in such a way that, in the end, we shall be able to place it in God's hands.[20]

In effect, the beauty of the earth and of creation becomes life-giving to the extent that God is at the center. To set God aside or in opposition to the beauty of the natural order does not result in freedom, but in enslavements of varied kinds. But once God is at the center, the true radiance of beauty shines out for all to see, and even the human being encounters beauty as liberation and ecstasy. The cry of joy of Augustine, his theological master, must certainty have resonated with Ratzinger:

> Late have I loved you, O beauty, so ancient and so new, late have I loved you. And see, you were within, and I was in the external world and sought you there, and in my unlovely state I plunged into those lovely, created things that you made. You were with me, and I was not with you. The lovely things kept me far from you, though if they did not have their existence in you, they had no existence at all.[21]

Again, we see the Augustinian-Ratzingerian leitmotif: If natural beauty is not rooted in God, it loses its efficacy and becomes rather an idol that is dull and boring. Obviously, then, beauty for Ratzinger is not mere aestheticism. It is essentially centered on the figure of Christ, with the dominant icon being the suffering face of Christ, the Suffering Servant of Isaiah, "He had neither beauty nor majesty, nothing to attract our eyes" (Is. 53:2). It is in the disfigured Face of the Suffering Servant that one finds the ultimate beauty, the beauty of love that goes to the very end, proving mightier than falsehood and violence.[22] This gives the Ratzingerian understanding of beauty a very Christological coloring. In the final analysis, if Ratzinger is concerned about theological aesthetics, it is because he sees the truly beautiful as the encounter with Christ who loves and suffers, and by so doing, saves the world. This is the sense in which one can say, perhaps with a Balthazarian tone, that beauty saves the world.

Eucharist, Priest, and Victim

Ratzinger shows particular interest in the action in which the priest offers his voice and his actions to Christ, acting *in persona Christi capitis*, at the most solemn moment of consecration. ***This is my Body which is given up for you****! Central to understanding this exchange stands the theology of the Cross. It is the self-immolation of the priest himself as well, a most profound radical identification between priest and the Crucified Lord. In the thought of the Fathers, especially of the East, the moment of the institutional narrative marks the moment of bloodless immolation, in which flesh and blood are torn apart. The Cross, therefore, is never missing in the life of the priest. There is an intrinsic relationship between the Eucharist, the Cross of Christ, and the priest who acts *in persona Christi capitis* in the celebration of the Eucharist. Benedict XVI writes in *Sacramentum Caritatis*, that "the intrinsic relationship between the Eucharist and the sacrament of Holy Orders clearly emerges from Jesus' own words in the Upper Room: 'Do this in memory of me' (Lk 22:19)". On the night before he died, Jesus instituted the Eucharist and at the same time established the priesthood of the New Covenant. He is priest, victim, and altar: the mediator between God the Father and his people (cf Heb 5:5–10), the victim of atonement (cf 1 Jn 2:2, 4:10) who offers himself on the altar of the Cross.[23] The celebration *in* *persona Christi capitis* places the priest in the very being and existence of Christ, and only in this Christ-like mode of being can the true fruitfulness of the words of consecration come alive and find their meaning and efficacy. As Ratzinger further clarifies:

> "This is my Body" is what is said now, today. But these words are the words of Jesus Christ. No man can pronounce them for himself. No one can, for his own part, declare his body to be the Body of Christ, speaking in the first person, the "I" of Jesus Christ. This saying in the first person—"my body"—only he himself can say. If anyone were to dare to say, on his own behalf, that he saw himself as the self of Christ, this would surely be blasphemy. No one can endow himself with such authority; no one else can give it to him; no congregation or community can give it to him. It can only be the gift of the Church as a whole, the one whole Church, to whom the Lord has communicated himself.[24]

Along this Ratzingerian line of thinking, it is therefore the case that at the center of the sacred power of consecration is the reality of a gift and a personal invitation from Christ to the priest-celebrant, who is called to enter into the very personhood of Christ. This appears to be the most challenging liturgical moment or action, for clearly, to enter into the priest and victimhood of Christ when the priest-celebrant speaks the words "This *is* my Body," cannot be any other thing than the self-gifting and self-offering that defined the historical action of the institution of the mystery of the most holy Eucharist in the Upper Room in Jerusalem. In effect, Holy Thursday, the day of the Eucharist, if it is to be fully understood and made fruitful, cannot be severed from Good Friday. Christ not only gives us his body. He likewise gives us his Cross. Like Christ, the priest who celebrates the Eucharist enters into that mystery of the Lord's Cross. And yet like Christ, the priest is called to offer himself daily, to give himself up, for the salvation of the world, bearing everything with patience, with the consciousness, as Benedict XVI said in the homily inaugurating his Pontificate in April 2005, that it is God's patience that saves the world, and that the world is saved by the patience of God and destroyed by the impatience of men and women.

Eucharist and Easter: Word, Death, and Resurrection

To Ratzinger, though the institutional narrative of the death of the God-Man are pivotal to the institution of the Eucharist, the words of institution and the death of Christ alone are not sufficient to bring about the Eucharist. The Eucharist is not borne from the Cross alone. The Eucharist flows out from both Cross and the Empty Tomb, for it is only with the resurrection that we find the Father's acceptance of the death of His Son. The resurrection is the Father's transforming the death of Jesus, an otherwise painful end and failure, into the door for new life. As Ratzinger explains, it is "out of this whole matrix—that he transforms his death, that irrational event, into an affirmation, into an act of love and of adoration."[25] It is only because of the conquering of death by the Father's action on Jesus that the Eucharist too is able to become a source of life for all. Without the resurrection, the Eucharist would have been a meal that immortalized a preceding death. But with the resurrection, everything changes. The new life of the resurrection becomes the new life of the Eucharist. As Ratzinger puts it, "out of such a death springs this sacrament, the Eucharist."[26] In a continent scarred by so many wounds of violence, war, and dehumanizing events, the understanding of the Eucharist as the source of new life clearly holds out hope for the continent of Africa, hope for a new life of justice, a new life of peace, and a new life of reconciliation.

Eucharist, Ecclesial Identity, and Mission in the Church

Another significant aspect of Eucharistic ecclesiology is that of the intrinsic unity of the Church. As Ratzinger says, "the Church does not arise from a loose federation of communities. She originates in the one bread, in the one Lord, and thanks to him she is first and foremost and everywhere the one and only Church, the one body that comes from the one bread."[27] Precisely because she emanates from the one bread of Christ, the unity of the Church transcends any human inventiveness.

A further noteworthy aspect of Eucharistic ecclesiology is the transformative potential that the Eucharist could unleash in the Church. **Ratzinger points out five transformations that come about with the Eucharist:** the bread of earth becomes the bread of God; secondly, through Jesus' act of self-giving love, the violence of death, of the act of killing, is transformed and conquered by love; thirdly, by partaking in the one bread and one cup, men and women are transformed by Christ's life-giving spirit (1 Cor. 15:45), in the sense that bodily existence and self-giving are no longer mutually exclusive but complementary. To live is to be a self-gift. Fourthly, these transformed men and women become united in the new life of the resurrection; and finally, through these new united persons, all of creation must be transformed, become new, "that God may be everything to everyone" (1 Cor. 15:28), hence the missionary dimension of Eucharistic transformation.[28] In a word, the Eucharist is an ongoing process of transformation, from what we are to what we are called to be in Christ, in the mystical body of the Church.

In all, the insights briefly covered above that shed some light on Ratzinger's rich Eucharistic theology are certainly not meant to be exhaustive. In all, they are meant to provide a context from which one could engage Ratzinger's treatment of the Eucharist in AM. What stands out from this rich fabric is the attentiveness that Ratzinger gives to this greatest gift of Christ to the Church, the Eucharist as the source and summit of the Church's life, as the Second Vatican Council rightly taught. Perhaps the more the Church in Africa allows itself to be caught up in the fruitfulness of Eucharistic amazement, the more she will be able to usher in a new era of justice, peace, and reconciliation that is called for by Benedict XVI in AM.

Ratzinger on Scripture

For Ratzinger, it is within the living faith of the Church that the Scripture becomes accessible, as already demonstrated by the example of the Fathers pointed out above. *Sola scriptura*, therefore, cannot be a meaningful option, for "resorting to the Bible in isolation as a mere historical document does not sufficiently communicate to us an insight into what is essential."[29] It is within the living context of the Church, wherein Scripture is understood and lived, that one can gain a meaningful understanding of Scripture. Ratzinger's approach to Scripture is therefore ecclesio-centric, with the Church as hermeneutical locus of Scripture.

Ratzinger, Scripture, and Revelation

What is typical about Ratzinger in relation to Scripture boils down to his understanding of Scripture via-a-vis the question of Revelation. Typically, Scripture, understood as the word of God, is construed to constitute Revelation. But things are quite different for Ratzinger. To him, Scripture, understood from his post-doctoral study of Bonaventure, is a witness to revelation but not Revelation itself. One can read the Scripture without experiencing the supernatural. The Bible can be read and has been read as a literary text by many. To Ratzinger, the Bible is a testament to revelation because Revelation is God's self-disclosure of God's self to human beings. God is the sole source of Revelation. The Bible is an account of God's revelation, first to Israel, and then, through the saving work of Christ, to the nations. Ratzinger explains:

> For revelation signifies all God's acts and utterances directed to man; it signifies a *reality* of which Scripture gives us *information* but that *is* not simply Scripture itself. Revelation goes beyond Scripture, then, to the same extent as reality goes beyond information about it. We could also say that Scripture is the material principle of revelation (perhaps the only one, perhaps one

of a number—we may leave that point open for the moment) but is not that Revelation itself.[30]

At the core of Ratzinger's theology of Scripture and Revelation resides the conviction that Scripture is information about Revelation, but cannot be identified with Revelation per se. In God's Word Ratzinger offers a clarifying and informative footnote in terms of just what he means when he asserts that Scripture as the written word is information about Revelation. As if to mitigate against any tendency at trivializing Scripture because one could no longer identify it with Revelation per se, Ratzinger says:

> This statement (that Scripture gives us information about Revelation but is not Revelation itself), is not intended to mean that Scripture is merely an account, without any substance, of facts that remain entirely outside of it. Rather (as, hopefully, what follows will show), the view that the reality of Revelation is a reality of the word—that in the word, the proclamation of the reality of Revelation comes to me—should remain fully valid. It nonetheless remains true that the mere word before us, available to us, is not yet itself the reality of Revelation, which is never just "available" to us. What is said here is simply intended to point to the difference between the word and the reality that occurs within it, a difference by the nature of Revelation as word.[31]

In effect, Ratzinger's intention is not to reduce the grandeur of Scripture as the written word of God, but to point to that which make Scripture come alive, namely, faith—living faith. Once faith is missing, there emerges the real possibility of having Scripture without having Revelation, for Scripture ceases to speak to the heart as the word of God. Without faith which makes Revelation come alive, Scripture easily becomes a dead letter.

As Ratzinger makes clear, the unbeliever "can read Scripture and know what is in it, can even understand at a purely intellectual level, what is meant and how what is said hangs together —and yet he has not shared in Revelation. Rather, Revelation has only arrived where, in addition to the material assertions witnessing to it, its inner reality has itself become effective after the manner of faith."[32] In effect, the reality of Scripture can only come alive when and if both what Ratzinger calls the "material assertions," namely, Scripture, and the receiving subject of the "material assertions," namely, the reader of Scripture, meet in the lively interaction that comes about thanks to faith on the part of the one who reads Scripture. It is faith that opens the eyes of the mind and heart to the reader of Scripture, enabling him or her to encounter in these words the voice of God that speaks. The picture is that of a trinity of Scripture, reader, and faith. Only faith opens the eyes of the reader to the revelatory presence of God that is witnessed to by Scripture.

And given that faith is essentially personalistic even as it is a gift from God, Ratzinger draws this conclusion: "Consequently, the person who receives it also is a part of the Revelation to a certain degree, for without him it does not exist. *You cannot put Revelation in your pocket like a book you carry around with you*. It is a living reality that requires a living person as the locus of its presence."[33] For Revelation to take place therefore, faith is an essential ingredient, faith that the one who is disclosing the self is God, who cares about me and wants my good. As Ratzinger learned from Bonaventure in his *Habilitation* work, without faith there is no key to throw open the book of Scripture: "This is the knowledge of Jesus Christ, from whom, as from a fountain, flow forth the certainty and the understanding of all sacred Scripture. Therefore, it is impossible for anyone to attain to knowledge of that truth unless he first have infused faith in Christ, which is the lamp, the gate, and the foundation of all Scripture."[34] Aquinas also asserts that "the letter, even that of the Gospel, would kill were there not the inward grace of healing faith."[35] In effect, no veil is removed if I do not believe that the one who speaks in the written word of Scripture is the loving Almighty God who is reaching out to me and inviting me into a living relationship with

Him. To summarize Ratzinger, Revelation transcends Scripture in that it always extends upward into God's action. There is more to it that cannot be exactly captured by the written text of Scripture, given the limitations that come with the human word that expresses the data of Revelation. Hence, Revelation extends beyond the mediating fact of Scripture, for Scripture is only a part of the greater reality of Revelation. In effect, only because there is a subject that receives Revelation can there be Revelation. Nothing is revealed if there is no receiving subject. No veil is removed if there is no one behind the screen to see the drama that is unfolding on the theatre stage. In plain terms, the human believing subject is crucial to God's self-disclosure. On this note, *sola scriptura* appears untenable as an intellectual position.

Ratzinger, Revelation, and Scripture as the Book of the Church

The above position on Scripture and Revelation certainly has a critical implication regarding how one understands the Church. Ratzinger's insistence that Scripture is a witness to Revelation and not identifiable with Revelation, as explained in the preceding section, brings to the radar the irreplaceable presence of the community called Church, the primary recipient of Scripture. But this leaves us with a much more crucial factor, namely, the relationship between Scripture and Church. The Second Vatican Council in *Dei Verbum* had reasserted the task of the authentic interpretation of Scripture to the College of Bishops as Successors of the Apostles. The Bishops, as shepherds and pastors of their particular churches, are to guard, interpret, and spread the message transmitted by the Scriptures. This implies that there has to be an ongoing and inimitable relationship between Scripture and Church, so much so that the understanding of Scripture flows from the living community of the Church. The Church is, therefore, the privileged space for the reception and the coming to life of Scripture. Herein enters the dynamism between Revelation, Scripture, and Church, at the bottom of which stands faith in the living God. Benedict XVI explains this relationship as a fundamental criterion of biblical hermeneutics, that is, to see the Church as that locus or setting in which the Scripture is read and comes alive, the Church as the hermeneutical principle for the interpretation of Scripture.[36] This is not to make the Scripture subservient to Church so much so that the Church becomes an extrinsic rule that exegetes must submit to. As Benedict XVI clarifies, the Church as the locus for the interpretation of Scripture is an awareness or consciousness that belongs to the very nature of Scripture itself.[37] The reality of the Church is not imposed on Scripture, placing an unbearable burden on exegetes. Rather, it is in the very nature of Scripture that Church be a part of its reality if Scripture is to be truly the living word of God. Such must be the case, for:

> Faith traditions formed the living context for the literary activity of the authors of sacred Scripture. Their insertion into this context also involved a sharing in both the liturgical and external life of the communities, in their intellectual world, in their culture, and in the ups and downs of their shared history. In like manner, the interpretation of sacred Scripture requires full participation on the part of the exegetes in the life and faith of the believing community of their own time.[38]

This certainly poses a challenge for exegetes, who must resist the temptation of seeing themselves as possessing an elitist or gnostic knowledge about the scriptural text. As they go about with the arduous task of biblical interpretation, it has to be the case that such commendable efforts should always take cognizance of the community called Church, of the believing community of the past and present, as we head towards the future. In a word, it is the faith of the living and believing community that recognizes in the Bible the word of God. Augustine's dictum captures this position with qualitative pointedness: "I would not believe the Gospel, had not the authority of the Catholic Church led me to do so."[39] Thus, the Bible, as the Book of the Church, was written by the

People of God for the People of God, and as the Second Vatican Council clearly articulated in *Dei Verbum*, under the inspiration of the Holy Spirit. Consequently, for Ratzinger and together with the Fathers, especially Jerome and Augustine, the ecclesial dimension of scriptural interpretation is not an extrinsic imposition on the Bible, for the Bible is the word of God because it is likewise the word of the People of God.

Conclusion: Church, Eucharist, and Scripture

Looking at Scripture and Eucharist from the Ratzingerian perspective, what emerges as the connecting thread is the reality of the Church as the locus, brought about by the former and the latter, and yet, in a typical Ratzingerian dialectical fashion, keeping the former and latter in an ongoing mutually enriching relationality. In effect, to the question whether the Eucharist and Scripture for that matter make the Church, it would be perfectly in order to respond in the affirmative, without overlooking the fact that the Church is likewise the gathering, or the community, that keeps both Scripture and Eucharist as a testimonial text for the former, and a religious ritual for the latter. In effect, it is not only the Eucharist that makes the Church. As a gift of and for the Church, the Eucharist is likewise from the Church. The Church, as the body of Christ with Christ as its head, this particular gathering in the liturgical assembly is the privileged locus that the Eucharist comes to birth. And what can be said about the Eucharist can likewise be said about Scripture, for without the believing community for whom Scripture comes alive as a witness to God's self-disclosure, Scripture can be construed like other great literature. The hope of this lecture is that understanding the Ratzingerian positions on Eucharist and Scripture spelled out above thus provides a richer context for comprehending and engaging the teachings regarding Eucharist and Scripture by Benedict XVI in AM. As shown above, Eucharist and Scripture are living realities precisely because of the living faith of the Church. Eucharist and Scripture, Sacrament and Word, constitute the two hands from and for the Church. As the Church in Africa continues along the path of justice, peace, and reconciliation, Eucharist and Scripture certainly constitute empowering sources of strength in the often complicated and complex task of building a just and peaceful Africa, for its peoples and for the world.

Preaching Reconciliation in a Divided Zone Mindful of *Africae Munus*

By Rev. Jude Thaddeus Langeh Basebang, C.M.F., D.Min.

Introduction

During his visit to Cameroon in 2009, Pope Benedict XVI described this country as a "beautiful country," "Africa in miniature," a "land of promise, (and) a land of glory!" Reporting on this visit, journalist John Allen confirmed that "especially by the standards of West Africa, Cameroon is peaceful, tolerant, orderly, and relatively developed."[1] The country has thus enjoyed long years of apparent peace and progress, and before November 2016, Cameroon distinguished itself in Central and West Africa like a paradise on earth, a land only akin to *"Alice in wonderland."*

Despite all the encomia, Cameroon currently faces an armed conflict between the government and separatists from the country's English-speaking minority. This conflict has witnessed many deaths and has brought about many refugees and internally displaced persons. This is happening when the war with Boko Haram in the country's Far North Region has taken many a life and triggered the rise of vigilante self-defense groups. The country is now subject to internal divisions based on tribe, language, social status, political affiliations, regions of origin, etc., that affect different fabrics of society.

How can this contrasting view of Cameroon be explained? How can the Church bring about reconciliation and propose a new political future? Our lecture will answer these questions. We will start by presenting Cameroon as a land of glories besieged with much division and thus in need of a clarion call for reconciliation. Secondly, we will delve into the theology of reconciliation, tapping from the African Synod of Bishops and *Africae Munus* to provide a roadmap for effective reconciliation in Cameroon. Lastly, we propose Cameroon's new political future based on a "new we" identity.

Cameroon, the Thorn-Crowned Glory of Africa
The Glories of Cameroon

It is not uncommon for the Cameroonian to hear her/his father-land being referred to as "Africa in miniature." Cameroon's rich subsoil deposits, its crude oil, rubber, the inestimable measure of natural resources that endow the country; the evergreen virgin forests, natural vegetation, fertile soils receptive to complex agri-cultural exploits; the beautiful landscape; the hospitable fluctu-ating climate; the spectacular touristic attractions that the country harbors... all these and much more make proud every conscious patriotic citizen of Cameroon. Pope Benedict XVI also observes the glories of this in these words:

> Cameroon is truly a land of hope for many in Central Africa. Thousands of refugees from war-torn countries in the region have received a welcome here. It is a land of life, with a Government that speaks out in defense of the rights of the unborn. It is a land of peace: by re-solving through dialogue the dispute over the Bakassi peninsula, Cameroon and Nigeria have shown the world that patient diplomacy can indeed bear fruit. It is a land of youth, blessed with a young population full of vitality and eager to build a more just and peaceful world. Rightly is it described as "Africa in miniature," home to over two hundred different ethnic groups liv-ing in harmony with one another.[2]

In addition to nature's generosity, the country is strategically sit-uated at Africa's armpit, opening wide her arms to welcome every intercontinental transaction by sea route. Above all, the dynamic inhabitants of a thousand and one origins (over 200 ethnic groups) enrich its cultural heritage. The originality of their genial productions: music (such as *makossa, njang, bikutsi, asiko,* etc.), arts and crafts, intellectual works, internationally acclaimed sportsmanship, etc.; their long past years of peaceful cohabitation—for example, Muslim and Christian, or people of different ethnic groups. In fact, there is no doubt that a panoramic view of Cameroon reveals it to be a microcosmic representation of its continent. Yes, Cameroon is Africa in miniature and a "Land of Glories." But curiously, a critical look at the other side of the coin also reveals some uncomfortable situations of division that can lead and are leading to greater woes because of lack of management.

Cameroon: A Land of Worries in Need of Reconciliation

At the same time as it stands glorious some have seen Cameroon as a country bleeding in silence. Many internal socio-political and ethnic crises do plague and divide the country, and they are degenerating into other fatal happenings because they are overlooked. From independence to the present times Cameroon has remained a nation in need of reconciliation. Jean-Marc Ela depicts that a few years after independence many young Cameroonians "were shut out of the job market and the numbers keep increasing. The hope of the nation, no less! The future of the young is as bleak as that of the intellectuals...."[3] Unfortunately, it so happens that the country suffers a host of multidimensional "spats" that stifle her progress and put her internal coherence to question:

- The current socio-political strife across the national territory, the recurrent Boko-Haram attacks causing insecurity in the North region of the country, and the belief that military violence and oppression will solve problems during strikes;
- The worsening situation of the "Anglophone problem" especially in the North West and the South West regions of Cameroon. In effect, "many contemporary accounts of

secessionist violence in Anglophone Cameroon begin with the protests and strikes by teachers and lawyers in the fall of 2016 that eventually escalated to demands for federalism and later secession… the secessionist claims can be traced to policies since the colonial period";[4]

- The despicable hardship and bloodshed, displacement of families, and the joblessness of the youthful population;
- The rather *non-dynamic* leadership. We can observe that ever since independence in 1960 the "democratic Cameroon" has produced just two presidents;
- Exacerbated corruption, misappropriation of public wealth, and the centralization of administrative structures and institutions;
- Ethnicity, tribalism, and "regionalism" hamper national unity.

As shown above, while Boko Haram and especially the Anglophone Crisis are the most contemporary issues in Cameroon, this country still suffers from many social, political, and ethnic problems of division. Many people turn to the Church for a solution to all kinds of problems. The people of Cameroon need "a church where real and fragile people embody the gospel. (For) Reconciliation is grounded in a story—the story of God's new creation."[5]

A Roadmap for Practical Reconciliation in Cameroon
Cameroon in Need of a Christian View of Reconciliation

Nowadays, reconciliation has become a popular notion. We hear much about it in the political realm, especially in countries where there is oppression of any kind, division, enmity, and the pursuit of nation-building and new societies. However, "the idea of reconciliation emanates from the Christian tradition. For many centuries, the concept was dealt with as a mere theological concept belonging to the field of systematic theology and the pious, mystical and spiritual experience of Christians."[6] But today, our world needs to have recourse to a Christian view of reconciliation,

111

especially as other prevailing versions have failed. Reconciliation must be rooted in Scripture and sustained by the Church.

Reconciliation is at the heart of God's plan for salvation. God created man and woman in God's image and likeness (Gen 1:26). With the Fall and the entry of sin into the world, one would expect to hear that all is lost. However, God promised to crush the head of the serpent (Gen 3:15). In the Old Testament, one understands the Great Day of Atonement (*Yom Kippur*) as implying reconciliation between humans and God through the intercession of the priest. In the New Testament, "reconciliation is at the heart of the Gospel."[7] Reconciliation refers to the relationship between human beings and God. Jesus explains, "Therefore, if you bring your gift to the altar, and there recall that your brother has anything against you, leave your gift there at the altar, go first and be reconciled with your brother, and then come and offer your gift." (Mt 5:23–24 NABRE). Saint Paul stands high as the best theologian and the principal resource for a biblical and Christian understanding of reconciliation (cf. Ephesians 2:12–19; Colossians 1:13–23 etc.). In addition, Romans 5:6–11 is the classic location for a Protestant theology of reconciliation, while 2 Corinthians 5:17–20 gives reconciliation a Catholic emphasis.[8] Robert J. Schreiter insists that "reconciliation is the work of God, who initiates and completes in us reconciliation through Christ."[9] Going further, Katongole insists that reconciliation is a "gift and an invitation into another world."[10] In effect, Pauline soteriology adds something fundamental to understanding reconciliation, namely "New Creation." Paul tells the Corinthians:

> Therefore, if anyone is in Christ, the new creation has come: The old has gone, the new is here! All this is from God, who reconciled us to himself through Christ and gave us the ministry of reconciliation: that God was reconciling the world to himself in Christ, not counting people's sins against them. Furthermore, he has committed to us the message of reconciliation. Therefore, we are Christ's ambassadors, as though God were

making his appeal through us. We implore you on
Christ's behalf: Be reconciled to God. (2 Corinthians
5:17–20 NIV)

Reconciliation, thus, is not only limited to spiritual atonement
or cleansing of a sinner's guilt "but a total reordering of creation,
an exchange of an old order of things, and the inauguration of a
new dispensation. Reconciliation is the process through which
the restoring of a broken creation is realized by God."[11] By proclaiming a new creation, Paul invites Christians to experience in
reality another realism and wear another lens to see the world
from a different angle. How important is this invitation to
Cameroon today? The Church's teaching will throw more light
on this point.

Africae Munus, a Spark of Hope for the Nation

Pope Benedict XVI's post-synodal apostolic exhortation, "*Africae
Munus,*" stands paramount in talking about reconciliation in
Cameroon. It is addressed to bishops, the clergy, consecrated persons, and the lay faithful of the Church in Africa, in service to reconciliation, justice, and peace. It goes without doubt that this
document, addressed "in a particular way to the Church in
Africa," casts light on the prevailing situation in Cameroon and
suggests significant paths leading to reconciliation, justice, and
peace in Cameroon.[12] In saluting the realistic and far-sighted contributions of African prelates that have demonstrated the Christian maturity of the continent, the Holy Father implicitly
underlines that the synod members are aware of their continent's
socio-political, ethnic, economic, and even ecological situations.[13]

Cameroon is no different, thus the need for the clergy to take
more conscious action in boldly responding to her prophetic mission of denouncing and decrying the ills, as mentioned above,
that plague the country. Despite the challenges the Church in
Cameroon faces, her ministers must remain "authentic servants
of God's word."[14] For this to be effective, the Church must become

more assiduous in listening to God's word, meditating on it, nourishing itself with it, letting this word penetrate the very being of its members. The word of God should be at the center of all preaching. Only so can the people come to be reconciled with God and with one another. This reconciliation is a necessary path for the construction—or rather the reconstruction—of communities. And giving priority of place to God's Word is simply a necessary recognition of the fact that Christ, the ultimate source of the reconciliation, justice, and peace which we seek, is at the heart of the realities of this country.[15]

Common Efforts Towards the Reconciliation of the Entire Country

In order to obtain the reconciliation preached, all people of goodwill must make constantly renewed efforts of hospitality, expressed in a language that proliferates unity, journeying together towards justice and peace, especially by respecting the dignity of the human person. Undoubtedly, the Church is the harbinger of this reconciliation, and everyone else must participate. In that light, it could only be providential that the entire second chapter of *Africae Munus* is consecrated to a proposal for the paths towards reconciliation, justice, and peace. An earlier observation explains this all the more: "men and women are shaped by their past, but they live and journey in the present and they look ahead to the future."[16]

With the dire need for general reconciliation across the country, the role of the family cannot be overlooked in this essential goal. In fact, "the family, as a natural and divine institution, has to be at the center of the Church's and the society's attention. It must be protected and preserved from the plagues of modernity."[17] Every member of the family ought to take up their responsibilities, therefore: the man fulfilling his duties as head or father of the family; the woman being respected and valorized beyond the circumference of maternity to which she is often limited; youths playing their role as the "energy of the society" for constructive changes; children benefitting from the cherished place that is their due, given their fragility that recommends protection, as well as the docility that makes them receptive to assimilate what they learn and could be exploited to teach them to be virtuous.

In a nutshell, every member of the Cameroonian society, particularly the Church there, has a role to play in the country's reconciliation. In preaching this reconciliation, bishops, priests, missionaries, permanent deacons, consecrated persons, seminarians, catechists, lay people—utterly everybody must be conscious and active in reflecting the Church as the presence of Christ who reconciled the world—men and women with themselves, with each other, and with God.[18] In fact, all of us are required to be preachers of reconciliation. If preachers succeed in this, we can build a new political future for Cameroon.

Role of Preachers in Building a New Political Future
The Church as the Harbinger of a New Political Future

In *Africae Munus*, Pope Benedict XVI invites all of Africa to reconciliation in these words: "Be reconciled to God" (2 Cor 5:20b). He draws from the Pauline soteriology that sees reconciliation in terms of a "New Creation" (2 Cor 5:17–20b). In that light, the Church in Cameroon must preach real reconciliation and propose new politics of a new "We." While not asking the Church to meddle with partisan politics, it is worth noting that the Church has a great platform to educate and form its faithful—Preaching—as it is evidently a very religious country. Through preaching, the Church can touch the lives of millions of Cameroonians daily. Many still have confidence in Church, and people come to Church for their salvation. From the very first chapter of *Africae Munus*, Pope Benedict XVI points out that in addressing the themes of reconciliation, justice, and peace, the synod was interested in the public role of the Church and her place in today's Africa.[19] Being a nation that needs healing from its deep brokenness, it is paramount for Cameroon to go back to the theology of reconciliation. Preachers should be bold enough to identify and address the social ills in Cameroon—the "spells" of the country today. These spells are difficult to discern and haunt one's present existence. Katongole insists that "only by naming those spells and setting out to exorcise them in protracted ways does one hope to live into a new future."[20] They can be anything: tribalism, crises, intertribal war, interethnic and linguistic struggles. Once named, we then look at what Christianity can offer in order to interrupt these spells. But alas! It's a pity that they are often mistaken for identity. Therefore, there is a need to define the real Christian identity.

Defining a New Identity for the Cameroonian

If you happen to ask an average Cameroonian: "who are you?" The tendency will be to rather respond to questions like "where are you from? To which tribe or ethnic group do you belong?" Though composed of more than 200 ethnic groups, Cameroonians can easily describe themselves as Anglophones and/or Francophones, relative to who was the former colonial master of their region of origin—Britain or France respectively. In the political field, we know the parties primarily for the Anglophones and those mainly for the Francophones. People group themselves socially and politically as Betis, Bamilikes Bamuns, Bassas, Sawas, Grassfielders, Nsos, etc. Worthy of note is the fact that all these appellations have become political identities, produced and reproduced through the political formation of modern Cameroon. This implicitly determines the events of the country. For example, a clash between the Ruling Party CPDM and the opposition party CRM becomes a serious tribal and ethnic problem between the Betis and the Bamilikes, which is taken even into Church. This situation has led people to naively assume that "one's national, ethnic, or racial identity is one's 'natural,' and therefore, primary identity, on which one's being Christian builds."[21] Some go as far as theologically backing this with Aquinas' dictum that "Grace builds upon nature" to suggest that:

Christian formation does not radically change or interrupt our natural identities but simply builds on these.
But such formulations do not allow for the full political
reality of Christian identity. For once it has been accepted that our biological, national, racial, or ethnic
identities are our primary identities, then the best that
Christianity might be able to do is to provide either
inner spiritual dynamism to bolster those so-called natural identities or ethical guidelines to civilize and check
the excessive tendencies of racism, tribalism, or nationalism. Christianity is left without any resources to question or interrupt the political goals and expectations
toward which these so-called natural identities are di-
rected.[22]

In other words, Christian identity has been confused with political identity and has become a sort of belonging, seeking to advance specific political visions of life and expectations.

Preachers and church leaders are easily caught in this trap,
thus the urgency to think about a new political future, a new
"We." Preachers are to encourage Christians to accept the recommendations from Romans 12:2: "Do not conform yourself to this
age but be transformed by the renewal of your mind that you may
discern what the will of God is, what is good and acceptable, and
perfect." Katongole's paraphrasing of this exhortation is necessary in Cameroon: "Brothers and Sisters (*Cameroonians*, emphasis
is mine), do not be naïve about the politics of your nation; do not
just fit within the forms of belonging as identified by your race,
ethnicity, language, or tribe, but be transformed by the renewing
of your minds, so that you learn to negotiate what is perfect, true,
and good."[23]

Negotiating a Political Future Based on a "New We"

As a preacher, I am always thrilled to celebrate and preach at wed-
dings between couples from two separate and even conflicting

tribes in Cameroon. It is always a cherished opportunity to tell people that "God is determined to form a new people in the world. Baptism and the entire range of Christian Practice are meant to reflect and to advance political reality."[24] On this note, there are many take-home messages from Saint Paul's letter to the Ephesians. God's purpose in Christ was to create, out of many, "one new man" (Eph. 2:15), so that Jewish and Gentile Christians now share "one Spirit" (2:18), "one hope" (4:4), "one Lord, one faith, one Baptism, (as they are all Children of) One God and Father of all" (4:56). The Christians in Ephesus, politically and culturally identified as Jews and Gentiles, are no longer separated. They are no longer "strangers or sojourners, but … fellow citizens." They have been brought together by Christ's death, who breaks down the separation walls. As an "Ephesian moment," they are no longer two separate communities; they are all members of one community in which they have a single body. Although historically and politically separated into different ethnicities, tribes, and languages (anglophones and francophones), Cameroonians must recognize the urgent need to have a new Christian identity in which we can live together, eat together, pray, and socialize together. This will help break the walls of division and create forms of catholicity that reflect and reveal the very height of Christ's full stature. The new political future will no longer be francophone or anglophone, Bamileke or Beti, but it will be a mixture of all, portraying real ecclesial solidarity in which "our membership in the Body of Christ is our primary identity."[25]

Conclusion

From the above presentation, we are convinced that Cameroon is a country that needs reconciliation at all levels. Reconciliation can be brought about through the state, traditional kings, NGOs, religious communities, etc. However, everyone in Cameroon knows the major influence of religion in the country. In all major state events, religious leaders are given privileged positions. Based on this, our work above has been to explore the magisterium of the

Church, hinging on *Africae Munus*, to show that it is the Church's mission to preach reconciliation. It is clear that the mission of the Church is not political but spiritual, and that immediate involvement in politics does not fall within the direct competence of the Church, but within the political sphere, whose principal mission is to build a just social order. Nevertheless, the Church can be the harbinger of a new political future, not by taking the place of politicians, but by making her voice heard through what she knows best to do, namely, preaching. Since Christians always find themselves located within other forms of belonging, such as, race, tribe, and ethnicity, instead of the waters of Baptism, there is a need to redefine Christian identity as a form of interruption within the existing political, national, ethnic, or racial formations. A new political future is possible for Cameroon especially if all citizens adhere to national reconciliation and opt for a new sense of belonging.

Challenge to Women as Peace Agents: *Africae Munus* in a Feminine Key

By Prof. Forbi Stephen Kizito, S.J.

> "Violence is a major variable that
> discriminates against women."
> (Rita Manchanda)

Introduction

Increasing female participation in post-conflict peacebuilding and reconciliation is still a challenge, even though there is growing agreement that female participation will enhance the chances for lasting peace. According to a study by UN Women, no woman has been appointed as a lead mediator in any UN-sponsored peace talks in Africa since 1992.[1] Women's participation has mainly been as part of a team of mediators in some talks sponsored by the African Union (AU) and other institutions. A positive case is the inclusion of the influential political figure, Graçia Machel, in a team of three mediators involved in resolving the 2008 electoral crisis in Kenya.[2]

According to another UN Women 2018 report, between 1990 and 2017 women continued to account for only 2% of mediators, 8% of negotiators, and 5% of witnesses and signatories of the main peace agreements. And, only 11% of the agreements signed in 2017 contain provisions relating to gender parity. This trend is similar to that observed between 2000 and 2016, where only 25 of the 1,500 agreements signed in this period addressed the role of women in the implementation phases.[3] The table below is a

synopsis of the participatory level of women in peace processes
from 2000–2011.

		Women Signatories	Women Lead Mediators	Women Witnesses	Women in Negotiating Teams
1.	**Burundi (2000) – Arusha** *Arusha Peace and Reconciliation Agreement for Burundi*	0%	0%	-	2%
2.	**Somalia (2002) - Eldoret** *Declaration on Cessation of Hostilities and the Structures and Principles. Principles of the Somalia National Reconciliation Process*	0%	0%	0%	-
3.	**Cote d'Ivoire (2003)** Linas-Marcoussis Peace Accords	0%	0%	0%	-
4.	**DRC (2003)** The Sun City Agreement ("The Final Act")	5%	0%	0%	12%
5.	**Liberia (2003) – Accra** Peace Agreement between the Government of Liberia, the Liberians United for Reconciliation and Democracy, the Movement for Democracy in Liberia and the political parties	0%	0%	17%	-
6.	**Sudan (2005) – Naivasha** The comprehensive peace agreement between the Government of the Republic of Sudan and the Sudan People's Liberation Movement Sudan People's Liberation Army	0%	0%	9%	-
7.	**Darfur (2006) – Abuja** Darfur Peace Agreement	0%	0%	7%	8%
8.	**Uganda (2008)** Juba Peace Agreement	0%	0%	20%	9%

9.	**Kenya (2008) – Nairobi** Agreement on the Principles of Partnership of the Coalition Government	%	33%	0%	25%
10.	**Central African Republic (2011)** Accord de cessez-le-feu entre l'UFDR et le CPJP	0%	0%	0%	-

Adapted from *Women's participation in 31 peace processes (1992 - 2011).*

https://reliefweb.int/sites/reliefweb.int/files/resources/03AWo menPeaceNeg.pdf

In any case this quantitative approach is not enough. It must go hand in glove with a qualitative approach: the parity objective must not overshadow the importance of ensuring that the designated women are given real decision-making powers that are not simply limited to care issues. It is within this backdrop that *Africae Munus,* as a hope-centered message on moral and spiritual issues, proposes its pervasive and revolutionary stance concerning gender-based discrimination.

Africae Munus challenges African women radically not to be sedentary in traditional roles as custodians of culture and nurturers of the family, but to venture into new tasks, particularly that of peace negotiations and post-conflict reconstruction efforts. However, while acknowledging that *"overall, women's dignity and rights as well as their essential contribution to the family and to society have not been fully acknowledged or appreciated,"*[4] Benedict XVI iterates that *"When peace is under threat, when justice is flouted, when poverty increases, you (women) stand up to defend human dignity, the family, and the values of religion."*[5] Women's contribution to peace is expressed in terms of *"the humanization of the society."*[6] Female participation in post-conflict peacebuilding and reconciliation is conditioned by two situations: a mental revolution, or *"evolution in thinking"* about women,[7] and a *"recognition and liberation of women, following the example of Christ's own esteem for them."*[8] The problematic of this lecture, inspired by *Africae Munus,* is: despite the violence perpetuated against women, how can they take their rightful place in post-conflict negotiations?

This lecture responds to the above question in three parts. First, it will review the new feminism. Second, it will investigate avenues for liberating women for peace mediation. Third, it will delve into the practical dimension of "human ecology" proposed by the *Africae Munus*.

The New Feminism

The fundamental condition for women's inclusion in post-conflict management in Africa starts with a paradigm shift from clichés and prejudices about women. This shift, which we designate as a mental revolution, is already in progress. This section sketches the problem of female political involvement and the progress that has been made thus far. The thrust of the "feminine genius" of Edith Stein, the "new feminism" of John Paul II, and the "feminine gift" of Benedict XVI all reject the phenomenological view of femininity as passive and out-dated. They aim at encouraging active participation of women in public and social life. The demand for the involvement of women in reconciliation, justice, and peace processes, in *Africae Munus*, is also founded on Gospel values, that is, *"following the example of Christ's own esteem for them."*[9] According to African Traditional beliefs and practices, particularly in matters relating to life, women are viewed as the ones who understand the sacredness of human life more than other members of the community. The reason being that a woman is the one who carries life in her womb, brings it forth, nurtures it, and defends it when it is threatened. As such, African women should be reserved a special role in stopping war. The *raison d'être* for this honour is that they are protectors and defenders of life. This clearly shows that by their specific *"feminine gifts,"* women in the Church in Africa ought to rightly seek participation in processes that foster reconciliation, justice, and peace.[10] After all, African Tradition agrees with the teaching of the Church that a woman is treasured as a God-given gift in crucial matters touching life. Indeed, Benedict XVI reminds the Church in Africa that God has made women channels for life— something that we need to have in mind in our service to reconciliation, justice, and peace.

The Progressive Mental Revolution

Favourable conditions for active participation in peace processes by women are necessary for this to happen. Among them Benedict XVI insists that we *"combat of all acts of violence against women, speaking out, and condemning them."*[11] Put positively, this means that *"we must recognize, affirm, and defend the equal dignity of man and woman."*[12] Benedict XVI is calling for a deconstruction of the concept that fosters violence and discrimination against women. A deconstructive stance or a mental revolution is a switch in thought, substituting traditional rules of thumb. As it concerns women, it is a change of attitude towards them concerning peacebuilding. Mental revolution aims at improving the thinking of women about themselves as well as by men. According to Edith Stein the essence of a mental revolution concerning women is to move from an enslaved stance that they are solely biologically determined to one that holds *"that being of female gender must not be a hindrance to a habilitation."*[13] According to *Africae Munus*, mental revolution designates *"initiatives which reinforce their (women's) worth, their self-esteem, and their uniqueness... so that they may assume their proper share of responsibility and participation in the community life of society."*[14] It is in line with this change of mentality that Benedict XVI argues for a move from negative anthropology to positive anthropology in which *"feminine gifts"* are valorised:

> The Church counts on you to create a "human ecology" through your sympathetic love, your friendly and thoughtful demeanour, and finally through mercy, values that you know how to instill in your children, values that the world so badly needs. In this way, by

the wealth of your specifically feminine gifts, you will foster the reconciliation of individuals and communities.[15]

As such, Benedict XVI is situated in the evolutionary thinking trajectory of the Church. The concept *"new feminism"* is from John Paul II's encyclical *Evangelium Vitae* or *The Gospel of Life,* where he stated that:

> In transforming culture so that it supports life, women occupy a place, in thought and action, which is unique and decisive. It depends on them to promote a "new feminism" which rejects the temptation of imitating models of "male domination," in order to acknowledge and affirm the true genius of women in every aspect of the life of society, and overcome all discrimination, violence, and exploitation.[16]

John Paul II's concept of a *"new feminism"* continues in Benedict XVI's rejection of the idea that women belong only in the private sphere. Positively, it agrees with his idea of meaningful involvement of women in public life, bringing with them their distinctively feminine psycho-physical gifts. *"When peace is under threat,"* says Benedict XVI *"when justice is flouted, when poverty increases, you stand up to defend human dignity, the family, and the values of religion."*[17] Meaningful participation in peace processes signifies the capacity of women to have an influence in these negotiations. The present theorizing on women will remain a sterile scepticism if it does not respond to and strive to influence social realities like peace-building. Women peace agents are not to be viewed as rivals of male peace agents, but as both fulfilling complementary roles.

The absence of women in peace-building processes is rooted in the fallacious statement that war has always been the prerogative of men. Benedict XVI advanced a self-evident truth according to which women have always participated in and have been affected by war. That is why the Sovereign Pontiff urges both men and women to collectively *"build this just social order by their responsible conduct"* thereby ensuring a just, more peaceful, and reconciled Africa.[18] According to Benedict XVI women have to ask themselves what they have to do in order to take their rightful place in justice, peace, and reconciliation negotiations. Getting women to participate in these processes will not only promote their dignity but also promote the principle of the common good as provided for in the Church's social teaching. This allows them to live their commitment to making the reign of God of peace a reality in the Church in Africa.[19]

Empowering Women for Mediation

Benedict XVI is not a voice crying alone in the desert for an increase in women's participation at the negotiating table as a precondition for lasting peace. The UN resolution 1325 of 2000, called for an *"increased representation of women at all decision-making levels...in institutions and mechanisms for the prevention, management, and resolution of conflict."* Advocacy groups for women's participation in peace processes abound on the African continent. There is the *Southern African Women Mediators* (SAWMS), hosted by the African Centre for the Constructive Resolution of Disputes (AC-CORD), in collaboration with the *United Nations Entity for Gender Equality and the Empowerment of Women* (UN Women). The editorial line of this group is to make the case that women's potential in mediation remains largely untapped and that organizations engaged in peace-making should improve their support for women's increased capacity and participation in peace processes. The rationale for this demand is that no category of victims should be left out of peace negotiations. Benedict XVI, while advocating for an increase in women's participation in post-conflict negotiations, acknowledges its materialization has been slow. What are some of the constraints to and opportunities for the inclusion of women from marginalized communities in peacebuilding initiatives?

Inhibitions to Women's Opportunities in the Peace-Building Process

An example of one obstacle to women's liberation are those structures that are insensitive to the effects that female devaluation and violence against women have on society. They are instances of resistance because they are slow or disinterested in the eradication of the social evil of women's subordination. Among these factors are patriarchal norms and attitudes, lack of support for women's rights organizations, devaluing women's role as peacebuilders, inequalities in education, and the responsibilities of women in the household.

Cultural norms: Women's exclusion from peace processes is justified by cultural norms and patriarchal customs that reduce women to the private sphere. The private sphere, as opposed to the public sphere, is that of deprivation of political life. This stance is also justified by the fallacious theory, as already mentioned above, that war and peace negotiations are the prerogatives of men. Another obstacle is women's "natural" tendency to self-exclusion from the public sphere on grounds that they are incompetent to participate meaningfully in peace processes. Pope Benedict XVI points to illiteracy as the explanatory principle of this incompetence:

> Illiteracy represents one of the principal obstacles to development. It is a scourge on a par with that of the pandemics. True, it does not kill directly, but it contributes actively to the marginalization of the person—which is a form of social death—and it blocks access to knowledge. Teaching people to read and write makes them full members of the *res publica* and enables them to play their part in building it up.[20]

The self-censorship by women is often due to a lack of technical capacity and social norms which identify women with *social* and not *peace* roles.

Structural rigidity: The system governing and structuring peace processes is old and is struggling to reform itself in the face of advanced thinking about women. Today, women hold ministerial positions, some are presidents of countries, etc. Why are they not considered by peace processes? Also, the rigidity and lack of inclusion of women in peace processes are found at the level of actors seated around the table. In many cases, rather than concern themselves with gender inclusiveness, they seek to achieve their immediate goal, namely, to urgently put an end to the conflict. Another level of resistance is found in the separation of formal and informal processes of conflict resolution. Despite the important role that women play in informal processes of reconciliation, and their role in crisis and conflict resolutions at local or community level, these informal processes are often overlooked by the international community and those involved in formal peace processes. In other words, there is under-reporting of women's peacebuilding work at informal levels. This neglect is prejudicial to the formulation of the peace results.

Lack of expertise and capacity by women's organizations for peace: Another obstacle to women's participation in peace-building is the incapacity of women's organizations to be impactful in peace agreements. This is due to their lack of technical expertise (language, specific measures and knowledge, legal aspects) when peace agreements are being negotiated, implemented, and monitored. In other cases, women are exposed to different types and levels of donor investment in their capacity-building, depending on when and where these women operate, resulting in women being given asymmetrical access to the knowledge and skills they need. This creates divisions among the "women's movement," aggravates a sense of grievance and inequality, and makes it more challenging to communicate across political lines. Thus, peacebuilding practitioners and international women's support organizations should not only offer opportunities for training of women but also exert what influence they can to level the playing field.

Logistic obstacles. It is impossible to ignore logistic obstacles to participation, which women face in terms of childcare, the cost of travel or lack of security to get to meetings, the access to advocacy opportunities, and therefore lack of ability to participate in the peace negotiations. Related to these logistical obstacles, it is worthy of note that the socio-cultural context and women's lack of empowerment limits both their physical and economic placement.

Lack of income is a significant barrier for women to take part in peace-building activities. They are unable to engage in peace-building or development activities due to a lack of time because of their domestic roles. In addition, women are marginalized economically as a result of low levels of education, lack of finances, and lack of experience in employment. Given a cultural tradition that previously marginalised women economically, women stated that they lack the confidence to engage in income generation or to speak up in public. The economic situation of households can hold back women's participation in peace-building. The multiple burden of caring for children and households, as well as contributing to income generation, leaves limited time for political engagement. Women are not able to take time away from income-generating activities and therefore cannot join initiatives that do not immediately and directly benefit their families.

Empowering Women

Women's peace activism tends to get obscured by the fact of their cultural experience of being disempowered—that is, protest strategies that use symbols of motherhood, mourning, or ritual cursing. However, by taking them into the public arena, women politicize and transform them. Pope Benedict XVI, in this context, urged the Church in Africa to move from a mere recognition of the dignity of women to their involvement in civil and social life. Within this context Benedict XVI challenges women to be the *"backbone"* in peace-building.[21] This can happen through strategic empowerment, gender enculturation, political will, etc.

Strategic empowerment designates innovative ways to enhance a meaningful participation by women at all levels of peace processes. According to Benedict XVI, there is need for a paradigm shift from one that considers women as victims of peace processes to one that considers women as peace-builders. This also resonates in significant leadership challenges. Also, in order to give greater visibility to women's advocacy groups for inclusive participation in peace processes, it is incumbent on women to de-compartmentalize their organizational structures to include youth and male activists. This strategy will give more resonance to their messages and circulate information to gain visibility and influence peace processes.

Benedict XVI is quite aware that in Africa the role of women in conflict prevention, resolution, and implementation of lasting reconciliation processes is almost absent. That is why *Africae Munus* exhorts women not to be passive and silent victims of violence and conflict. Women must "*make their voice heard and express their talents*" in peace processes.[22] Women must participate in their own emancipation.

Strategic enculturation. In the context of feminism, strategic or gender enculturation "designates the process of integrating a strategic and social understanding of women as a distinct group, thereby incorporating women's cultural experience and including a commitment to the emancipation of women into enculturation."[23] Enculturation, here, is not understood in the sense of dialogue between the Gospel and local cultures but as the political and economic emancipation of peoples, particularly women.

Benedict XVI calls on the African Church to discern aspects of African culture that promote the values of women. Without downplaying enculturation theologies Benedict XVI encouraged gendering enculturation in the sense of political emancipation. This immediately calls to mind the participation of women in reconciliation, justice, and peace. Within the thrust or this triptych, the Pope is arguing that there can be no African cultural beauty in the midst of blatant political and social injustice against women. Gendering enculturation is liberative in the sense of a growing social consciousness about issues of gender and social justice. It is a challenge to address the deeper cultural issues, especially the impinging exclusion of women from post-conflict negotiations. In the African culture, the value of life is synonymous with women since it is they who give forth life and it is, therefore, incumbent on them to protect and preserve this life.

Political will, awareness, and responsibility of organizations and actors involved in peace processes: This is what Benedict XVI calls a *"political culture"* which he opines is *"needed for development and for peace."*[24] This is a question of *"civic responsibility."*[25] It is, therefore, incumbent on mandated organizations and mediators of post-conflict management to adopt strict measures to ensure the participation of women in a transversal and effective way. It is equally imperative to promote the participation of women in peace processes in Africa by putting in place binding mechanisms that ensure parity at all levels. For example, mediators refusing to take part in peace process if women are not invited to the negotiating table.

This political will must also be adopted by regional, national, and international organizations like the African Union, CEDEAO or CEMAC, as well as by economic and development partners who invest in conflict-ridden countries. The commitment of these key players is critical to ensure the participation of women in peace processes. Concretely, a "code of good conduct" can be drafted to ensure active participation of women at the negotiating table. Among those who can uphold such a code, Benedict XVI mentions the following: political leaders, political groupings, decision makers, citizens in political life, etc.[26]

Many armed conflicts or incompatibilities that involve the government of a state and other armed groups within or without the state are usually designated as *male public violence*. As such, peace-building processes are gendered as the male domination is commonly upheld and women's exclusion is considered normal. The demand for an increased participation of women in peace-building and negotiation processes is founded on the democratic principle which presupposes a system of governance in which diverse interests and grievances are accommodated by negotiations and compromises. Democratization and peace-building have been thought of as mutually beneficial processes. For a peace process to be just and sustainable, it has to be placed on a sound legal framework and to include women in an equal manner as negotiators, mediators, and observers. Legislation should guarantee gender equality in all areas of life.

Women and Humanization of Society

Although the inclusion of women in peace-building processes has gained momentum in policy discussions over the last 15 years, the number of women in decision-making positions remains relatively small. While these legal frameworks have increased awareness of how conflict impacts women specifically, many peace negotiating organizations and institutions have not been successful in rolling out their strategies for women's participation in peace processes. However, it is the firm conviction of Benedict XVI that women's inclusion in peace-building processes and security apparatus will have a pacifying and "humanizing" effect. Peace-building is the foundation for creating sustainable human security and equitable development in countries emerging from conflict. To address this "discriminatory" stance à propos of women Benedict XVI suggests the putting in place of a "human ecology."

Human Ecology

The expression *human ecology* was used by John Paul II when he advocated the putting in place of *"moral conditions for an authentic human ecology."*[27] Human ecology is the prevention of man's auto-destruction. Just as environmental ecology has been identified as a pressing need to prevent the destruction of our natural environment, so too, human ecology calls for an adopted approach to life that protects and promotes every human life. Due to the lack of the moral conditions for the preservation of every human life, the human being has developed a culture of self-destruction by losing his grip on the correct methods of complete stewardship of human life.

Benedict XVI picks up the theme of *human ecology* in his message for the celebration of the World Day of Peace on 1st January 2007. In his message he creates an inseparable link between the "ecology of peace" and "human ecology":

> Thus, there is an urgent need, even within the framework of current international difficulties and tensions, for a commitment to a human ecology that can favour the growth of the "tree of peace." For this to happen, we must be guided by a vision of the person untainted by ideological and cultural prejudices or by political and economic interests which can instill hatred and violence. It is understandable that visions of man will vary from culture to culture. Yet what cannot be admitted is the cultivation of anthropological conceptions that contain the seeds of hostility and violence.[28]

Among the ideological prejudices that instill hatred and negative anthropological conceptions that constitute sources of violence are the: "*inadequate consideration for* the condition of women *(which) helps to create instability in the fabric of society... the exploitation of women who are treated as objects*" and the cultural subordination of women "*to the arbitrary decisions of men, with grave consequences for their personal dignity and for the exercise of their fundamental freedoms.*"[29]

Four years later, Pope Benedict XVI develops the theme of *human ecology* in *Africae Munus*: "*The Church counts on you to create a 'human ecology' through your sympathetic love, your friendly and thoughtful demeanour, and finally through mercy, values that you know how to instill in your children, values that the world so badly needs. In this way, by the wealth of your specifically feminine gifts, you will foster the reconciliation of individuals and communities.*"[30] *Human ecology* is concerned as well with interrelationships between humans. It seeks a holistic or comprehensive understanding of these interactions. In the case of *Africae Munus*, it addresses issues of injustice against women in public life. There can be no peace without democratic participation or political justice for women. From the standpoint of women, therefore, we can understand Benedict XVI's study of *human ecology* as probing the vulnerability and resilience of women in the socio-political sphere in Africa. Vulnerability designates women as passive victims whereas resilience considers them as active agents. So, in the reckoning of Benedict XVI, vulnerability and resilience co-exist. His thinking is aimed at the reduction of female political vulnerability by integrating them in the mainstream of public and political life.

Conclusion

One area of the social mission of the Church in Africa which carries much promise, according to *Africae Munus*, is harvesting the gifts of African women. This is relevant in the context of present "political *feminicide*." Feminicide is *"misogynist killing of women by men"* with impunity.[31] It is a radical and systematic obstruction to the integral development of women. It is inhibiting their ability to embrace their full personhood. Benedict XVI's *Africae Munus* raises, in very strong terms, the question of the role of women and gender equity. This seems the mature version of his thought on women since at the Synod of October 2009 when Benedict XVI wrote: *"The Church has a duty to contribute to the recognition and liberation of women, following the example of Christ's own esteem for them."*[32] The treatment of women in *Africae Munus* has a dual purpose: firstly, to increase the visibility and recognition of women from marginalized communities to stakeholders in peace- and state-building activities, as actors who both disrupt ("spoilers") and work toward ("facilitators") peace and security; and, secondly, to raise awareness about strategies and practices to enhance their political participation and representation.

Peace processes are *kairos* occasions for the societies that have been affected by armed conflicts to put an end to direct violence. It can also serve as a lever for more profound transformative processes. In this sense, peace processes can be incomparable scenarios for the alteration of the structural causes that led to armed conflict and for the design of policies aimed at addressing issues such as exclusion, poverty, or democratization. Nevertheless, both women and a consideration of gender exclusion have been largely absent from these processes. The presence of women in negotiating teams that have taken part in peace talks has been, at best, anecdotal.

In order to increase women's participation in post-conflict peacebuilding it is imperative to invest in and support the formation of women in preventive crises and preventive diplomacy. The development of competences by women in areas in which traditionally they have had no access like defence, security, and good governance is an important prerequisite for them to participate meaningfully in peace-building. Also, it will be profitable to decompartmentalize women's associations through collaboration and communication among them, among women's and men's associations, etc. Furthermore, as the Church in Africa continues to foster justice, peace, and reconciliation in the letter and spirit of *Africae Munus*, it will be worthwhile to develop peace platforms that bring together women beyond national borders, women's political affiliations with a view of discussing and supporting their respective actions, and promoting African cultural values such as tolerance, sharing, and hospitality.

Health Care in the Light of *Africae Munus*: From a Merely Biomedical to a Holistic Paradigm of Health Care

By Rev. Giles Ngwa Forteh, Ph.D.

Introduction

In her doctrinal formulations and pastoral action, the Church has always considered the care of the sick as an integral part of her role, since it is engraved in "Christ's saving mission" itself.[1] In the Gospel of St. Luke, Jesus tells his disciples, *"Whenever you enter a town and its people welcome you, eat what is set before you; cure the sick who are there and say to them, 'The Kingdom of God has come near to you.'"* (Lk 10:1,8–9). The healing of the sick was one of the major signs which accompanied Jesus' own proclamation of the reign of God. Inspired by his example and teaching, the Church understands the care of the sick as the continuation of Jesus' compassionate ministry to the sick and suffering of this world.[2] Consequently, she earnestly desires that the care of the sick provided in her health care institutions, in ecclesial communities, and in families should bring people to experience the "touch" of the divine, a sense of the "beyond," and should enable patients to transcend their present realities and "be called forth into new dimensions of personhood."[3] Employing various descriptions of deep theological and pastoral significance, such as "Ecclesial mission,"[4] "Church's maternal vocation to the needy,"[5] "messianic mission of mercy, healing, and forgiveness"[6] to describe health care, the Church transmits a vision of the care of the sick which derives from fraternal love, invites and engages all the followers of Christ, takes into consideration the total reality and experience in which patients are embedded, and emphasizes a relational and personalised perspective of health care.

In the Post-Synodal Apostolic Exhortation *Africae Munus*, Pope Benedict XVI embodies this vision of health care when he makes a strong appeal to health care institutions and all their personnel *"to see in each sick person a suffering member of Christ's Body"* and to *"bring Jesus' compassionate love to those who suffer."*[7] In the present epidemiological and therapeutic context, marked by persistent calls for a radical shift from a merely disease-centred to a patient-centred approach to understanding health, illness, and health care, one that combines technical competence and interpersonal skills, the Pope's appeal provides a venue for a deeper reflection on how to perceive the complexity of the reality in which patients, especially those with chronic diseases, are embedded and the approach to healthcare that will adequately respond to their multidimensional needs. The Pope describes the sick person as a "suffering member of Christ's body," in need of compassionate love. Here we find a significant hint on the need to consider the total reality in which the sick person finds him or herself, and the type of care that will be adequate. Apart from the physical brokenness or the physiological abnormality with which a purely biomedical model will be concerned, patients, especially those with prolonged illnesses, are usually at the centre of intense emotional, psychological, and spiritual needs, hardly answered by a mere perfunctory diagnosis and administration of drugs. A chronic illness is one that lasts for an extended period, usually six months or longer, and often throughout the person's life.[8] It confronts the patient with a wide spectrum of needs and involves an on-going management over an extended period of time.

This paper reads the recommendation of *Africae Munus* in the context of new paradigms and constant research in the fields of medicine and the social health sciences (medical sociology and medical anthropology), to provide holistic healthcare by placing the human person at the centre of therapeutic efforts.[9] The technological advances of the past century initiated a significant shift in the focus of medicine from a caring, service-oriented model to a technological, cure-oriented model, which often pays only sparse attention, if any at all, to spiritual or compassionate care with its focus on serving the whole person—the physical, emotional, social, and spiritual.[10] Our presentation will comprise four parts: Firstly, a description of the methodology; secondly, a review of current epidemiological situation of chronic illnesses; thirdly, an exploration of the patients' "world" in order to understand their experience of suffering and discern their needs; and lastly, the implication of the understanding of health care as bringing "Jesus' compassionate love" to those who suffer. Attention will be paid to how the concept of "compassionate love" enriches the biocultural and biopsychosocial models of health care with its powerful emphasis on the relational and personal dimensions of care.

Methodology

This paper combines an integrative literature review and qualitative research. To understand the situation of suffering in which the sick person is embedded, a qualitative approach was suitable for it focuses on meaning-making and allows for rich descriptive accounts of the participant's subjective perspective.[11] It enables the researcher to explore the behaviours, perspectives, feelings, and lived experiences of patients.

Sampling was purposive and snowballing proved very helpful. Our observations focused on 50 patients with the following four chronic diseases and frequencies: diabetes (15), cancer (12), high blood pressure (9), and HIV/AIDS (14). The research participants were heterogeneous with regard to their ages, gender, and states of illness. We preferred chronic diseases because they produce complex trajectories, whose duration and the dimension of uncertainty have perceptible effects on the way people think of themselves, and their place in the world in relation to other people. Data was gathered through in-depth interviews and Focus Group Discussions, and was analysed using an interpretative phenomenological analysis, based on the outline for thematic analysis recommended by Braun and Clark.[12]

138

Our study adopts an interpretive approach based on the theory of social constructionism. The choice of this theory is informed by our primary research focus which is about meaning-making in the complex relationships, behaviors, and interactions that illness and the response to it often generate. The social constructionist approach highlights the roles of social and cultural processes in defining, interpreting, and responding to maladies.[13] It seeks to explain the ways in which people develop, through their experience and social interactions, knowledge, perceptions, attitudes, and behaviors about a given phenomenon, such as illness. It should be noted that we will consider the moderate form of social constructionism, which admits of ontological truth.

Epidemiology of Chronic Illnesses

The Pope's message and indeed the perennial teaching of the Church on the care of the sick today acquire urgency and special relevance from the current epidemiological context. Chronic conditions cover a wide range of health problems such as cardiovascular disorders, diabetes, lung disease (e.g., asthma), HIV/AIDS, mental disorders (such as depression and schizophrenia), disabilities and impairments such as musculoskeletal disorders and cancer.[14] The global burden of chronic diseases is on a constant rise, posing considerable challenges to health systems, communities, and families.[15] In 2002, the leading chronic diseases—cardiovascular disease, cancer, chronic respiratory disease, and diabetes—caused 29 million deaths worldwide.[16] In 2005, chronic diseases, such as cardiovascular disease, cancer, respiratory disease, and diabetes caused 58 million deaths worldwide.[17] According to the 2011 World Health Organization Global Status Report, of the 57 million annual global deaths—a staggering 36 million or over 63% are due to chronic diseases.[18] Four non-communicable diseases—namely cardiovascular, cancer, diabetes, and chronic respiratory diseases— emerge as the leading cause of mortality in the world, accounting, respectively, for 17, 7.6, 4.2, and 1.3 million deaths based on the latest available global epidemiology data. It was predicted that by 2020, global deaths due to chronic diseases are projected to worsen by at least 15–20%. Estimates indicate that the above-mentioned four diseases will be responsible for 75% of worldwide deaths by 2030.[19]

Africa bears a significant proportion of the global burden of chronic diseases. The World Health Organisation (WHO) projects that over the next ten years the continent will experience the largest increase in death rates from cardiovascular disease, cancer, respiratory disease, and diabetes. In 2015, communicable disease condition in Africa accounted for 5.2 million deaths (56.4%) and non-communicable diseases accounted for 3.1 million deaths (33.5%), rising from 29.4% in 2010. The World Health Organisation estimates that the prevalence of non-communicable diseases in Africa will increase by 27% over the next ten years.[20]

Although the epidemiological situation of non-communicable diseases is poorly documented in Cameroon, the Health Sector Strategy 2016–2027 of the Ministry of Public Health provides some indications of the prevalence of chronic diseases.[21] In 2012, 14,000 new cases of cancer were diagnosed and about 25,000 people lived with the disease.[22] 1n 2013, the contribution of some chronic diseases to the national disease burden stood as follows: cardiovascular diseases (4.57%), cancers (2.02 %), chronic respiratory diseases (1.38 %), and chronic kidney diseases (0.76).[23] In 2015, the national prevalence of High Blood Pressure stood at 29.7% and that of diabetes was 6.6%.[24]

The implication of the foregoing data is that sooner or later, every family will have to deal with the problem of caring for a chronically ill patient. This task cannot be satisfactorily carried out without a clear understanding of the multidimensional implication of illness, in a context in which persons are no longer seen as paramount value to be cared for and respected, especially when they are poor and disabled, not yet useful—like the unborn, or no longer useful like the elder and the very sick.[25]

The Multidimensional Experience of Chronic Illness

Illness, as a social phenomenon, sets in motion a chain of actions and reactions, which generate and modify behaviors and relationships among people in society. According to Kleinman, the experience of any given condition of illness is not only an individual matter, but an "inter-subjective" experience.[26] Illness experience emerged as a major subject of scientific enquiry during the 1960s and 1970s when social scientists provided an expanded interpretation of Parson's (1951) conception of illness and the sick role with reference to chronic illnesses.[27] These studies paved the way to substantial reviews which dealt principally with patient's "subjectivity" and the meanings that individuals gave to their illness through the use of metaphors, cognitive representations, and images which they developed around their condition. Much emphasis was laid on the notions of stigma, sense of shame, and the loss of self as essential dimensions of the illness experience.[28] In exploring the illness experience, due attention is to be paid to people's everyday lives, living with and in spite of illness, the social organization of the sufferer's world, and the strategies used in adaptation.[29]

Apart from their biological details, chronic illnesses have social, psychological, and spiritual dimensions which the caregiver must understand in order to provide care that can be termed holistic. In our interaction with patients, we discovered four principal dimensions of the social experience of illness, namely, the perception of bodily threat, the transformation of the familiar world, threat to personal integrity and autonomy, and spiritual anguish deriving from guilt. It is all about the interaction of the environmental, biological, and social factors to create the patient's world and experience.

The Perception of Bodily Threat

Concerns about the appearance and functionality of the body have a deeply felt impact on the experience of long-term illnesses.

Chronic illnesses create a feeling of vulnerability as one's body appearance is deformed, and the illness breaks through our everyday complacency to remind us that we are radically dependent on (and interdependent with) our bodies. The lived experience of bodily breakdown is often accompanied by the awareness that the malfunctioning body directly threatens or undermines one's continued physical existence. As the situation becomes severe, one feels oneself at the mercy of one's body, powerless in the face of the body's intransigence, and captive to physiological processes which have the potential to disrupt one's life.[30]

Long-term illnesses are likely to have a damaging effect on the body. Our interviews with patients suffering from cancer depict the significant influence of socially constructed standards of beauty and body shapes on the interpretation and experience of illness. The fear of disfigurement of body appearance and image as a result of the abrasive effects of illness or the side-effects of treatment, contributed to structure the perceptions of illness, as the following narrative demonstrates:

> The doctor has spoken to me about the side-effects of chemotherapy. He says that I will lose my hair and my complexion will change. The color of my skin may change from fair to dark. This is exactly what happened to my cousin who died from cancer five years ago. What is a woman without her hair? I will now look like a man. The complexion I have kept throughout my life will be lost. I will become a caricature, a shadow of myself. That will not be me again.[31]

Body image refers to one's perception of one's body or of the bodies of others, and one's feelings about that perception. It includes perceptions of how the body ought to be or should be according to the parameters established in the sociocultural contexts and how people feel about their bodies.[32] For close to five decades, anthropologists and sociologists have adopted embodiment as a theoretical framework for the understanding of experience.[33] Several studies have demonstrated that a body image dissatisfaction is related to psychological and physiological agony,[34] and often results in negative symptomatology, including anxiety and depression.[35]

The Transformation of the Patient's Familiar World

In their illness narratives, a good number of patients mentioned the experience of a significant change and limitation of their familiar world as a result of their illness. This change was presented as a major determinant of the way a particular illness is experienced. With the ability to carry out everyday activities extremely diminished or disrupted, the subjective experience of distance changes precisely because dimensions and distances such as near or far, high or low, are closely related to bodily capacities and limitations. One patient who got blind as a result of acute diabetes gives meaning to her condition in terms of her being confined to a limited space: "For fifteen years, I have suffered in the hands of diabetes. It has deprived me of my eyes. Now I only circulate between the room and the parlor. This is my own world. I can no longer go about as freely as I used to do."[36]

Limited mobility produced both a challenge and a call for different forms of adaptation to a new mode of life. In her work, *Good Day, Bad Day: The Self in Chronic Illness and Time*, Charmaz (1991) has made a similar observation of how the world of some individuals shrinks when they are immersed in the day-to-day aspects of managing a chronic illness.[37] Becoming increasingly cut off from the routines of conventional life, a good number of participants see both their social sphere of influence and physical space tremendously reduced. They view themselves as being forced into or imprisoned in a mode of life which interferes with the expression of their dignity and vitality. The loss of the capacities on which the sense of self is built takes away hope and when there is apparently nothing to look forward to time may be experienced as being fixed.

Feeling of Loss of Self and Autonomy

The loss of the sense of control was found to be an important dimension of the illness experience. A sense of control occurs when patients feel that they have the power and capacity to influence their life or their illness. Patients who lost a sense of control over their illness were reported as connecting the loss of control with unpredictable deterioration in health, loss of independence, financial security, and the ability to participate in decision-making. Various restrictions placed on them were interpreted in terms of imprisonment and this often resulted in feelings of helplessness, powerlessness, and the conviction that premature death was unavoidable. This acute and gnawing sense of loss of autonomy and selfhood is echoed by a grandmother who, before she became blind as a result of diabetes, was a very successful traditional healer:

> I was a great herbalist, and many people came to me for help. I knew and used herbs and barks of trees and could cure a good number of illnesses. Now my grandchildren are sick, and my blindness makes me incapable of going to the forest to fetch the herbs. I feel the wickedness of my condition each time I hear any of my grandchildren crying and I am told that he or she is ill. When I hear that a relative is suffering from the illnesses I used to treat, I feel very miserable and useless.[38]

Disruption of Social Life

Patients had the tormenting sense of being cut off from conventional routines—unable to work, spend time with family, socialize with friends, and move about freely. Community events such as funerals and marriages are special occasions for self-expression, and not being able to take part in them increases the burden of one's illness and can easily lead one to feel the oppressive and debilitating character of his illness. Such is the lot of one of our informants who is almost completely immobilized by prostate cancer:

> When I hear the sound of the talking drum during funerals, I am reminded of the fact that I am no longer who I used to be. I was a good dancer, and everyone admired me. I always returned home with gifts after a dance. At times when I hear the beating of the drum from this position where I am lying, the most I can do is to shake my head and wish that I was not carrying this burden. This is the existence of a shadow.[39]

The foregoing views are consistent with the assumptions of Charmaz who argues that as a disease progresses, individuals may develop visible disabilities resulting in stigmatized identities, or may suffer from discreditation of their identity due to reduced participation in everyday life.[40] Bury's 1982 work, *Chronic Illness as Biographical Disruption* was groundbreaking in research on illness experience.[41] Chronic illness can break an individual's social and cultural experience by threatening his self-identity. Habits and perceptions of life change, social networks may be disrupted (loss of friends), and more time, energy and finances may need to be mobilized by the family. Studies undertaken by various scholars have highlighted social isolations as a principal component of illness experience.[42]

A Sense of Guilt and the Fear of Stigma

Reality is composed of societal definitions and interactions, and the media provides a means for conveying definitions and facilitating interaction, thus shaping perceptions of phenomena.[43] Media discourse on the causative elements of diseases has an enormous potential to contribute to the sense of blame and stigma that may surround such diseases. Media reports, for example, which propound a strong causative association between lifestyle and behavioral factors and HIV/AIDS create a perception of the disease as a form of "divine" retribution for the sin of sexuality.[44] When this happens, people with HIV/AIDS are seen as victims, often deserving of their predicament.[45] Following this line of argumentation, the disease comes to be viewed as an illness afflicting people who willfully violated the moral code and is considered a punishment for sexual irresponsibility.[46]

According to Huber and Gillapsy (1996), HIV/AIDS-related terminology is a means of organizing the body of knowledge.[47] A socio-linguistic construction which employs such metaphors as plague and pollution to describe HIV/AIDS, focusing on the terminal, debilitating and stigmatizing consequence of the disease, and lays heavy emphasis on people dying from AIDS rather than people living with HIV invariably creates a sense of self that is helpless and hopeless.[48]

A discourse of war has been pervasive in literature about cancer and HIV/AIDS.[49] Like cancer, HIV/AIDS has become a symbol of death and extinction, incorporating a fear of being overwhelmed by the "other" and portraying an image of decline.[50] Cancer cells are said to "invade" or "infiltrate" the body and patients are "bombarded" with radiation in the hope of "killing" the cancer cells during treatment. HIV/AIDS has been positioned as the "enemy" against which campaigns are mounted in order to fight the adversary. Information, education, and sensitization on prevention are presented as the weapons of choice in the battle.

Putting the Human Person at the Center of Healthcare: the Element of Compassionate Love

The previous section of this paper has demonstrated the extent to which chronic diseases can cause psychological, emotional, and spiritual disruptions in the lives of patients and families. Some studies on the experiences of asthma, cancer, diabetes, and sickle-cell anaemia in sub-Saharan Africa show that the social experiences of patients are characterised by depression,[51] chronic unhappiness, spiritual distress,[52] "psychiatric disturbance,"[53] and "suicidal ideation."[54] The patient standing in front of us is not a mere container of a disease, a body, a case to be a fixed, but a human person with emotions, fears, expectations, experiences, and hopes. All these dimensions interact to form the experience of illness and the care of the sick should integrate them. The reductionist approach of biomedical care has been criticised for its neglect of the social and environmental context of health and illness, and its treatment.

On several occasions, particularly in their message on the World Day of the Sick celebrated annually on the 11th of February, which is also the feast of Our Lady of Lourdes, the Popes have compared patients to the people "lying, as it were, on the edge of the road, sick, injured, diseased, marginalised, and abandoned … in dire need of Good Samaritans who will come to their aid."[55] This image conveys not only the vulnerability and suffering of patients, the desperate condition in which particularly patients with chronic and terminal diseases often find themselves, but also urges the solicitude, human warmth, and personalised approach that should characterise the care of the sick in health care institutions and in families.

Pope Benedict XVI describes holistic care as bringing *Jesus' compassionate love to those who suffer.*[56] The quality of compassion relates to the whole person to whom help is given. From its etymology, the noun "compassion' is a combination of two Latin words: *"cum"* (with) and *"passio"* (to suffer), "compassion" means *to suffer with*, co-*suffering*. Compassion involves "feeling for another" and is a precursor to empathy, the "feeling as another."[57] Compassion motivates people to go out of their way to help the physical, spiritual, or emotional hurts and pains of another. It involves recognizing suffering and understanding it as a human experience, allowing ourselves to be moved by suffering, and experiencing the motivation to help alleviate and prevent it. Acts of compassion are defined by their helpfulness. The qualities of compassion include patience, kindness, perseverance, warmth, and resolve. In concrete terms, compassion means physical presence, encouragement, assistance to the patient, and action in the direction of searching for a solution. It includes both action and attitudes.[58]

In addition to technical competence that is to be guaranteed by proper training and certification for those who work in health care institutions, a combination of Christian attitudes and approaches will be required for the care of the sick to be holistic, whether it is given in the hospital, within the Christian community, or the family. This paper highlights four aspects of compassionate care.

Effective Interpersonal Communication

Practicing compassionate care means being fully present and attentive to patients and being supportive to them in all of their suffering: physical, emotional, and spiritual; and listening to patients' fears, hopes, pain, and dreams. In their suffering, patients are in dire need of someone who can listen attentively to them and carefully explain their illness and treatment to them. The ability to listen empathically, to use friendly and soothing words which suggest sympathy and involvement, and kind gestures, contribute to building trust, which is an essential element of therapy. Interpersonal communication takes a combination of forms—verbal forms (oral or written), nonverbal (gestures, mimics, posture, movement, appearance) and paraverbal forms (by voice attributes accompanying the words, such as intonation, the inflection of voice, tone, rhythm and verbal flow). "As I was struggling to enter the room, the doctor noticed that I had a lot of difficulty. He rose from his seat and helped me to walk to the consultation table, offering very kind words of encouragement and consolation to me. He said to me 'courage, it will be fine.' I really felt welcomed. As I walked out of the room, I felt better."[59]

Patients are particularly sensitive to actions, words, and gestures which convey such values as kindness, patience, and compassion, considered to be integral to holistic healthcare. Many of the patients were concerned about the attention which they received especially at the first encounter, the amount of time that was given to them, the nature of the language used to address them, and other gestures that showed that their case was being taken seriously. A good number of studies have linked interpersonal communication in healthcare to improved patient outcome, including: high patient satisfaction, improved adherence to treatment and real therapeutic alliance, reduction in psychological effects (depression, anxiety), increased patient confidence or self-efficacy, improved quality of life, and increased survival rates.[60]

Social Support

There is a strong relationship between the social environment, the quality of social relationships in which patients are embedded, and the way they understand, interpret, and experience the phenomenon of illness. Social support is the perception or actuality that one is cared for, receives assistance from other people, and that one is part of a supportive network. The concept of social support embodies four principal dimensions: 1) emotional support: the offering of concern, empathy, affection, acceptance, encouragement, constant care, warmth, and nurturance;[61] 2) tangible or instrumental support in the form of financial assistance, material goods, and services;[62] 3) informational support: the provision of advice, guidance, counseling, suggestions, or useful information that will help the patient to seek solution to his health problems;[63] and 4) personal appraisal or companionship support which creates a sense of social belonging and is marked by the active presence of companions in the life and activities of the patient.[64]

In their interactions (therapeutic and social) with family members, friends, and health personnel, the interpretations which patients formed of their condition depended on whether the discourses, attitudes, actions, and reactions of the significant others strengthened their capacity to cope with the illness or caused psychological stress. Statements made by some of the patients suffering from HIV/AIDS or cancer or diabetes such as—"My brothers and sisters make sure I am present for all major family events; I am treated like a queen," "My brother joyfully pays for all my treatments and constantly tells me not to be worried about anything," "My children are always around me, providing all my needs," "My friends visit me regularly and bring me gifts, etc.,— indicate that social support, as a context, provides a sense of belonging, acceptance, personal dignity and worth, values whose presence or absence can make a huge contribution to the subjective definition and experience of chronic illnesses. Patients who received empathic care in a hospitable social environment made up of committed relatives and neighbors as well as enabling health personnel, reported that they found their condition to be less burdensome.

On the contrary, patients whose social environment was hostile, characterized by blame, rejection, isolation, and even stigmatization developed a very negative and punitive perception of their illness. This generated or aggravated in them the feelings of the fear of loss of self-esteem and loss of control over body and emotion, of exposure of formerly private things to public view, and of being different, deficient, abnormal, or unattractive. Such feelings and thoughts were major contributing factors in the representation and definition of their condition, as it is exemplified in the following narrative: "When I was diagnosed with tuberculosis and AIDS, the attitude of my family members changed drastically. They told me that I caused my problem through my immoral way of living and should face whatever comes to me. I feel at times like a plant uprooted and flung away because they seem not to want to have much to do with me anymore. Some even told me that I was on my way out of life and needed to repent immediately."[65] In all, social support constitutes an indispensable element of the social structure in which patients are embedded in an interactive process that constructs the social significance of illness.[66] It frames the subjective experience of the patient and determines strategies for coping with illness.

Confidentiality

In the context of healthcare, confidentiality entails the protection and proper use of sensitive or private information concerning someone's illness and treatment. Sensitive information can be manipulated as the basis for disqualification, stigma, and social exclusion. A person's or his family's social image is a great value which has to be preserved or promoted. Information which seems to suggest that members of a given family may be prone to certain biological deformities can do great cultural harm.

It should be noted that confidentiality does not require absolute secrecy but rather that information be revealed only as necessary for proper medical care. The potential sources for leaks of private and very sensitive medical information include the physician, other medical personnel, and those who keep medical records within medical and insurance institutions. The potential concerns include personal or economic harms that might result from disclosures to family or friends, or to employers or insurers, inappropriate or disrespectful discussion among medical personnel, or a generalized sense of losing control over information about one's self as it enters the social media arena and other public spheres. With the expansion of social media today, concerns about confidentiality have become extremely important.

Spiritual Outlook

The Church desires that her healthcare institutions, families that care for the sick, and ecclesial communities become more and more the "inn" of the Good Samaritan who is Christ (cf. Lk 10:34), that is, a home where patients encounter His grace, expressed in closeness, acceptance, and relief. Similarly, those who care for the sick are to be the Good Samaritans, moved by fraternal charity, and helping patients to look beyond their illness to a greater horizon of new light and fresh strength for their lives in Jesus Christ. This kind of care is rooted in fraternal charity which suggests the right approach to the different situations, enabling the Christian caregivers to perceive the particular features of each person and to respond to them, in keeping with the call of Christ: "Just as I have loved you, you also should love one another" (Jn 13:34), "Whatever you did for one of these least brothers of mine, you did for me" (Mt 25:40).

In all, Catholic health ministry sees care for the sick as a sacred ministry pursued in fidelity to the example and teachings of Jesus Christ, dedicated to the relief of suffering within the constraints of the divine law, and giving primacy to the spiritual destiny as well as the temporal well-being of human beings. Fraternal love in Christ necessarily generates a community of healing, a community that leaves no one behind, a community that is inclusive and welcoming, especially to those most in need. In it the care of the sick becomes an encounter, an interpersonal relationship, in which God's gift finds a response in the faith of those who accept it. The care of the sick consists also in spiritual and religious assistance. "Meaning" is an essential dimension of spirituality and it enables patients to have a sense of relatedness to dimensions that transcend the self in such a way that empowers and does not devalue the individual.[67]

Conclusion

The pastoral solicitude of Pope Benedict XVI as expressed in *Africae Munus*, and indeed that of the Church, is for a total attention and sensitivity to the needs of the sick and for an approach which considers them as persons with emotions and hopes, upholds their dignity, and accommodates their supernatural calling. For therapy to be effective, it must have a relational aspect, for this enables a holistic approach to the patient. Laying emphasis on this aspect can help families, doctors, nurses, professionals, and volunteers to feel responsible for accompanying patients on a path of healing grounded in a trusting interpersonal relationship.[68] This understanding and approach is sure to create a covenant, a therapeutic alliance, between those in need of care and those who provide that care, a covenant based on mutual trust and respect, openness and availability.[69]

In Christ, every human being is our brother or sister, much more must the sick, the suffering, and those in need of care be at the centre of our attention, so that none of them feels forgotten or marginalized.[70] There has to be human warmth in the approach of health care. What is needed is a personalized approach to the sick, not just of curing a body but also of caring, in view of an integral human healing. In experiencing illness, individuals not only feel threatened in their physical integrity, but also in the relational, intellectual, affective, and spiritual dimensions of their lives. For this reason, in addition to therapy and support, they expect care and attention.[71] In the final analysis, an overarching culture of care for the sick constitutes an integral part of the fostering of reconciliation, justice, and peace in Africa, as per the spirit of Benedict XVI's *Africae Munus*.

The African Concept of Person:
A Source of Renewal in *Africae Munus*
By Rev. Dr. Peter Takov
and Bello Nicodemus Maimo

Introduction

The pride of the human being is deeply rooted in the logic of creation, where man and woman were fashioned in the "image and likeness of God" (Gen. 1:26–27). Whether by myth, by faith, or reason, the dignity of the human being is indisputable. The dignity of the person remained central in Christ's Mission. Human life is sacred because the human person is the most central and clearest reflection of the image of God. "This dignity is not based on any human quality, legal mandate, or individual merit or accomplishment; it is inalienable."[1] It is on this score that Christianity at large has always embraced this mission of reaching out to humanity by enhancing, protecting, and defending the invaluable, fundamental rights of all. The human person has been central to the African world view and especially from the African Christian perception. Benedict XVI remains optimistic about African Christianity when he points out the growth and accomplishments of the Church: its maturity, the reverence of life, and the vitality it holds for the future; and how as a spiritual lung, this praiseworthy description can inspire the rest of the world and the Universal Church.[2] African discipleship should take the form of "salt of the earth."[3] Now that African communities and countries are embroiled in depersonalizing and dehumanizing conflicts where the dignity of the person in the "image and likeness of God" has been mortgaged on the altar of materialism, it takes

154

the faithful courage to persevere in their faith, especially in the face of hatred, violence, injustice, and ethnocentrism. Where else can the notoriously religious African turn to than the Ubuntu?

In Ubuntu philosophy, care and love are personified.[4] Aranda sees the Ubuntu Culture as the last resort of the African when all is lost. Ubuntu can become the "saviour/redeemer" of the unitive spirited element of the African. Mwalimu Nyerere (President: 1964–1985) calls this, "the African spirit of brotherhood." Sedar Senghor (President: 1960–1980) aptly describes it as Negritude— "l'ensemble des valeurs culturelles du monde noir, telles qu'elles s'expriment dans la vie et les œuvres des Noirs."[5] All this beauty of the African has been rocked by a litany of dehumanizing crises. In the face of the crises, Benedict XVI exhorts *Ecclesia Africana* to rediscover, reshape, and promote a concept of the person and his or her nexus with reality that is the fruit of a profound spiritual renewal and hope. We tend to ask ourselves whether this exhortation is a celebrated achievement, or a project that we are called to live with renewed strength, ten solid years after it was promulgated? Is this another lot in the list to fill our shelves, collections, and/or libraries? This is the problematic of this paper. We will first trace a historico-analytical development of Ubuntu personhood and argue how its proper interpretation serves as an opportunity for renewal and hope in Africa in the face of the myriad crises bedevilling the *Ecclesia Africana* and the African personhood. In order to better situate the invaluable place of the human person in the African culture and Church, it will be useful if we have a careful analysis of the Ubuntu as the heartbeat of what is *per se cum in se* African.

Ubuntu Conception of Personhood

The concept, Ubuntu, has its roots in the *Nguni-Bantu* term meaning "humanity." It is sometimes translated as, "I am because we are" (also as "I am because you are") or "humanity towards others" (in Zulu: *umuntu ngumuntu ngabantu*). The Zulu phrase literally means that a person is a person through other people.[6] In

Global Citizen, Hlumelo Siphe points out that Ubuntu is essentially about togetherness, and how all of our actions have an impact on others and on society.[7] It is generally argued that one of the greatest 21st-century exponents of Ubuntu philosophy was Archbishop Desmond Tutu (b.1931–d.2021). He is said to have invoked an Ubuntu ethic to evaluate South African society. In some circles, he is described as the High priest of Ubuntu considering his arguments and quotes: "I am because you are, because we are." Above all, "I am because I belong, and I have chosen to belong." "I am a person through other people. My humanity is tied to yours."[8]

According to Kete, the word consists of the augment prefix: *u-*, the abstract noun prefix: *bu-*, and of the noun stem: *-ntu*, meaning person.[9] This word is found in most Bantu languages and shares the same root, or phonetics, or similar concept. Most Bantu ethnic groups use a phonological variant of the word, but its meaning, worldview, and application are universal to the indigenous people of Africa South of the Sahara. For instance, the Swahili-speaking people of East Africa use the word: *Utu*; the Kikuyu people of Kenya use the word: *Umundu*; the Chagga of Tanzania use *Undu* and the Sukuma people of Tanzania use the word *Bumuntu*.[10] In the Cameroons, Ubuntu according to the *Nso* worldview has been submitted to mean: *M'dze Bi'wiri*—transliterated as "I live and exist because of others." This is best explained by the phrase: *wiri' shiy bi' amo'oh*, meaning: "the survival of a person rests in the hands of others." Among the indigenous people of the Lebialem this statement: *Ma'vinka'wehabunkam* sums up the Ubuntu philosophy. It is translated as: "I exist and survive because of the others." Among the Mbum clan, Ubuntu is translated as: *wehja'me – me' ja'we*, which carries the same translation as: "A person survives and lives because of others."

Besides the rich etymological trajectory of Ubuntu, it has to be acknowledged that the Ubuntu philosophy of personhood has existed for centuries. Historically, it cannot be dated since it lives and vibrates in the heart, soul, mind, and the spirit of the African. Geographically, it cannot be located except in nexus to the terminology: Ubuntu. By terminology, we can describe it as a sub-Sahara African concept that refers to respectful treatment of all persons as in sharing, caring, and living in harmony with the rest of creation. It aptly describes the *modus vivendi cum modus operandi per se et in se Africana*. The spirited element of oneness, unity, togetherness, and being one's keeper: socially, morally, culturally, religiously, and above all in relationship to healthcare. Ubuntu is in the nature of the African. As a cultural philosophy it is transmitted from one generation to the other. As a socio-moral philosophy, it is lived. As a religious philosophy, it is revered and adored. The African child was therefore nurtured with the Ubuntu values like: the harbinger of sharing, caring, love, justice, symbol of peace and truth. Every attempt to move away from these realms was shunned and viewed with contempt. The aim of which was to harness and enhance the spirit of communal life. Fonlon asserts that the aim of the African system for the upbringing of children was the moulding of the person, the individual endowed with humanness and virility. The aim of this personhood education, therefore, was to harden, to instill discipline, fearlessness, endurance, and other socio-moral values.[11] Munyaradzi (b.1988) articulates that according to the Ubuntu philosophy, an ideal and meaningful life is a product of inner peace, resulting from harmonious relationships among individuals, between individuals and society, and between people and their environment. What does this personhood entail?

In this light, the philosophy of Ubuntu personhood presents a communal mind-set for socio-ethical decisions whereby individuals, communities, and the world are interconnected. Why does this inter-connection prevail? It is based on the fact that individual welfare is subsumed into the communal welfare. This can be summed up as the philosophy of "gross communal happiness." The commonwealth of persons in the African perception has one fundamental goal *cum finis*: a flourishing life tailored at begetting the happiness of all. That is Ubuntu par excellence. The philosophy of Ubuntu personhood provides insights about the nexus of a community of persons amongst themselves, with the surrounding communities, and with the world that enables this indigenous African ethics to contribute to global ethics.

In all, this shared world-view of the culture of Ubuntu is articulated by Broodryk as, "a comprehensive ancient African worldview based on the core values of intense humanness, caring, sharing, respect, compassion, and associated values, ensuring a happy and qualitative human community life in a spirit of family."[12] However, though ancient, Ubuntu transcends the garb of ancient days and is still very visible about us today. In fact, Ubuntu has now attained universal underpinnings. That is why Asante, Miike, and Yin describe the Ubuntu worldview as multi-dimensional, representing "the core values of African world views: respect for all human beings, respect for human dignity and for human life, collective shared responsibility, obedience, humility, solidarity, caring, hospitality, interdependence, and communalism, to list but a few."[13] In Louw's words, Ubuntu is interpreted as both a factual description and a rule of conduct, describing personhood as "being-with-others" and prescribes what "being with-others" should be all about.[14] In sum, Ubuntu is the capacity in African culture to express compassion, reciprocity, dignity, harmony, and humanity in the interests of building and maintaining community with justice and mutual caring. It is not just an African philosophy but the spirituality and the ethic of African traditional life. What then are the essential characteristics of Ubuntu shared and expounded by *Africae Munus*?

The Triple Character of the Ubuntu

The African Ubuntu is said to be: **Anthropocentric-Cosmocentric-Theocentric** in character. It cuts across these three realms of life: the person, the universe of things, and the divine. The notion of God is both transcendent and immanent. Although our people (men, women, and children) often pray to God directly, they usually do so through intermediaries because these are believed to have better access to God. Such intermediaries would include ancestors and benevolent spirits.[15] Mzeka and Bujo explain this view when they note that "One who pays heed to the dignity of the human person also pleases God, and the one who acts against the human person offends precisely this God."[16] African ethics treats the dignity of the human person as holistic, including the dignity of the entire creation; so that the cosmic dimension is one of its basic components.[17] Consequently, African ethics can only be properly understood from the perspective of being Anthropocentric and Cosmocentric. It is founded on love, truth, happiness, eternal optimism, and inner goodness, which are the essential values shared by the African. Ubuntu is the essence of a human being, the divine spark of goodness inherent within each being and which is shared with other beings. A person's life and existence are inseparable from others, the world-here and the world-hereafter, and above all with the author of life.

Christianity too shares these triple characteristics of the Ubuntu: Anthropocentric, Cosmocentric and Theocentric as expressed in *Africae Munus*. A person in Africa is not an island. The notion of the commonwealth of persons is indispensable and inseparable from other realities in the cosmos. The individual lives together with others, and other communities such as plants, animals, ancestors, spirits, divinities, *et al.*, share in the universe of reality. As articulated by Bujo, each member of the community and the community as a whole must guarantee the promotion and protection of life by specific moral codes. Life is the highest principle of ethical conduct.[18] Whatever is against life is unethical; whatever favours life is ethical. Although human life is the centre of all life on earth, all life is sacred since all life is considered interdependent with origin from God, the creator. This creative power fashioned the universe in order, not in chaos. Mofor lucidly articulated this argument thus:

> The principle of hierarchy, considered above focuses attention on an underlying conception of order in the structure of reality. On the one hand, order is based on the downward tendency, characterizing the relation of *Nyuy-Mbom* (God the creator) and the spiritual

realities in the invisible world, (*Mbo'lah*) to realities in the visible world (*Nsay*). On the other hand, the inclination of realities in the visible world to greater realities in the invisible world represents how order is understood."[19]

We cannot therefore destabilize this created given order, without harming our progeny and the Creator. Christianity, and in particular, the Church in Africa, shares this view which is the core and heartbeat of Ubuntu.

The exhortation of Benedict XVI, *Africae Munus*, therefore, expounds this notion that together as a family, the Church can forge ahead. One invaluable tenet of this exhortation is the necessity of interdependency which is best described in the *Nso* saying mentioned above: *kiwo kilo' yoh kibiiy, kibiiy ki'a yoh kiwo*—when the palm/hand oils the thigh, the thigh oils the hand. This is aptly expressed by St. Paul in his first Epistle to the Corinthians when he describes the unity and diversity in the body politic. "The eye cannot say to the hand, I don't need you! And the head cannot say to the feet, I don't need you! On the contrary, those parts of the body that seem to be weaker are indispensable...so that there should be no division in the body, but that its parts should have equal concern for each other. If one part suffers, every part suffers with it; if one part is honoured, every part rejoices with it..." (1 Cor. 12:21–26). This is the spirited element that *Africae Munus* exhorts the African and in particular, the African Church to renew, review, and live. The spirited element of dependency cum interdependency cuts across all layers of the Ubuntu cultural philosophy. This explains why these triple characteristics of the Ubuntu are inseparable. Closely woven with these values is the interdependency feature of the African person.

Persons in African Worldview are Interdependent

Ubuntu observes a network of interdependence of persons and relationships between such persons that are divinely ordained

160

to promote, sustain, and foster life. A human person can neither be defined, nor can they survive, if separated from the society and the cosmos that enables that person's existence. Tumaini Chuwa, interpreting the Ubuntu flourishing spirited element, argues that, "Ubuntu has one loaded principle: Whatever one does to another, s/he does it to herself or himself. 'I am who I am because you are who you are,'" is a universal maxim that forbids malicious action to either humans or non-human parts of the universe.[20] It is a matter of sustainable justice to care for other persons from the day of conception to the natural end as well as taking care of other lives and the non-living beings that are part of the cosmos.

Len Holdstock (b. 1926 – d. 2001) describes this African perspective of reality as holistic. He notes that for an African, everything belongs together; humans and the world around them belong together. Causing harm to the environment is indirectly hurting oneself. Persons are perceived as a vital force, which is interrelated with and contingent upon other vital forces around them. To explain this mind-set among the peoples of sub-Sahara Africa, Donna Richards writes that, "the traditional African view of the universe is as a spiritual whole in which all beings are organically interrelated and interdependent. The cosmos is sacred and cannot be objectified. Nature is spirit, not to be exploited. All beings exist in reciprocal relationship to one another."[21] However, Richards notes that there is tension in reality which underlines individual self-determination without negating the ideal of harmony in reality. She also notes the same interdependence between spirit and matter. She states that "the mode of harmony which prevails does not preclude the ability to struggle. Spirit is primary, yet manifested in material being."[22] This essentially leads us to another key feature of Ubuntu which is mutuality. What is mutuality? Besides the necessity of a revival of the Ubuntu spirit of interdependency among Africans, and above all Christians, another spirit in need of a revival is the spirited element of mutual co-existence exhorted in *Africae Munus.*

Mutuality and Ubuntu Personhood

One prominent idea in *Africae Munus* is that of social cohesion. Individual and common societal realization requires human mutuality. The spirited element of togetherness and brotherhood which cuts across Julius Nyerere's *Ujamaa* (1962) is described by Chuwa in his book, "Interpreting Ubuntu," as: "Ujamaa as praxis of Ubuntu reciprocity."[23] The notions of dependency cum mutuality remain salient in the Ubuntu. Mutuality is defined as the sharing of feelings, action, or a relationship through co-operation.[24] It does not overlook individual needs, rather it places individual needs within an essential relational context that views "fulfilment of self in and through the flourishing of others."[25] Authentic personal fulfilment happens in collaboration and co-operation with others. Personal fulfilment contributes to the good of the society as a whole. That mutuality is captured in the *Nso* Man's proverb: *"kiwo kilo' yoh kibiiy, kibiiy ki'a yoh kiwo"* as quoted above.[26] Mutuality is recognizing equality and overcoming our natural inclination to ego-centricism. In both Catholic tradition and Ubuntu culture, human action has dual characteristics. It is at once for-self and for-the-society. Catholic tradition is inspired by Christ's giving of himself for humanity. Ubuntu is inspired by the fact that all that a human person claims is what he has received. Giving back is a matter of course. Human life is about constant giving and receiving. This situates what Pope Benedict XVI himself taught about mutuality.

The theme of Benedict XVI's *Caritas in Veritate* is the undeniable fact of the centrality of truth in the Christian faith. Even though the main message of Christianity is charity, charity must be founded on truth. God is love and God is truth. God's Love is the truth without which nothing makes sense. Benedict XVI analogically equates that, "a Christianity of charity without truth would be more or less interchangeable with a pool of good sentiments, helpful for social cohesion, but of little relevance."[27] A genuine sense of truth is *sine qua non* for authentic development. Without truth "the social action ends up serving private interests and the logic of power, resulting in social fragmentation."[28] Even though the Church may lack the

technical solutions to offer, she does have "a mission of truth to accomplish" for, and about, human society which "is attuned to man,
to his dignity, to his vocation."[29] African Ubuntu has as her central
tenets, love and truth as well.

Addressing the scandal of hunger in the world, Benedict XVI
calls for a "network of economic institutions" to work together
for resolution of this problem which is a terrible scandal. He believes that the solution lies in "employment of relevant and effective techniques of agriculture and land reform in the third world
countries."[30] In this encyclical, personhood should always be protected from the shame of hunger and starvation. Benedict XVI reminds us, especially of the Church in Africa, that economic life is
not free from the principles of ethics and morality. If our development "is to be authentically human," it has "to make room for
the principle of gratuitousness," especially with regard to the interplay of market principles of supply, demand, and profit max-
imization.[31] Benedict XVI urges African nations especially to work
together in addressing the problem of immigration because of the
human dignity of the immigrants. Immigrants, like other citizens,
possess "fundamental, inalienable rights that must be respected
by everyone and in every circumstance."[32] A similar call is re-
echoed in *Africae Munus* § 91.[33]

Benedict XVI mentions the importance of bioethics in safe-
guarding human dignity. In his view, bioethics is of crucial importance as it functions as a battleground between the
"supremacy of technology and human moral responsibility."
However, bioethics has to be inspired and motivated by faith
since "reason without faith is doomed to flounder in an illusion
of its own omnipotence." The Pope then exhorts the human race
to have a "new heart" in order to rise "above a materialistic vision
of human events."[34]

Reconciling the Views

Once again, Benedict XVI's views explored in *Caritas in Veritate*
reflect the shared perspective between Ubuntu and Catholic

Social Teaching concerning human dignity; the necessity of safe-guarding the truth about human dignity; precedence of ethics and morals over materialism; and a worldview of connectedness of the human species as one family whose familial bonds have to be preserved and protected as a matter of ethics. Along these same lines, the Pontifical Council urges political leaders to rethink the urgency of addressing the fact that the "present economic, social and cultural structures are ill-equipped to meet the demands of genuine development." Political participation and social justice are necessary for lasting peace. Solidarity "must be made an integral part of the networks of economic, political, and social interdependence that the current process of globalization tends to consolidate."[35]

Furthermore, the Pontifical Council for Justice and Peace promotes morality as an "absolute necessity" for political or public service. Every person needs to live and act in accordance with his or her conscience. If one fails to follow the dictates of his conscience or contradicts his conscience, he can achieve neither happiness nor authentic fulfilment.[36] However, morality is not only a matter of personal conscience, but also social. Actually, in Africa, every society has a fund of moral principles. A complete rejection of moral principles annihilates society. One important question is whether the principles in place or imagined by a people are objectively ethical. For instance, unlimited presidential mandates in a country like Cameroon, some Church ministers clinging fast to certain positions and giving the impression that they are indispensable, and others holding parishes hostage thereby hijacking the affairs of the parish as if it were their family heritage. Many such cases abound and tend to build a new mission of the Church which is un-Christ-like. This is anti-Ubuntu and an un-Christian mission.

In sum, the human person is an organism within a bigger organism, the society. Human society is a part of the biosphere and the cosmos. God is both transcendent and immanent in the sense that he pervades reality while at the same time remains separate from it. Somé observes that the close relationship between people

and place is symbolized by the bond that indigenous people recognize between a person and his or her place of birth, and also in
the fact that any ritual that is performed is viewed as being tied
to the geography where it takes place.[37] Comprehensively therefore, Ubuntu is a loaded term which is defined in a variety of
ways. Whichever way Ubuntu is defined, it reveals the African
culture and tradition, beliefs and customs, and value systems.[38]
Ubuntu is the bond that underlies the cultural diversity and various value systems of most African ethnic groups. What then is
our assignment?

Human Persons in Need for Otherness

Ubuntu takes cognizance of the fact that an individual can only
become conscious of his/her existence along with its rights as
well as obligations towards the self, other persons, and the universe by the medium of the presence of others. In other words,
cut off from all others, no individual personal life is possible, let
alone personal consciousness.[39] Such personal consciousness is
based not only on the living members of the society, it is based
also on the deceased persons from whom the present members
descended. The culture of Ubuntu recognizes that the present
generation is a product of past generations. Many past generations have paved the way and made it possible for the current
generation to exist. Current generations, therefore, stand on the
shoulders of past generations.[40] Because of its "other-oriented"
worldview, Ubuntu is communitarian. Logically, it takes more
than three to make a community; it is hardly two. Mbiti expresses
this interconnection between individuals in praxis when he states
that in the Ubuntu culture whatever happens to the individual
happens not just to that individual but to the community in which
the individual is a member.

    Our usage of the term "culture" is analogical. "The root word
culture, thanks to analogy, is now reserved for a higher kind of
tillage: today, when we use the word culture, we mean almost ex-
clusively the cultivation of man."[41] Fonlon articulates this, that

"just as tillers of the soil aim at producing the perfect plant, in like manner, tillers of men aim at rearing the perfect human being."[42] For while the former is a biological metaphor, the latter is an analogical metaphor. Likewise, whatever happens to the community impacts other members. When an individual rejoices, "he rejoices not alone but with his kinsmen, his neighbours and his relatives whether dead or living. The individual can only say, 'I am, because we are; and since we are, therefore, I am.'"[43] Gyekye notes that most Bantu languages acknowledge that a person is "inherently a communal being, embedded in a context of social relationships and interdependence, and never as an isolated, atomic individual."[44] No individual can survive where there is an independent spirit away from or inimical to the community.

Since the community enables individuation and its basic rights, duties, and obligations, the individual owes the community just as the community owes the individual. Neither of the two survives without the other. The community is a product of her numerous individuals just as the individual is a product of many members of the community. The interdependent mutuality between the community and its members can neither be denied nor overstated. In his *African Traditions and Religions* basing that argument on findings in sub-Saharan Africa, Mbiti explores the symbiotic relationship between sub-Sahara Africans and their respective ethnic communities. He notes that individual existence is only possible within corporate existence. Consequently, any particular individual is simply "part of the whole." Separation from the community is not only impossible; it is inconceivable.

It is an essential duty of the community, therefore, to make, create, or produce the individual; for the individual depends on the corporate group. Physical birth is not enough: the child must go through a rite of incorporation so that it becomes fully integrated into the entire society.[45] The role of the corporate community is constant on-going creation, for the individual commands reciprocity in the form of individual co-operation in the life of the community. The phrase "being with others" in Ubuntu is of central importance. It is not limited to human beings. It includes the biosphere and the cosmos since human action affects both humans and the non-human universe. Human beings are not only dependent on one another; they are dependent on the biosphere and the cosmos. Human existence is rooted in, facilitated by, and constantly related to the biosphere and the cosmos. Ubuntu as a culture connotes a litany of taboos and/or prohibitions geared at ensuring mutual coexistence.[46]

Ubuntu and Unity: No Dichotomy

Due to its steadfast belief in the importance of unity as a fundamental value, Ubuntu personhood is not interested in separating, defining, and distinguishing. Kasanene expresses this worldview in his work, *Ethics in African Theology*, when he argues that in African religions, there is no separation between religion and ethics, between one person's beliefs and one's actions towards other persons. Ethics is an integral part of religion.[47] Mbiti notes that religion is part and parcel of the lifestyle and all activities of traditional African persons. In Mbiti's words, "because traditional religions permeate all the departments of life, there is no formal distinction between the sacred and the profane, between the religious and irreligious, between the spiritual and the material areas of life." Mbiti insists that wherever the African is, there is his religion.[48] Whether a traditional African is happy or sad, s/he is religious. Religion cannot be separated from the person of the believer. Thus, the daily normal activities of persons are at the same time acts of worship.[49] Bujo summarizes this holism when he writes: "no dichotomy exists in Black Africa between body and soul, or between theory and praxis, or in the present instance between the body and knowledge."[50] Reality or existence is a function of unity.

A definition of a human person which excludes the community is deficient of the necessary components that define personhood; the most important of which concerns his relationality, need for community and unity.[51] For instance, in *Nso*, "personhood" is: *Dze-wir* and this is employed to signify a human, male or female, who is: caring, loving, considerate, just, a trouble-shooter, and kind. The opposite is a beastlike person: *wir-yiimo' kuura*, or *wir vən dze nyamkwa*, or *"wir woo foter"* (Bamfem proverb). The first proverb is translated as, *the person's actions are like that of a wild beast*. The second is translated as, *this person is a "forest-beast" as opposed to the domesticated animal*. The last stands to describe a person of no valour or value.

Ubuntu healthcare for the terminally ill illustrates this familial unity. The aging and terminally ill are considered as a shower of blessings to one who nurses them unto their natural end. On the 1st of January 2021, Pope Francis set aside a day for the grandparents and the elderly. This is to be celebrated every year on the fourth Sunday of July. This shows the invaluable place they hold in the nuclear family, the extended family and the community. The Ubuntu culture shares this view, even though we are now fashioning special homes for the grandparents and elderly. Such a novelty is not only anti-Ubuntu but un-Christian. The community should instead accompany the elderly, sick, and/or dying; giving them, as Bujo notes, "the feeling and the awareness that they are included in the process of personal growth even as their physical strength declines, the sick and the dying find fresh courage and learn to face suffering and death with greater human dignity."[52]

This positive perspective on death and the participation of the community in the process is a great help not only to the dying but also to the living. It is ascertaining both dying with dignity and a healthcare lesson for the community. The living members of the community learn to prepare and to go through this inevitable natural initiation with courage when their turn comes. This is well enshrined in the *Nso* folk wisdom that "he who mourns for a dead person is also mourning for himself."[53] Sometimes we copy and/or emulate the wrong things from other cultures in the name of acculturation. Where Westerners delight in fashioning homes for the old because they are a burden and a nuisance, the anti-Ubuntu African sees this inhumane western system as laudable. Old persons' homes are being carved out as a blessing to the

African Church, which is *neo-Africanization* and at large falls short of the spirited elements of Ubuntuism.

Ubuntu's major objective is provision of the optimum good for all individually, communally, and above all universally. This is aptly expressed in the philosophy of King Jigme Singye Wangchuck (4th King of Bhutan) when in 1972 he coined "Gross National Happiness" as the logic of life in his Kingdom. No one should be left behind in crossing the Rubicon of life. It seeks to provide quantitatively and qualitatively the best of life for humanity. In the words of Wangchuck, sustainable development should take a holistic approach towards notions of progress and give equal importance to non-economic aspects of wellbeing. Life is not only the interplay of the market forces. Money! Money! Money! is not that which gives life but that which takes away life. There is more to life than materialism. A flourishing life, wellbeing, and happiness can be gotten somewhere else. This is the central objective of Ubuntu. Has this been achieved so far? The exhortation: *Africae Munus* gives us a response.

Relevance of the Ubuntu Worldview *Vis á Vis Africae Munus*: Contribution to Renewal

Being a product of many centuries of human existence in relation to nature, the culture of Ubuntu personhood is discovered or spontaneously observed rather than invented. Individuals find themselves already bonded with each other, the cosmos, and the Divine as a matter of necessity. The rationale for this bonding together is a product of many centuries of cumulative experience-based survival wisdom. Such wisdom is passed on by ancestors via elders.[54] In antiquity, ancestors are said to be the custodians of the culture of Ubuntu who bequeath and dispense this culture to individuals and the community. Benedict XVI perceives that this is a legitimate source of renewal, and there is hope for the universal Church in the way our African cultures respect life in every stage until natural death. Is this pious preachment of Benedict XVI not like a sermon preached to an empty church in Africa?

A sermon sent to the wrong audience or congregation? Let us look at a few case studies in the African continent.

The most dangerous plague vis-à-vis Ubuntu is genocide, traceable to actions from colonialism and neo-colonialism. The African has become the enemy of the Ubuntu culture. In recent times, a series of cases abound, such as the outbreak of the Arab Spring in North Africa from December 2010 to December 2012 and the massacres in Libya during and after the fall of Tripoli to the Western organized and funded rebels on 20th August 2011. Muammar Gaddafi was the brainchild of Ubuntuism. He was killed by Africans; his own people opened the Libyan corridors of his death to our enemy. As if that was not enough, Libya has not known peace to date. The civil war in Sudan pitting Muslims in the North and Christians/Animists in the South still remains fresh in our memories including the slaughter in genocidal proportions in Darfur. For decades Africans were killing each other in Sudan for mundane gains. This civil war was fought for 22 years and after the independence of Southern Sudan, peace is still a luxury. The genocide in Rwanda in 1994 is still fresh in our minds. This was a historic genocide: Hutu Africans versus Tutsi Africans. We cannot minimize the case of the Central African Republic where the government, rebels from the Séléka Coalition, and the anti-Balaka militias, all Africans, are at daggers drawn and slaying each other since 10th December 2012 and to date the Central African Republic has known no peace. Cameroon is not left out. We are living witnesses to the violence, killings, and massacres in the North-West and South-West Regions with no solution in sight. This is a fresh genocide based on cultural and linguistic differences. It is five years running, and both within and out of the Cameroons there are many fan clubs who are thriving from the violence, killings, and slaughter. Northern Cameroons are not left out with the extremist Islamic group Boko Haram and other groups killing, maiming, burning, slaughtering, and wreaking havoc. Thus, Africa has been plagued by a catalogue of genocidal civil and tribal wars that have been sponsored from abroad and mustered from within.

Ubuntu might have been asleep, or the custodians might have been on a pilgrimage to the gods. It is like Ubuntu has been carefully embalmed in books and stored on shelves everywhere. Bring it down from the shelves like Aristotle did to the Forms of Plato. Where has Ubuntu been? What is new in *Africae Munus*? The most fundamental question is: how many Church leaders have seen, touched, opened, and read this famous exhortation, ten years after its publication? *Africae Munus* may be good music without dancers and listeners. The African Church, and in particular her leadership, appears to be asleep. Do we need an African Oscar Arnulfo Romero y Galdamez of El Salvador (15th August 1917 – 24th March 1980) to lead and castigate the social injustices and violence amid the escalating conflicts where the men and women in uniform often turn against the civilians they are trained to protect and instead protect obnoxious leaders? How, when the people who ask for their basic needs, development, and their rightful due are labelled as terrorists, charged with treason, and sentenced to death? The Church leaders are silenced with cash and gifts. Do we need another Desmond Mpilo Tutu (7th Oct. 1931 – 26th Dec. 2021), the revered anti-apartheid and human rights outspoken activist? We are only good and at our best creating commissions or ministries without portfolios in all efforts to embezzle, rather than to guarantee the basic and fundamental needs of the suffering lot.

Individualism and egoism have upset the apple cart of the culture of Ubuntuism which is intrinsically African. These vices have been majestically enthroned and worshipped in the place of this blessed cultural value of Ubuntuism. Justice, love, and truth have become the opium and pie in the sky. Other values are almost dead and buried. People go out singing the language of love and peace without justice in praxis. There is an African-Nso saying that: *wan yilo' tong, a lohti vin'ni*. Which is translated as: *whenever the child cries, we supplicate with breast milk*. When the people are starved of their basic needs, we cannot beat, arrest, torture, imprison, and kill them. This is the exact opposite of what Jesus, retorting the pharisees and scribes in the Gospels (Mt. 7:9–12 and

171

Lk 5:36–39), said: "Which of you, if your son asks for bread, will give him a stone? Or if he asks for a fish, will give him a snake? So, in everything, do to others what you would have them do to you ... (He sums up the roots of African problems thus): No one tears a piece out of a new garment to patch an old one. Otherwise, they will have torn the new garment and the patch from the new will not match the old. And no one pours new wine into old wineskins. Otherwise, the new wine will burst the skins; the wine will run out and the wineskins will be ruined. No, new wine must be poured into new wineskins." That is exactly the way leadership is managed in most African Churches, societies, and countries, and especially in Cameroon. It is by panel-beating the rotten and obnoxious existing systems and/or cosmetically shifting and postponing the time bomb. The spirited element of the Ubuntu culture is often far-fetched. This important truth is best explained in Benhabib's work: *Situating the Self: Gender, Community, and Post Modernism in Contemporary Ethics* where he argues that: Because the identity of the self is inter-subjective; the "I" can only become an "I" in the context of a "We." Individuation does not precede association; rather it is the kind of associations which we inhabit that define the kinds of individuals we become.[55]

There is the tendency for modern day Africans, therefore, to copy individualism from the West. Individualism retards, regresses, and brings in egotistical behaviour. *Africae Munus* sets the ball rolling by reminding us of this source of renewal. The world can learn from the Church that is in Africa if and only the ecclesial authority leads without partaking of midnight meals with the obnoxious leaders. Church leadership in the then Democratic Republic of the Congo, Zaire, had set the pace whereas elsewhere and in particular the Cameroons, they are dragging their feet and divided. In the mandate Christ stipulated, "Blessed are you when people insult and persecute you and falsely say all kinds of evil against you because of me. Rejoice and be glad because great is your reward in heaven; for in the same way, they persecuted the prophets who were before you (Mt. 5:11–12)." How apt and realistic this mission has been and lived within the confines of the culture of the Ubuntu in *Ecclesia Africana* has been problematic. Individualism and tribalism, nepotism and godfatherism have watered down this culture. Now that it is in the mortuary, where and when is the burial? The only hope and sure faith is a total renewal and revival of our worldview and perception prescribed by *Africae Munus*. It is not completely lost, as we can see in recent strides in the continent. The case of Rwanda and Paul Kagame (president since 2000 – to date) is laudable. He is described as a no-nonsense leader who is not reading the Ubuntu culture but living it in his country. Like him are the presidents: Hakainde Hichilema (August 2021) of Zambia, Nana Akufo-Addo (January 2017) of Ghana, Uhuru Muigai Kenyatta (April 2013) of Kenya, Wavel Ramkalawan (politician and priest-since Oct. 2020) of Seychelles, Prithvirajsing Roopun (December 2019) of Mauritius, et al. They have left their legacy in the living and praxis of the Ubuntu. The encyclical *Laudato Si* (of Pope Francis, 24th May 2015) if read culturally, offers a lot of hope to Africa, for we share the earth, our common home, with flora and fauna and these creatures, like us, dwell in the community.

Essentially, Benedict XVI argues that a human person cannot exist as a monad in African societies. That explains his description of the understanding of the human person in Africa as really the "spiritual lung" of the Universal Church. Solitary human existence is self-contradictory. To be human means to simultaneously be a member of the human community, to actively participate as a member of the present human community, and to take one's place in the on-going chain of human history, which must be passed on to future generations. This approach to meaning and significance of human life is shared both by the Christian Social Teaching and Ubuntu, and the Church in Africa stands on strong feet to witness the love of life, such that we of this Church can boast of the generational gap being narrowed between the old generation (grandparents) and the iPhone generation (grandchildren). This, in principle, has been celebrated by Pope Francis, in creating a day for the elderly. They must not be confined in solitary houses or cubicles in the name of "retirement homes" or residences. When a priest, a priest for life till death swallows the human priest from his duties. Such a novelty is not African and not found in the Ubuntu dictionary. It is difficult to discover under this mess of corruption, materialism, egoism, among other prevalent ills, anything of the original Bantu philosophy of Ubuntu personhood or *Bi' Wiri'* worth redeeming. *Africae Munus* challenges those dark and evil influences of many adherents to discontinue, so that Africa becomes really the spiritual lungs of the Universal Church. Otherwise this potential fails to translate into those areas in people's lives. If this potential remains hidden in literature, human flourishing will not be enhanced in our cultures, but held captive by a backward philosophy that is foreign to Ubuntu personhood.

Conclusion

The post-synodal apostolic exhortation by Benedict XVI, *Africae Munus*, is a strong encouragement to the Church in Africa and a challenge to her leadership. This has been described as a shot in the arm for the Church in Africa. In the words of Benedict XVI, Africa is the spiritual lung for a humanity that appears to be in a crisis of faith and hope. *Africae Munus* can therefore be described as practical guidelines for pastoral activity for the coming decades of the life of the Church in Africa. It is on these words: "practical guidelines for pastoral activity" that our last word is based. The leadership of the African Church is being called upon to harness and exploit her cultural values which serve as the cornerstone for the Gospel. Values deeply embedded in the Ubuntu philosophy unknown to the African Church leadership need to be harnessed and exploited. Drawing from the Gospel of Matthew (5:13–15) *Africae Munus* has realized that the Church in Africa is bedevilled by a litany of human disasters, owing in large measure to poor leadership. The cultural philosophy of Ubuntu could be harnessed and employed to make the Church in Africa, "Salt of the Earth...Light of the World."

If we misconstrue the exhortation as an affair of the Church and not of the African *per se* and *in se*, then we run the risk of paralysis of analysis. We are first and foremost Africans before being Christ-like in our *modus operandi cum vivendi*. That is why the exhortation is a challenge to the African and to the African Church as a perfect example: salt of the earth...light of the world. This can only be achieved and attained if Ubuntuism is lived in and out of the Church. If this challenge is coming from without, it means the church leadership is drowning and may sink. What does *Africae Munus* set to renew that was old and unfashionable? I am afraid we have to keep our cassocks on the altars and talk to the hearts and not minds of the suffering lot out there. Let us look straight into the signs of the time.

After a Mission Station, Parish, or Diocesan feast, where and what do the priests and religious eat? What type of lifestyle do they lead? What type of cars do they ride in? Who do they associate with? Without belabouring the point, let us meditate on these two famous sayings: *show us your companion(s) and we shall tell you who you are. By your fruits, we shall know you.* As African/family leaders, where is the Ubuntu in us? As Christians/Church ministers, where is the Christ in us leaders and witnesses to the gospel mission? For instance, in the heart of the Southern Cameroon Crisis which we will prefer to call a catastrophe, we tend to become experts in Canon Law and what do we say: the Church is apolitical. The catastrophe is staring in our faces, and no one can be indifferent. We are all affected directly or indirectly. Where is Ubuntu? Leave Ubuntu aside. Where is the logic of God's creation of humans (you and me) in his image and likeness?

If the African has been failed by Ubuntu, Christ cannot fail us. But one last hope, *Africae Munus,* as an exhortation remains relevant. It is often said among our people that: *Wir yohyi yen ndzem rhə—one cannot see his or her back. Africae Munus* may be coming at a time good enough to wake us from slumber. *Africae Munus* may be coming at the right moment to reawaken the African communal spirit of Ubuntu and above all living it in the spirit of the Gospel. The Ubuntu at the national level ushers in the wellbeing, happiness, and a flourishing life for many. The African Church has to take her turn and flourish from the level of the Mission Station, Parochial, Deanery, Diocesan, and Ecclesiastical Provinces. The spill-over will be enormous. A renewal with the spirit of total commitment as prescribed by Christ and exhorted by *Africae Munus* may clean the church filled with cobwebs of injustice and other ills. With a firm hope and conviction that it is not just another exhortation and a project but a slap on our leadership to emulate the examples of our ancestors and Christ, *Africae Munus* is a necessary exhortation for us. One last word: An unjust Church is doomed to fail. We may have the most beautiful sermons, projects, schools, Christians and churches; but if the waters of justice do not wash the shores of each individual Christian, then we are chasing the shadow of Christ and searching for God in shades and shadows.

The African Concept of Person:
A Source of Renewal in *Africae Munus*
by Peter Takov and Nicodemus Maimo

A Critical Response by Stephen Kizito Forbi

One of the anthropological challenges that *Africae Munus* proffers is to *"rediscover and promote a concept of the person and his or her relationship with reality that is the fruit of a profound spiritual renewal."* It is in response to this challenge that Dr. Peter Takov and Bello Nicodemus Maimo opt for an analysis of the African concept Ubuntu as personified care and love for the human person. It contains the germs of hope sought for by Benedict XVI for Africa. His problem with Ubuntu centres on the debate whether it is an achievement or a project.

Ubuntu, as an operational historical concept, is a triptych composite. First, it is anthropological, because it focuses on the dignity of the human person in a holistic manner. Second, it is theocentric, because it focuses on the vertical and transcendental aspects of the human being and the immanence of the Supernatural Being. The importance of this orientation is divine-human appeasement. Third, the cosmocentric dimension which highlights human social solidarity in which each member of the community and the community as a whole guarantee the promotion and protection of life by specifying or ordaining ethics and morality. These dimensions are held together by an ethics focus and interpersonal relationships.

Ubuntu is an African spiritual worldview in which all beings are organically interrelated and interdependent. Also, the cosmos is sacred and cannot be objectified. Nature is spirit, not to be exploited. All beings exist in reciprocal relationship to one another.

However, there is tension in reality which underlines individual self-determination without negating the ideal of harmony in reality. The mode of harmony which prevails, according to the Ubuntu understanding, does not preclude the ability to struggle.

The principal methodology that spans the paper is that of a historical analysis. It is historical in that it considers the concept of Ubuntu in some geographical areas of Africa (Cameroon, Kenya, Tanzania). It is analytical in that it compares and contrasts the points of views of a garden variety of African thinkers in the like of Bernard Fonlon, Kete Asante, and D. J. Louw.

The underlying philosophical principle of Ubuntu is alterity. A person is both ontologically and socially a product of other persons. Ubuntu is based on two maxims. The first is "a person is a person through other persons," enunciated in the Nso proverb: "A person can only be successful thanks to the assistance of others."[1] The second maxim is a translation of the same statement that underlines the need for diversity and plurality. Mutuality is defined as the sharing of feelings, action, or a relationship, through co-operation. It does not overlook individual needs, rather it places individual needs within an essential relational context that views fulfilment of self in and through the flourishing of others. Authentic personal fulfilment happens in collaboration and co-operation with others. Personal fulfilment contributes to the good of the society as a whole.

The merits of this paper are manifold. The concept of Ubuntu fittingly captures and encapsulates salient aspects of Catholic Social Teaching embedded in *Africae Munus*. For example, the teaching on safeguarding human dignity, working for world solidarity. This approach to meaning and significance of human life is shared both by Christian social teaching and Ubuntu.

Also, the paper puts into focus the datum that human beings are social beings by nature as propounded by Aristotle who affirms that "man is a political animal." In other words, the ultimate personal moral obligation is to become fully human, which in Ubuntu means entering into community with others without losing one's individuality. Cut off from human community, personal consciousness, development, and actualization is impossible. Social participation is a constitutive element of human identity.

However, the paper romanticizes Ubuntu, and this does not do justice to the "animality" of man as evidenced in some philosophers like Thomas Hobbes, for whom man is a wolf for the other, and Jean Paul Sartre for whom the other is my hell on earth. Does Ubuntu develop any theory of how to tame this aspect of the *humanum*?

In my opinion, this paper responds to the demand of *Africae Munus* that calls for the rediscovery of the African personhood. It is this knowledge that is quintessential to solving the woes of Africa given that knowledge is power.

Christians in the City:
The Political Commitment
According to *Africae Munus*
by Jean-Paul Tagheu

A Critical Response by Stephen Kizito Forbi

The conference of Rev. Jean Paul Tagheu starts by tracing the genesis of the last two Synods on Africa, namely, *Ecclesia in Africa* and *Africae Munus*, to Vatican II. In a concise comparison of the two documents, he affirms that the focus of the former was enculturation theology, while that of the latter is Christian political engagement. From thence, he announces the problematic of *Africae Munus* in the form of serial questioning: "*Can we reconcile Christian life and political life in the society? How can someone be a Christian in socio-political context like that of* Africae Munus? *To which extent can a Christian be involved in political affairs? What are the calls for Christian political commitment in* Africae Munus?" These questions are answered in three sections sandwiched by an introduction and a conclusion.

Among the arguments marshalled to elucidate his points are:

a) The *Historical* argument: According to the author, *Africae Munus* is credited for considering or addressing the "African memory" or historicity. These include: slave trade and colonisation; the fallacious wind of democracy; civil wars, genocide, social dislocation, political instability, economic crisis, devaluation of *Franc cfa*, etc. It is in this dramatic and tragic historical context that the Christian is called to live his or her Christian faith. *Africae Munus* calls African Christians to be engaged in a two-fold reconciliation between God and humans on the one hand, and between humans themselves on the other hand.

180

b) The *Biblical* argument: The author evokes the leitmotif of Scripture: reconciliation that sums up the life and mission of Christ, justice that elucidates the will of God, and peace which is the pristine state of human existence. These are the triple dimensions, or orientations, of the political commitment of a Christian outlined by *Africae Munus*.

c) The *Political* argument: It spells out in concrete terms the social engagement of a Christian. It takes the form of a *cura personalis*, the engagement in living harmoniously of all the different strata of the population and communal dialogue. The author describes these actions as "political theology" which he defines as *"a theology at the service of justice, reconciliation, and peace, and which gives us to think of a political, economic, legal, and social theology."*

This paper has the following *merits*: Firstly, it is evident that the author's reflection is closely tied to the texts. The abundant citations from *Africae Munus* attests to this. Secondly, the underlying arguments are pertinent in the context of Africa. The actualisation of the text of *Africae Munus* to speak to people ten years later is very significant. Thirdly, the distinction made by the author of the divine and human realms and his affirmation that both are not antithetical, but dovetailed, embellishes the credit due to the paper.

Some areas that have to be looked into that may constitute some drawbacks of the paper are: A good number of the authors cited predate *Africae Munus* (2011). For instance Tibor Mende – 1972, Jean-Marc Ela – 2003, Dom Helder Camara – 2009, Edgar Morin – 2010, etc. (Si ces documents étaient évoqués pour mettre en exergue l'historicité de l'Afrique l'on comprendrait. Quelle est donc leur pertinence par rapport à *Africae Munus* ?)

In my opinion, this paper is both an invitation and a challenge to Christians to give a practical dimension to their faith. This has been couched in many ways in the history of thought; faith and works, contemplative in action, work, and prayer, etc. It is a challenge to alterity. A Christian is called to live a mixed life in which one's spiritual life and social life should mutually improve on one another. It is an invitation to be aware of a disincarnate spirituality that can take the form of fideism. Jean-Paul Tagheu's paper does justice to the prophetic call of *Africae Munus* to Africans which is that of giving hope to Africans. Practically, to give hope is to recognize the need for the world to be "otherwise." It is to recognize the need for action, to recreate the values and structures that are antidotes to injustice, poverty, hunger, hatred, violence, and suffering in Africa.

The Task of the Church in the Process of Peace and Reconciliation: Perspectives from *Africae Munus*

By Valentine Banfegha Ngalim, Ph.D.

A Critical Response by Bello Nicodemus Maimo

Introduction

The author is chiefly concerned with the crucial question of politicking that is peculiar to Church ministers in Cameroon flirting with the political outfit. Without attempting to name any Church minister, for that would appear as "piercing the tadpole in the eye" (Lamnso proverb), Ngalim gives his impression that justice and peace may not be served if religious leaders are actively wielding political power.

Politicians have the tendency of requesting Church ministers to stay away from politics. Their often point to the complexities of the political world in their exhortation to Church ministers to not meddle in politics. Consequently, they should *only* preach the Word of God and remain spectators of the political drama in their respective countries. This approach, based on a Thomas Hobbes mindset, is criticized as being unrealistic. He rejects the cliché "fasting from politics." Fasting from politics is misleading because Church leaders are part and parcel of the *polis* as enunciated by Augustine and Aquinas whom he has profoundly consulted. The people of the *polis* are entrusted into their care and Church leaders have the moral obligation to help these persons live good and holy lives.

This is situated in the task set by *Africae Munus,* as it is, somewhere between immediate engagement in politics which lies out of the Church's direct competence and the potential for withdrawal or evasion, and present in a theological and spiritual speculation, which could serve as an escape from concrete historical responsibility.[1]

What is the Role of the Religious Leader in Politics?

The task of Church leadership in establishing justice, peace and reconciliation in the society obliges her to be directly involved in political matters. What needs explanation is the extent to which religion, which is within the competence of the Church leadership, ought to intersect with politics. Following the assertion from *Africae Munus*, no. 23, this task of the Church is not easy because of the challenges involved in defining the boundaries within which the Church has to be engaged in politics in order to distinguish it from what the Church is not expected to do.

From this segment, I therefore concur with William Talla's articulations and thoughts that our bishops today need to "explain to their flock whether they still intend to defend the cause of justice in pursuit of peace, real peace, rather than supporting the false proposition being advanced by the political authorities that there can be peace in the absence of justice or through oppression and humiliation."[2]

Ngalim sets the ball rolling and maps out as well as defines these boundaries by pinpointing the role of the Church leadership in its religious preoccupations on moral education, raising questions of justice, condemning evil practices like embezzlement of funds, promotion of the common good, electoral manipulation and fraud, and the oppression and exploitation of the poor and the youth by repressive regimes. These issues indicate that the Church has to be necessarily involved in politics within the set ambit. It is the Church's duty to ensure the well-being of the citizens in the State, primarily because these citizens constitute the body of Christ. Ngalim thus refreshes that primary duty to continue the prophetic call in these key areas. He does not recall concrete historical or existential instances where the Church in

184

Cameroon has either succeeded or failed in this assignment, within the delineated boundaries.

From the foregoing in setting the boundaries of politics for religious leaders, he argues that religion ought to offer concrete steps to ensure the establishment of justice, peace, and reconciliation in times of crises in the State, like the ones we are experiencing in the Anglophone regions. Some nagging questions he poses beg for answers: Should the Church simply stay away from all political discourses and preoccupy herself with preaching the Good News for the salvation of souls? Should the preaching of the Good News not have a bearing on the practical experiences of the people, including politics? Is salvation possible without an appropriate healthy, happy, and good life on earth? These questions, he hopes, are meant to provoke thought and to present the Church/religion as an institution capable of providing practical solutions to the daily problems of the citizens as well as Christians in the *polis*.

Church as Distinct From the State and Politics

Ngalim's paper offers boundary grounds for the Church to keep away from partisan politics. The interference of religious leaders or the Church hierarchy on some partisan political issues raised here is unacceptable and against the autonomy of the State. The thesis he defends is that the State is secular, and it is unacceptable for the Church hierarchy to interfere in some purely political matters. He takes his clue from *Africae Munus* which asserts that partisan politics "lies out of the Church's direct competence." It is on this note that he specifies key areas that are inimical to the Church hierarchy to desist from. Those areas include: Keeping away from membership in political parties, holding office of responsibility in civic life without prior permission of the local ordinary, or universal hierarchy, the Supreme pontiff, perpetuating electoral fraud through uncritical political discourses, abuse of the Pulpit with sentimental politics, hate speech, and hasty expression of motions of support.

185

These citations have noteworthy instances in the Church that is in Cameroon. What Ngalim could address are instances where those breaking these boundaries are Bishops or their immediate collaborators themselves. We could put some flesh on these seemingly gratuitous assertions for a concrete pedagogy. In his writing "Church and Party Politics," Paul Verdzekov (editor, *Cameroon Panorama* as he then was), gave this succinct distinction of the role of the Bishops in partisan politics: "Knowing that no political party is a communion of saints, but an organisation of sinful men as we all are, she cannot be so certain that a party is not paying mere lip service to human rights while in fact flouting those rights. And so, the Church cannot simply come forward uncritically 'to promote party objectives' as she has been summoned to do in some countries. Rather she must seek to maintain her independence in her proper domain, the religious domain, which also mean her autonomy in religious matters, together with respect for the political authority."[3] This prophetic voice of Paul Verdzekov' remarks (then a priest) "Meddling in Politics," which appeared in the editorial in *Cameroon Panorama* in September 1969, pinpoint, in a clinically lucid style, the place of a Bishop or his immediate collaborators in partisan politics in Cameroon.[4]

How is the Church hierarchy to stay off partisan politics? Partisan politics to Ngalim here refers to militant participation in a particular political party by religious leadership. Christians come to Church with diverse political opinions, and it could be very scandalous for them to follow religious teaching that shows sympathy to some political ideologies to the relative neglect of another political party, maybe an opposition party. There are several ways in which Church hierarchy and ministers could fall prey to this prohibition of Canon Law. A Church minister whose sermons highlight the ideals of one political party on the eve of elections to the relative neglect of the other is guilty of partisan politics. Canon 375 § 1 of C.C.L. directs that "by divine institution, Bishops succeed the Apostles through the Holy Spirit who is given to them. They are constituted Pastors in the Church, to be the teachers of doctrine, the priests of sacred worship and the ministers of governance."[5]

When a Bishop is appointed to work in the strictly partisan body called ELECAM, this is not sanctioned by *Code of Canon Law*. The two offices are incompatible, and anyone who holds both offices is a divided person, for you cannot serve both God and mammon. Canon Law and A.M. advocate neutrality in political matters of this sort on the part of Church ministers. Consequently, sermons have to serve as pedagogic pieces to enlighten Christians on right choices without necessarily expressing one's sympathy for a particular party's political slogan. In this context, religion is a strong pedagogic means for good political choices without degenerating to partisan politics.

Secondly, Church hierarchy are to refrain, according to Ngalim, from accepting appointments in political life without the prior permission of their Local Ordinary or higher, the Supreme Pontiff. This perspective is also expressed in the *Code of Canon Law*, for Canon 152 states that "Two or more offices which are incompatible, that is, which cannot be exercised at the same time by the same person, are not to be conferred upon anyone."[6] He argues that such permissions could only be granted in case of extreme necessity, and there has not been any such extremity yet. For a Church minister who receives this appointment must be excluded from exercising religious duties. This is the context in which he argues for the distinction between the State and the Church. Here, he sees no blueprint where there can be an intersection, as both bodies operate on parallel lines. In Cameroon, there are instances on the part of our religious leaders becoming partisan.

Thirdly, he warns that Church ministers should be wary of being accomplices to electoral fraud. Here, sermons with political pronouncements on the day of elections are unacceptable. He fears that this attitude could breed hatred and violence thus compromising transparent elections and has a direct bearing on lasting peace, a fruit of justice. This point is also discernible in a context where Church ministers use Church property to escape with stuffed ballot boxes for egoistic interests. Should Church premises host political elections, rallies, or balloting? There ought to be a distinction between the sacred and the profane. This direct participation in the political process is inimical to good conscience. This attitude could compromise the moral authority a Church minister enjoys within the community as well as a fatherly role.

Furthermore, Ngalim is not happy with sentimental political pronouncements and hate speech from some Catholic pulpits. The Church is critical, and her ministers ought to exercise sensitivity and good judgment within the political drama of their country. This is distinct from silence in the face of injustice.

Lastly, he condemns a hasty expression of motions of support by bishops or their immediate collaborators. This practice which has been recurrent amongst Church ministers should stop. We are not unaware of the reception of some monetary envelopes by the hierarchy from the political outfit. Christian Cardinal Tumi confirmed that most of our bishops received that monetary gift, except few like Archbishops Wouking and Verdzekov of blessed memory. Why do bishops accept that money? Will they be sincere in condemning embezzlement of the common fund if they participate in the spoils?

It is not the place of the Church to express popular will on partisan political matters especially within doubtful electoral proceedings. This attitude does not promote peace and unity, but it is divisive in its nature. Church ministers should be neutral because such political participation lies out of the competence of the Church hierarchy, like what we saw in the appointment of our Bishops in the Communication Department or ELECAM.

For instance, Msgr. Befe Ateba, then Chairperson of the National Communication Council, refused to acknowledge the fact that the media outlets, particularly *Cameroon Tribune* and C.R.T.V, both being the Cameroon version of *PRAVDA*, which sought to outdo each other in providing a Soviet-style processing of information, had allotted more than 90% of their time and space to the campaign adverts of candidate Biya.[7]

In condemning this cunning spirit of the hierarchy, Talla concludes in his *Open Letter* that "some feeble minds had speculated

188

that the Catholic Church might have been influenced by corruption and the buying of people's consciences which happens to be the stock in trade of the government. Some others, more caustic in their remarks, had expressed the hope that the Church dignitaries would enjoy the proceeds of their exploits."[8] Talla tips off a bombshell therefore, that "I shall reserve the right to endorse any such speculations until irrefutable evidence is adduced."[9] And true to this spirit, no evidence has been adduced to the contrary from the Episcopal Conference to refute this claim, unfortunately. *Africae Munus* reminds our religious leaders to draw the line between partisan politics and the care or governance of the people of God. Essentially, a religious leader, bishop, pastor, or priest should not wield political power, just like the State should not wield any religious power.

Africae Munus on Catholic Education as a Precious Resource for the Transmission of African Values: Creating the Bonds of Peace and Harmony in the Society

by Nelson Shang

A Critical Response by Prof. Valentine Banfegha Ngalim

Dr. Shang places his paper within the context of the rapid spread of secularism, moral relativism, materialism, atheism, and hedonism in the world and in Africa in particular. He asks the fundamental question: How do Catholic schools balance the demands to achieve quality in secular terms while, at the same time, upholding Catholic educational principles? This is because to him, Catholic schools have a mandate, informed by Gospel values, to maintain a distinctive Catholic ethos and identity. He argues with Pope Benedict XVI that Catholic education is a precious resource for the transmission of cultural values such as a sense of hospitality, a sense of the sacred, the sense of the sanctity of life, the Ubuntu spirit, respect for elders, etc. These, for him, are prerequisites for creating bonds of peace and harmony in the society.

Education is, thus, treated in the paper as the matter of justice for each child, as a means of transmitting African cultural values (and here he defines education as the process of transmission and renewal of cultural values from older to younger generations. Education in this sense is a threefold process: receiving cultural values from the past, renewing them in the light of our present context, transmitting the renewed version to the next generation). Conscious that we are a very unfortunate generation to be living

190

in the "Post-Truth Era," Dr. Shang equally treats Education as process of passing down knowledge full of truth. Conscious of the ambiguous power of technology he warns against a reductionist approach to education simply as the transmission of "mere know-how," arguing with Pope John Paul II that science and technology should be tempered by conscience (hence the trilogy: science, technology, conscience). As a Whiteheadian, Dr. Shang follows his master Alfred North Whitehead in arguing that Education should be the transmission of genuine knowledge full of life. For Whitehead, the teacher and students should be alive with thoughts, so as to avoid the transmission of dead knowledge or inert ideas. The African continent needs a transformative education, not a banking system of education. The last section of Dr. Shang's presentation examines the role of Catholic education in an Africa that is plagued by the rapid rise of secularism.

He concludes his paper by advocating for a form of education within the African context that will help Africans to eliminate certain mentalities: the colonial mentality, tribal mentality, mentality of laziness and mentality of sorcery / witchcraft. Africa should seek techno-scientific knowledge that is best suited to the geographical, climatic, cultural and historical circumstances of Africa. Thus, Dr. Shang is against the blind transportation and transplanting of technologies from the West to Africa because these will fail just as the transportation and transplantation of states from the West to Africa have left Africa with failed states.

The strength of this paper lies in its ability to emphasize the primary role of the Church in the education of children. Education is a fundamental right, and it is very interesting that Dr. Shang addresses this issue in the paper. At the same time, quality education within the realm of sustainable development goals includes the dimension of educating all, that is, inclusive education, taking into consideration persons with disabilities. This is the perspective that Dr. Shang needs to include in order to emphasize quality and equality in education. Apart from this suggestion, I think this is a well-researched paper worthy of consideration.

191

An Examination of *Africae Munus* in View of the *Tria Munera* of Canon 204§ 1
by Rev. Denis Tameh

A Critical Response by Rev. Joseph Clifford NDI, STAMS Bambui

Rev. Tameh's paper is structured in three chapters, with an introduction and a conclusion. His introduction gives us an orientation into his plan of work, highlighting at this initial stage the different subthemes that he intends to focus on. The fundamental norm on which the paper is based is Can. 204 §1 which gives us a definition of the term "*Christifideles.*" It is based on the understanding of this canon that he proceeds, first, in chapter one to elucidate the implication of these *Christifideles*, in respect of their distinctive canonical status, in the work and mission of the Church, at the service of reconciliation, justice, and peace; then in chapter two, to highlight the juridic effect of baptism; and finally, in chapter three, to demonstrate to us why we should see the call of *Africae Munus* as a juridical obligation.

Coming back to chapter One, the paper reminds us that the concept *Christifideles* (Can. 204 §1), which translates as Christian faithful, is an identity that is assumed at baptism and by virtue of which we become sharers in the *tria munera*, that is, the priestly, prophetic and kingly office of Christ. In order to clarify what the paper considers a common misunderstanding of this concept, it goes ahead to say that all those who have received a valid baptism, as defined in canon law, effectively belong to this family called the Christian faithful. Thus, the misunderstanding being corrected here is that the term *Christifideles* does not apply to

Catholics only. Rather it includes all validly baptized persons, whether they share full or only a partial communion with the Catholic Church. This brings on board members of non-Catholic ecclesial communities, meaning, as the paper says, that *Africae Munus* is not only addressed to the Catholic faithful, but also to non-Catholic Christians. But there is another perspective which it goes further to highlight, that is, the fundamental equality of all of Christ's faithful by virtue of baptism, thus referred to as the ontological effect of baptism. The affirmation of this fundamental equality effectively means that the distinctions made between Clerics (ordained ministers) and lay faithful is not to be over-stretched to the detriment of the innate right and obligation that every baptized person has to be part of this mission of the African Church at the service of reconciliation, justice, and peace.

Chapter two aims at elaborating the point that besides the on-tological effect of baptism, there is also a juridic or legal effect pro-duced by baptism, referred to as "personhood" within this ecclesial community. The emphasis here is on the fact that one au-tomatically becomes a subject of rights and obligations in the church by virtue of their baptism. Can. 96 is the reference point in this regard. As such and unless other factors should intervene, such as sanctions imposed on the individual, a rupture of ecclesial communion or even the age factor, the exercise of one's rights and obligations remains inviolable. A part of these includes a partici-pation in the *tria munera* of Christ, as already stated above. And one of the ways of doing so is by promoting social justice and as-sisting the poor from their own resources (Can. 222 §2).

Chapter three tells us that *Africae Munus* is more than just an exhortation. It is a juridical obligation. An obligation, first and fore-most, because the interpretation of Can. 222 mentioned above im-plies that. Secondly, because the Church cannot be a true promoter of reconciliation, justice, and peace to the people beyond her bor-ders if she is not capable of witnessing to these same virtues from within. It must begin by shining the light among her own children, before taking the light to others. Going forth from these premises, he now lists the different functions, corresponding to the three offices of Christ, in which all of Christ's faithful are invited, and have the right as well as the obligation, to participate, that is: the function of governance, of sanctifying and of teaching. And he concludes with a reminder that the Church in Africa should first of all be at the service of its own members, in order better to be at the service of the non-ecclesial community.

My very first appreciation about the paper is that it is well researched and touches the core elements. The author's intent is to help us see the connection between the exhortation given to us in *Africae Munus* and the normative instruction contained in the Code of Canon Law, starting with canon 204 §1—on the concept of the *Christifideles* and the three functions which they are mandated to carry out—as the fundamental base of his lecture. In this endeavor he remains focused on the principal theme of *Africae Munus* which is reconciliation, justice, and peace, while at the same time exploring the dispositions of the law which make the action of Christ's faithful imperative, if the exhortation is to bear fruits.

Canon law is essentially a juridic expression and extension of Church doctrine, meaning that the law cannot command what doctrine has not approved. In this regard, we are able to recognize the sound theological basis on which Rev. Tameh builds up his exposé. When he talks, for example, of the effect of baptism as being the basis of the new ecclesiology of *"communio"* and the reason for the personal configuration to Christ, in whose *munera* we are called to participate; it becomes easier to understand why every one of Christ's faithful, by virtue of their baptism, shares in that responsibility, whether by right or by obligation, of working for reconciliation, justice, and peace. However, the attempt at elaborating this concept of the common priesthood turns to overshadow the other doctrinal and juridical reality, which is no less important, namely the ministerial priesthood. Actually, we observe that part II of *Africae Munus* dwells on the roles to be played by each one of Christ's faithful in accord with their canonical status, beginning with Bishops, then priests, missionaries, etc. Of course, it is understood that what Rev. Tameh seeks to emphasize is the fact that the lay faithful must radically come on board and assume their responsibilities in response to the exhortation given to us in *Africae Munus*. He recognizes the fact that they can do a lot more by their engagement because the lay faithful interact more closely with the secular world and are thus capable of sanctifying the world by the witness they bear of the gospel values, above all, by being promoters of reconciliation, justice, and peace.

This, in effect, is part of the continual emphasis he makes about the rights and obligations of Christ's faithful. What I would have loved to see, precisely in chapter three of his paper, is the practical application of the obligations in particular. Under the three distinct *munera* which he outlines, the *munus regendi, munus sanctificandi* and *munus docendi,* a lot more is said about the rights of the faithful, of which a corresponding obligation is demanded of the sacred ministers. It is an expectation that is legitimate and necessary. However, it is equally necessary that the lay faithful develop a stronger awareness of what the Church expects of them; that they continually feel the sense of being part of this mission entrusted by the Church to the African people; and that they constantly find new ways of accomplishing the obligations given to them for the growth of the Church in Africa, above all, in the project of promoting justice, consolidating the process of reconciliation, and thus ensuring that true peace reigns in our communities.

I personally find the presentation enlightening, empowering, and thus commendable.

Ratzingerian Hermeneutics of Scripture and Eucharist Considering *Africae Munus* 39 – 41

by Rev. Maurice Agbaw-Ebai

A Critical Response by Rev. Charles Berinyuy Sengka

This is a profound and dense presentation, emanating from one who has exquisite mastery of Ratzinger's theology, especially in the light of *Africae Munus*. The word "Eucharist" appears thirty times in the exhortation. Specifically, in chapter two, titled: "Paths Towards Reconciliation, justice, and peace," we find in the second part the topic: "The gift of Christ: the Eucharist and Word of God."[1] The Holy Father here underscores the fact that "word and Eucharist are so deeply bound together that we cannot understand one without the other." Basically, wars, conflicts, tensions, infighting arise from the boundaries we set up among ourselves: boundaries of religion, of culture, of race, of language, of ethnic group etc. Sad to say, these boundaries and walls of division are gradually being experienced in our local Church, such that we fail at times to see in a Bishop, Priest, or Religious, not as a Servant of God but instinctively, someone from this tribe, from that region; and if we do not act fast in implementing the demands of *Africae Munus*, the crises that the Church in the recent past has gone through in neighboring Nigeria may be our lot. God forbid! The Holy Father, Benedict XVI, thus indicates that we "must really open these boundaries between tribes, ethnic groups, and religions to the universality of God's love" and then we shall understand that "men and women, in the variety of their origins, cultures, languages, and religions are capable of living together in harmony."[2]

196

To understand Ratzinger's theology of the Eucharist and Scripture, two essential elements are underlined. First, his return to tradition, to the Fathers and Doctors of the Church, to the sources of Christian thought, and that explains why Pope Benedict XVI is not popular among or loved by the so-called Progressivists who labeled him "Conservative." During his papacy he advocated a return to fundamental Christian values as an antidote to the increasing secularization of many western countries, characterized by what he calls a dictatorship of relativism, where each one wants to subjectively determine what is true, a culture in which the truth is established on the basis of the majority, the social consensus. He, however, admits that he is progressive, so long as being progressive entails remaining faithful to the deposit of the faith. This is revealed in his recent biography written by Peter Seewald. This is how the Church Fathers understand the development of doctrine. It is not about inventing novelties to satisfy the unseemly curiosity of many, but about presenting the truth handed down in tradition. St. Vincent of Lerins taught about this in the phrase: *non nova sed nove*. It is not introducing new things but presenting the same deposit in a new way.

The second thing that helps us to understand Ratzinger's teaching on the Eucharist and Scripture is to consider the context, what and who provokes particular reflections, what or whom he is dialoging with. From a philosophical perspective, it is good to note that after WWII many questions arose about the human person, about the world, about religion, about Christianity, and about life in general. Rev. Agbaw-Ebai makes reference to the fact that after the war approaches to the understanding of the human person and of life, hitherto followed by philosophers like Thomas Hobbes, Karl Marx, Hegel, and Nietzsche, received new impetus. Nevertheless, I would like to specify that there are twentieth-century philosophers who are contemporaries of Ratzinger that had a more direct and more profound influence on his thought, such as renowned Existentialists Jean Paul Sartre and Gabriel Marcel, the great Personalist Emmanuel Mounier, and the Phenomenologist Maurice Merleau Ponti. Their views on the human person and life in general provoke Ratzinger to proffer ideas and reflections that correct the erroneous views lived in his time. Let us highlight a few issues related to the Eucharist.

The message of *Africae Munus* remains relevant today as so many parts of Africa are still devastated by wars and violence. We are living this concretely. On account of this seeds of division and discord have been sown among us; erstwhile friends have become the bitterest of enemies living in total enmity and acrimony, hearts filled with a desire for vengeance and vendetta. Cardinal Sara in his *The Power of Silence* describes the situation of war as experienced by him in Guinea Conakry, a description that fits neatly in our context:

> War is always an enterprise of unacceptable destruction, elimination, and humiliation. The other is no longer worth anything. He becomes mere matter doomed to death. When a country, a government, or a coalition tries to subject and annihilate men or nations, barbarism is never far off. Hatred, jealous interests, the bulimic compulsion of the rich and powerful nations to seize the natural resources of weak poor nations by military violence, the will to dominate and avenge, are at the origin of so many wars. The other no longer has the right to life. Indeed, war is an enterprise because the devil, who detests pity, triumphs with delight (…) How many families are displaced, reduced to inhumane poverty, exile, and cultural uprooting? How many sufferings in these lives of continuous wandering and flight, how many atrocious deaths in the name of liberty, another Western goddess? How much blood is shed for a hypothetical liberation of peoples from the chains that supposedly keep them in the yoke of oppression? How many families are decimated in order to impose a Western concept of society?[3]

We are torn apart by war. But the Eucharist is called, *Communion*. In the celebration thereof, the Lord who prayed that all might become one seeks to gather his scattered children as we pray in the Eucharistic Prayer: "Gather to yourself all your children scattered throughout the world." Some are scattered by war. The body of Christ we receive is called "Communion." It is, therefore, a contradiction for one to receive the Eucharist and soon after that be an agent of division, an instigator, either proximately or remotely, directly or indirectly of conflict or war. Rev. Agbaw-Ebai brings out two aspects of transubstantiation that occur during the Eucharist: that of bread and wine becoming the body and blood of Christ but also that of the human person. We often focus on the first. To say a word about the second, the Eucharist unites one more intimately with Christ through a spiritual transformation. One, by sharing in the body of Christ becomes one as well, that is, united with other persons that share the same Body of Christ which is one. Again, where there is the Eucharist, there is love, a genuine desire to enter into another person's world, to see in the other, a brother and a sister to be loved, even if one naturally does not have a liking for the person. By participating in the Eucharist, I am promising that as I leave the celebration, I continue to live the Eucharist through concrete acts of love, and that is when the Eucharist bears fruit in our lives. At the end of Mass, we are all sent on mission: *"Ite, missa est."* Reflecting on this, Pope Benedict XVI states, "In antiquity, *missa* simply meant 'dismissal.' In Christian usage, however, it gradually took on a deeper meaning. The word 'dismissal' has come to imply a 'mission.' These few words succinctly express the missionary nature of the Church."[4] The Eucharist, thus, becomes the source of every act of love, being the "source and summit of the Christian life."[5] At the Last Supper, the evening of the institution of the Eucharist, Jesus knelt before his disciples and washed their feet, a task reserved for the most lowly of servants. By this, he was reminding his disciples, his closest friends, that he did not come to be served, but to serve. He taught them to wash each other's feet, as a Eucharistic people. Mother Teresa of Calcutta encouraged people to get closer to the Eucharist for, according to her, unless we believe and see Christ in the appearance of bread and wine, we will not see or recognize him in the poor. The saint tells us what it means to be a Eucharistic person.

Talking about the Eucharistic mystery and beauty, I strongly wish to make reference to the scandal of the Cross. When we talk about the Eucharistic beauty, it is not about esthetic beauty, but about the beauty of the heart, a beauty manifested in the highest disfigurement of someone, and that is the peak of love—the man of sorrows, acquainted with grief, one from whom men hide their faces. The beauty of the Eucharist leads us to the beauty of the cross, hidden behind the gory, sorrowful, bloody face of the anguishing Jesus. Yet it is this face that we seek as when the Psalmist says: "It is your face O Lord that I seek, hide not your face" (Ps 27:8–9). There is the loving invitation to enter into the mystery of the cross. God turns the excruciating event of the cross into the perfect display of a scandalous, unmerited love for the underserving, paying a debt that he did not owe because we could not pay the debt that we owed. This is because the Cross is the definitive revelation of love because on the Cross, Jesus becomes the worst of sinners, the cross acting as a symbol of torture and cruelty. Yet on that cross, we see the apex of love. No wonder John Chrysostom, regarding the Eucharist and the Cross, teaches that first, the cross stood for contempt, but today has become something venerable, having moved from being a symbol of condemnation to that of hope, the hope of salvation.

Regarding Scripture, one important fact is that the Scriptures are a witness to revelation, unlike the Quran, which the Muslims consider to be the paramount form of divine revelation. For Islam, revelation is onto-theological. Another dimension the Holy Father warns us against is that Scripture should be understood in the context of the hermeneutics of faith, together with Tradition and the Magisterium. From the growing number of Pentecostal groups springing up daily in our neighborhoods preaching a *sola scriptura* doctrine, there is the urgent call to intensify our catechesis.

In all, Ratzinger's reflection on the Eucharist and Scripture remains a relevant message to all Africans, especially as the Church in Africa works on implementing *Africae Munus*.

Preaching Reconciliation in a Divided Zone Mindful of *Africae Munus*

by Jude Thaddeus Langeh Basebang, C.M.F.

A Critical Response by Rev. Joseph Awoh Jum (Ph.D), Vice Chancellor, CATUC

Summary

Cameroon, like many other African countries, is besieged by dis-satisfaction, tensions, and armed conflict. As a result, reconciliation was one of the major challenges identified by the Second African Synod which focused mainly on *reconciliation and peace through addressing the root causes of conflicts, wars, division based on religion, ethnicity, political, economic, and social and cultural differences*. The presenter, Rev. Langeh Jude Basebang, has examined *Africae Munus* with a view to proposing how the Church can be a harbinger of reconciliation and healing to a wounded people like us in Cameroon and our brothers and sisters elsewhere in Africa. His presentation is divided into three parts. Part I paints Cameroon as a land of glory and promise (blessed with human and natural resources) besieged by numerous divisions, frustrations, and dissatisfaction. Part II presents the Christian perspective of reconciliation as the most viable launchpad to reconciliation between the tribes, regions, parties, and languages of Cameroon, since he believes that reconciliation must be rooted in the Scriptures and sustained by the Church. Part III emphasizes the role of prelates and ordained ministers in preaching reconciliation and mapping out a new identity for Cameroonians, not based on tribe, or region, or language, or political affiliation, but on the Christian message that we are all brothers and sisters in Christ, sons and daughters of God. In this way we can all forge a new future for Cameroon, where "our membership in the Body of Christ is our primary identity."[1]

The Strong Points of the Presentation

The presenter has been faithful to his topic and stayed as close as possible to *Africae Munus* in discussing the role of the Church in developing the theology of reconciliation and preaching reconciliation in a divided Cameroon/Africa. His many citations from *Africa Munus* attest to this. He likewise provides a scriptural/theological understanding of reconciliation, which enables him to take the reader/listener along with him, so to speak. He presents a roadmap for reconciliation in Cameroon, which is what Pope Benedict XVI prescribed in *Africae Munus* when he appealed to African theologians to come up with "transforming theology" which can bring about "concrete pastoral ministry" to meet the challenges facing faith and life in Africa.[2] Pope Benedict XVI gave African theologians a serious challenge of moving African theology forward from mere principles, proof-texting, and accumulation of data, regurgitation of Western theological categories and terms, etc., to concrete and transformative African theological praxis.[3]

Preaching, for Rev. Basebang, does not simply mean explaining the word of God to people and trying to get them to live more Christ-like lives. While forming Christ-like Christians would bring about a change of heart and subsequently reconciliation, Rev. Basebang believes that when pastors become authentic preachers of the word of God and let that word incarnate the words and deeds of their Christians, then we will become reconciled to each other and to God. It is in this way that we will forge a new identity for Cameroonians, the "new WE."

Additional Thoughts on the Presenter's Roadmap to Reconciliation

While I think that preaching is one of the ways in which we, as pastors, can pass across our message of reconciliation, heal wounded hearts, and restore peace in our communities and country, I also think that this preaching must do two things in order to be effective in our situation. First, it must move our people to be both lovers and seekers of peace. And second, it must call out unjust words, actions, and situations no matter where they come from. As Marcel Uwineza, S.J. says, the Church must speak out against "selfish treatment of others—which includes clinging to power, accumulation of wealth, corruption, tribalism, and a refusal of dialogue," because this is "in opposition to the Church's social teaching, which emphasises the intrinsic dignity of each person and the search for the common good."[4]

Next, in addition to preaching, *Africae Munus* encourages us to engage in dialogue with our Protestant brothers and sisters, adherents of African Traditional Religion, other ecclesial movements, Muslims, and those with other faiths.[5] Can the Catholic Church take the lead in facilitating dialogue and seek input from people of other faiths in view of achieving reconciliation? As *Africae Munus* no. 11 states, the challenge for African bishops and pastoral leaders is how to "dialogue with the various constituencies within the church and society,"[6] to embrace the contributions of all members of the family in justice and peace so that the Church can transform theology into pastoral care.[7]

Third, preaching reconciliation has to go with prayer, as reconciliation is ultimately the work of the Holy Spirit. *Africae Munus* encourages African countries to "celebrate yearly a day or week of reconciliation, particularly during Advent or Lent."[8] As we know, prayer goes with action. We need to organize workshops and seminars to discuss guidelines and propose the process of implementing *Africae Munus* so as to revitalise the Church's commitment to the promotion of reconciliation, justice, and peace.

The New WE and our Political Future

Rev. Basebang proposed a new identity for the new political future of Cameroonians and that proposal insinuates that the "new WE" would have " a new Christian identity...membership in the

Body of Christ [would be] our primary identity."[9] My suggestion would be that reconciliation needs a change of heart and mentality based on the Social Teachings of the Church, especially the dignity and equality of the human being, justice and peace, the search for the common good, and our stewardship of creation. *Africae Munus* proposes that we need to work on authentic reconciliation which, as we know, is built on truth and justice.[10] The Church needs to preach justice and peace and be seen to be at the forefront of the quest for truth and justice. Sadly, as Frantz Fanon says, there are those among us who, "possessing the exceptional privilege of being able to speak words of truth ... have taken refuge in an attitude of passivity, of mute indifference, and of cold complicity."[11]

Conclusion

Africae Munus is encouraging all the members of the Church in Africa to take their specific role in committing themselves to building a reconciled, just, and peaceful society. In line with the demands of *Africae Munus*, Rev. Basebang has presented his thoughts on what it means to preach reconciliation in a divided country/continent like our own. SECAM President, Cardinal Pengo thinks that "the Exhortation should give the Church in Africa a new impetus to build a more reconciled Africa by pursuing the paths of truth, justice, love and peace."[12] And I think this paper provides a possible roadmap as to how we should be doing so through preaching.

Challenge to Women as Peace Agents:
Africae Munus in a Feminine Key
by Prof. Stephen Kizito Forbi, S.J.

A Critical Response by Dr. Vivian Bongka Tah

This paper has examined from a feminine perspective the Church's provision in the mediation of peace and reconciliation. It evaluates the apostolic exhortation of Pope Benedict XVI's *Africae Munus* on the engagement of Africa in challenges they face, which also affect the Church as a principal actor and reveals that women's participation in post-conflict peace-building and reconciliation is still a challenge, irrespective of their vital role in enhancing authentic peace and justice. The paper thus investigates antagonistic forces that impede women as active participants in peace reconstruction and also highlights the need to create inclusive platforms that mitigate subjugation and promote egalitarianism especially in a peace-building process.

The feminist theory is used to corroborate analysis in this study as it underscores that patriarchy must be deconstructed to enhance female participation in an African society which is in dire need of peace. The study as a result is buttressed by innovative feminist perspectives emphasized in Edith Stein's concept of "Feminine Genius," John Paul II's "New Feminism," and Benedict XVI's "Feminine Gift." These points of views stress the importance of female active participation in public and social life, especially as it is in relationship with *Africae Munus'* prescription that upholds unity as Christ is the whole that holds all irrespective of sex or any other criterion. The importance of women cannot be undermined for they are the bearers and protectors of life. Consequently, women must participate in reconciliation, justice, and peace, for they understand the sacredness of human life.

The empowerment of women for mediation thus demands the integration of women in key post-conflict processes. Benedict XVI in this effect pushes forward that the Church in Africa needs to shift from only recognising female dignity to concretely involving them in civil and social lives. Both men and women are challenged to participate in peace-building processes collectively and actively. This study highlights that this can occur through channels like strategic empowerment, which shapes ground-breaking models to improve on genuine female participation in negotiating and mediating peace from all standpoints; strategic enculturation, which promotes the political and economic emancipation of peoples, predominantly women who must be inclusive in reconciliation, justice, and peace processes; and a political will adopted by regional, national, and international organizations as well as other stakeholders to guarantee the active participation of women in negotiating peace.

This paper further demonstrates that the immediate inclusion of women in peace-building processes and other security areas, as Benedict XVI upholds, will certify an appeasing and humanizing result, so he recommends the establishment of "human ecology" which denounces self-destruction of the dignity of the person as created male and female in the image and likeness of God. Against such a destructive ideology, Benedict XVI encourages the respect and preservation of human life. This study thus discourages "feminicide" which in a systematic way, relegates and keeps women perpetually passive and silent. It advocates for female inclusion and active participation in reconciliation, justice, and peace processes. It calls for collective commitment in complementary agencies that include women, men, and youths. This study is significant because it underlines the Church's contribution to creating general awareness of the importance of female active participation in leadership roles. The study could not only serve as an important tool to stimulate female consciousness to be empowered and create an authentic voice in mediation procedures, but encourages complementary gender roles that negate biased platforms that sanction conflicts and war in Africa. Finally, this study has integrated both the qualitative and the quantitative research methods to reach at its finding that women's participation in negotiating reconciliation, justice, and peace in most African societies was insignificant. Therefore, stakeholders like states and other international bodies could use results obtained here to derive inclusive policies that promulgate reconciliation, justice, and peace. Marguerite A. Peeters maintains that "All human beings are born free and equal in dignity and rights," therefore equality remains a supreme value in societies that desire to flourish in peace and harmony.[1]

Health Care in the Light of *Africae Munus*: From a Merely Biomedical to a Holistic Paradigm of Health Care

by Rev. Dr. Giles Ngwa Forteh

A Critical Response by Rev. Herbert Niba, John Paul II Institute of Theology, Buea

The paper entitled "Health Care in the light of *Africae Munus*: From a merely Biomedical to a Holistic Paradigm of Health Care," by Dr. Giles Ngwa Forteh, is situated along the lines of the social questions raised by *Africae Munus*. Given that the Church is an agent and catalyst of socio-political, economic, cultural, and ethical transformation, the vast fields of education, health, gender, etc., provide the social contexts where Christianity has to play a role in bringing about reconciliation, justice, and peace. This paper therefore enriches the reflection of this conference by plunging us into the world of healthcare, which is a world everyone should be concerned about. That being said, the central argument of Dr. Forteh's paper can be presented in this syllogism:

Premise 1: Pastoral care of the sick, which is an extension of the saving mission of Christ, targets the whole person: body, soul, and spirit.

Premise 2: The reality of Africa shows an increasing prevalence of chronic diseases, which not only harm the patients physically, but cripple them psychologically, ostracize them socially, and depress them spiritually.

Conclusion: For healthcare to be efficient, it must be holistic, and in line with Benedict XVI's recommendation in *Africae Munus* no. 140, it must bring Jesus's compassionate love to those who suffer, by effective interpersonal communication, social support, confidentiality, and spiritual assistance.

The above syllogism is an attempt to translate this work into a philosophical category. Yet the work was done with the research methods of Social and Cultural anthropology. An assessment of this must therefore target an examination of the data collection, the sample audience interviewed and their credibility, the analysis of the results obtained, and the conclusions drawn from that analysis. It is these criteria that show the first strength of this paper, namely, its methodological rigor. The combination of literary review and qualitative research makes the paper as holistic as its title, just as the interview selection and sampling among 50 patients with four prevalent chronic diseases (diabetes, cancer, high blood pressure, and HIV-AIDS) make the research very pertinent to our local reality.

A clue to establishing the pertinence of holistic health care as brought out in *Africae Munus* is to find out how consistent this idea is with Pope Benedict XVI's oeuvre and ministry. The evidence shows that the idea of holistic care is not an isolated teaching of Benedict XVI, as it is spread in his various messages on World Day of the Sick. Integral health care that targets the total person in his total environment is almost a leitmotif for Benedict XVI's pastoral ministry. Some of the boldest utterances made by him in the field of ethics touched on this integral understanding of health care. One key example is worth mentioning. On board the flight to Cameroon on March 17, 2009, a French Journalist, Philippe Visseyrias from France 2, criticized the Church for its denial to permit the use of condoms to reduce the spread of HIV-AIDS. This position, according to the journalist, was both unrealistic and ineffective to a continent so afflicted by the pandemic. With customary clarity, Benedict XVI replied that the problem of HIV-AIDS could not be overcome merely with money, necessary though it could be, nor with the mass distribution of contraceptives. On the contrary, that could rather increase it, by increasing the level of promiscuity that will come along with the false assurance of the 100% efficacy of prophylactics.[1] The holistic solution, for Benedict XVI, has to do first with the fostering of responsible behavior, which will bring out the truly human dimension of sexuality, that is to say a spiritual and human renewal inwardly, and second the extension of true friendship offered to those who are suffering, and the willingness to make sacrifices to be alongside the suffering. The secular press has never forgiven Pope Benedict XVI for that statement, and the other tragedy was that the entire trip to Cameroon (which was Benedict's first to Africa after assuming the Petrine office) became eclipsed by the media chagrin that developed from his words.

That said, we find in this interview the same position the Pope will later develop in *Africae Munus*. Health care must be holistic or integral; it should target the entire human being. If it is true that ordinary human health care is greatly supported by effective interpersonal communication, social support, confidentiality, and spiritual assistance, then this must be felt especially in mission-run hospitals. This would make them an extension of Christ, who upon healing a paralytic said, "Your sins are forgiven" (Mk 2:5), to spell out a divine truth that beyond the cure of physical infirmity, there was the need to re-establish reconciliation or communion with God.

Although the author does not explicitly mention it, one of the recommendations of *Africae Munus* no. 141 concerning holistic health care is that each health care institution ought to have a chapel. My personal experience as a chaplain to the Limbe Mile One District Hospital is that although I minister to the sick on their hospital beds, the presence of the chapel reminds hospital staff (management, physician, and nurses) as well as the sick themselves that God alone is the Lord of life and death.

The call to holistic health care invites health care institutions to recognize that the value of life is not measured only by physical ability and ephemeral standards of what beauty is. It calls for a rediscovery of the prolife vocation of the medical profession, and to see in the human being an image of God, not just a bundle of veins and tissues.

The call to holistic care challenges administrators of health institutions to avoid the temptation of making hospitals a source of enrichment from grant moneys or making them the locus of a network of corruption. The call to holistic care also invites caregivers to understand that hospitality is even a first remedy in hospitals before diagnosis, and that compassion not only helps the afflicted, but uplifts the caregiver.

A tradition born on African soil identifies the Good Samaritan with the Lord Jesus himself and issues an invitation to hope. *Africae Munus* quotes one of the Fathers of the Church as follows: "Who more than he, took pity on us, when by the princes of darkness, we were all but mortally wounded by our fears, lusts, passions, pains, deceits, and pleasures? Of these wounds the only physician is Jesus."[2] When health care is integral, it is Christ-like, for it is an imitation of what Christ did. It is also meritorious, for Christ also said: Whatsoever you do to the least of my brethren, you do it to me (Mt 25:40).

Endnotes

Introduction

1   Benedict XVI, Pope. Post-Synodal Apostolic Exhortation, *Africae Munus*, The Holy See, Dicastero per la Comunicazione - Libreria Editrice Vaticana, no. 163. Accessed December 2021. https://www.vatican.va/content/benedict-xvi/en/apost_exhortations/documents/hf_ben-xvi_exh_20111119_africae-munus.html

2   Benedict XVI, *Africae Munus*, nos. 22, 49.

3   Benedict XVI, *Africae Munus*, no. 13.

4   Benedict XVI, *Africae Munus*, no. 11.

5   Benedict XVI, *Africae Munus*, no. 10.

6   Benedict XVI, *Africae Munus*, nos. 4–5.

7   Benedict XVI, *Africae Munus*, no. 56.

8   Benedict XVI, *Africae Munus*, no. 57.

9   Benedict XVI, *Address to Members of the Special Council for Africa of the Synod of Bishops* (Yaounde, 19 March 2009). See also Benedict XVI, *Africae Munus*, no. 137.

10 Benedict XVI, *Africae Munus*, no. 13.

The Theology of Law of Joseph Ratzinger/Benedict XVI: Pastoral Perspectives for the Church in Africa in the Light of *Africae Munus*, Ten Years Later

1   Joseph Ratzinger, *Salt of the Earth: The Church at the End of the Millennium, An Interview with Peter Seewald,* translated by Adrian Walker (San Francisco: Ignatius Press, 1997), 66.

2   Benedict XVI, *Africae Munus*, no. 22.

3   Alan Watson, "Book One," In *The Digest of Justinian, Volume 1*, Revised edition., 1.1.1. University of Pennsylvania Press, 1998. http://www.jstor.org/stable/j.ctt3fhn70.11.

4   Justinian, *The Digest of Justinian, Volume 1*, ed. by Alan Watson. Revised edition., 1.1.1. University of Pennsylvania Press, 1998. Accessed December 2021. http://www.jstor.org/stable/j.ctt3fhn70.11.

5   Thomas Aquinas, *Summa Theologiae* II-II q. 57, a.1.

6   Bernard Murphy, *The Philosophy of Positive Law: Foundations of Jurisprudence* (Yale: Yale University Press 2005), 62.
7   Javier Hervada, *What is Law? The Modern Response of Juridical Realism: An Introduction to Law* (Montréal: Wilson & Lafleur, 2009), 25.
8   Benedict XVI, Address to Bundestag. Accessed December 2021. https://www.vatican.va/content/benedict-xvi/en/speeches/2011/september/documents/hf_ben-xvi_spe_20110922_reichstag-berlin.html
9   Benedict XVI, Address to Bundestag.
10 Cicero, Marcus Tullius. *De Re Publica De Legibus*, trans. by Clinton Walker Keyes, 1.18–19. Cambridge, MA: Harvard University Press, 1928. With the exception of Cicero, who had a very broad understanding of lex, his definition of lex is the reverse of what other jurists taught. Here is his definition: "lex is the highest reason, inherent in nature, which orders what ought be done and forbids the contrary. That same reason, when it is secured and completed in the human mind, is law" [lex est ratio summa, insita in natura, quae iubet ea quae facienda sunt, prohibetque contraria. Eadem ratio, cum est in hominis mente confirmata et perfecta, lex est]. And so, they judge that lex, whose business is to prescribe acting rightly and to proscribe doing wrong, is practical wisdom (prudentia).
11 Justinian, *Digest*, 1.1.0.
12 Gaius, *Institutes of Roman Law*, I, nos. 3, 25.
13 Thomas Hobbes, *Leviathan* (London: Penguin Classics 1982) 14, 3.
14 Aquinas, *Summa Theologiae*, II-II, q. 57.
15 Justinian, *Digest*, 1.1.1.4.
16 Aquinas, *Summa Theologiae*, I-II q. 95.
17 Aquinas, *Summa Theologiae*, I-II q. 91. a.1.
18 Aquinas, *Summa Theologiae*, I-II q. 93. a.1.
19 Caesar Flavius Justinian, "The Institutes of Justinian," trans. J. B. Moyle, 1.2.1. Project Guttenberg's The Institutes of Justinian. Release date 11 April 2009. Last updated 6 February 2013. Accessed December 2021. https://www.gutenberg.org/files/5983/5983-h/5983-h.htm#link2H_4_0003
20 Merely ecclesiastical laws bind only those baptized in the Catholic church or those who have been received into it and possess the use of reason. C. 11. *Codex Iuris Canonici auctoritate Ioanis Pauli PP. II promulgatus* (Vatican City: Libreria Editrice Vaticana, 1983) c. 208. English translation from the *Code of Canon Law, Latin-English Edition: New English Translation*. (Washington, DC: CLSA,1998).
21 Benedict XVI, *Address for the Inauguration of the Judicial Year of the Tribunal of the Roman Rota*, 21 January 2012.

22 Benedict XVI, Address to Bundestag.

23 Ibid.

24 Ibid.

25 Ibid.

26 John Paul II, *Natural Law is Sure Foundation of Human Rights*, accessed December 2021. www.catholicculture.org/culture/library/view.cfm?id=826.

27 Benedict XVI, *Address at Westminster Hall, City of Westminster*. https://www.vatican.va/content/benedict-xvi/en/speeches/2010/september/documents/hf_ben-xvi_spe_20100917_societacivile.html

28 Benedict XVI, Address to Bundestag.

29 Marta Cartabia & Andrea Simoncini, eds. *Pope Benedict XVI's Legal Thought: A Dialogue on the Foundations of Law* (New York: Cambridge University Press, 2015), 79.

30 Benedict XVI, *Address for the Inauguration of the Judicial Year of the Tribunal of the Roman Rota*, 29 January 2010.

31 Benedict XVI, *Address for the Inauguration of the Judicial Year of the Tribunal of the Roman Rota*, 40.

32 Benedict XVI, *Africae Munus*, no. 91.

Christians in the City:
The Political Commitment According to *Africae Munus*

1 See John Paul II, Post-Synodal Apostolic Exhortation *Ecclesia in Africa. On The Church in Africa* (Nairobi: Daughters of St Paul, 2005).

2 See Benedict XVI, Post-Synodal Apostolic Exhortation *Africae Munus. Africa's Commitment. On The Church in Africa in Service to Reconciliation, justice, and peace* (Roma/Kenya: Liberia Edict rice Vaticana/Daughters of Saint Paul, 2011).

3 John Paul II, *Ecclesia in Africa*, n. 2: "The Second Vatican Ecumenical Council can certainly be considered, from the point of view of the history of salvation, as the cornerstone of the present century which is now rapidly approaching the Third Millennium."

4 John Paul II, *Ecclesia in Africa*, no. 141.

5 Id., nos. 63, 85.

6 These themes, even though already present in *Ecclesia in Africa*, were not prioritized by the Fathers and theologians of the First African Synod. Cf. *Ecclesia in Africa*, nos. 79, 105, 110, 113.

7 Benedict XVI, *Africae Munus*, nos. 10, 17.

8 Tertullian, *Apologia*, no. 18.

9   See Augustine of Hippo, *The City of God*, XIV, 28. Translated by Marcus Dods, D.D., in *Nicene and Post-Nicene Fathers*, Series I, Volume 2, edited by Philip Schaff (Grand Rapids, Michigan: Christian Classics Ethereal Library, 1995).

10   Voir Edgar Morin, *Les Sept Savoirs Nécessaires à l'Éducation du Futur*, in *http://www.agora21.org/unesco/7savoirs* (consulté 14/01/2010), chapter 3.

11   Claude Rivière, "La religion au péril de la (post)modernité," in *Cultures et Sociétés. Sciences de l'Homme*, n. 6, April 2008 ("Visages du religieux dans le monde contemporain"), p. 37–44. See p. 38 for the reference.

12   Benedict XVI, Exhortation Apostolique sur l'Église au Moyen-Orient (14 Septembre 2012), no. 29.

13   Dom Helder Camara, *Essential Writings (Modern Spiritual Masters Series)*, edited by Francis McDonagh, (Maryknoll, New York: Orbis Books, 2009). Also see John Dear, *Peace Behind Bars: A Peacemaking Priest's Journal from Jail* (New York, Sheed and ward: 1995), p. 65.

14   Benedict XVI, *Africae Munus*, no. 17.

15   Second Vatican II Council, The Pastoral Constitution *Gaudium et Spes*, On the Church in the Modern World, 76, no. 2, in *Vatican II Council: The Conciliar and Post Conciliar Documents Volume 1*, edited by Austin Flannery, O.P. (Dublin: Dominican Publications, 1975).

16   See *Gaudium et Spes* 76, no. 1.

17   *Gaudium et Spes*, 76, no. 3.

18   *Gaudium et Spes*, 76, no. 1: "It is very important, especially where a pluralistic society prevails, that there be a correct notion of the relationship between the political community and the Church, and a clear distinction between the tasks which Christians undertake, individually or as a group, on their own responsibility as citizens guided by the dictates of a Christian conscience, and the activities which, in union with their pastors, they carry out in the name of the Church."

19   Benedict XVI, *Africae Munus*, no. 103. In no. 102, he further said: "Do not waste your human and pastoral energies in the vain search for answers to questions which are not of your direct competence, or in the twists and turns of a nationalism that can easily blind."

20   Jean-Marc Ela, *Repenser la théologie africaine. Le Dieu qui libère* [Rethinking the African Theology. The God Who Sets Free] (Paris : Karthala, 2003), 30. "C'est au cœur de cette historicité que la Révélation nous atteint."

21   Jean-Marc Ela, *Repenser la théologie africaine*, p. 11.

22   Benedict XVI, *Africae Munus*, no. 9.

23   Id., no. 81.

24 John Paul II, *Ecclesia in Africa,* no. 110.

25 Jean-Marie Roger Tillard, *Church of Churches. The Ecclesiology of Communion.* Translated from French by R. C. De Peaux, O. Praem (Collegeville, Minnesota: The Liturgical Press, 1992), 244.

26 Benedict XVI, *Africae Munus,* no. 155.

27 Id., nos. 20, 155.

28 Id., no. 21.

29 Id., no. 169.

30 Benedict XVI, *Africae Munus,* no. 22.

31 Id., no. 25.

32 Id., no. 26.

33 Id., nos. 26–27.

34 Id., no. 83.

35 Benedict XVI, *Africae Munus,* no. 18.

36 Id., no. 18.

37 Id., nos. 32–41.

38 Id., nos. 42–68.

39 Id., nos. 69–87.

40 Tibor Mende, *De l'aide à la recolonisation. Les leçons d'un échec* (Paris: Seuil, 1972).

41 Benedict XVI, *Africae Munus,* nos. 88–96.

42 Read on this Elga Sarapung and Corrie Van der Ven, "From Religion as Part of the Problem to Religion as Part of the Solution: Case Study on Multi-religious Engagement for Peace and Conflict Solution in Indonesia," in *The Ecumenical Review,* 68.4 (Religion and Development), December 2016, p.433–43. See also, Xavier Dijon, "La contribution de la religion au projet politique de l'Europe," in *Nouvelle revue théologique.* Tome 140, no. 2 (Avril-Juin 2018), 276–94.

43 This is a rephrasing of Edgar Morin who said : "*La science est une affaire trop sérieuse pour être laissée entre les mains des scientifiques.*" Edgar Morin, *Méthode 6, Ethique* (Paris: Seuil, 2004), p. 80.

44 Conseil Permanent de la Conférence des Évêques de France, *Dans un monde qui change, retrouver le sens du politique* (Paris: Bayard/Cerf/Mame, 2016), p. 20–21.

45 Conseil Permanent de la Conférence des Évêques de France, *Dans un monde qui change, retrouver le sens du politique,* p. 21.

46 Voir François Daguet, "Chronique de théologie politique et de doctrine sociale," in *Revue thomiste* 110/3 (Juillet-septembre 2010), 515–28.

47 François Daguet, "Chronique de théologie politique et de doctrine sociale," 518–19.

48 Benedict XVI, *Africae Munus,* no. 22. And also, Benedict XVI, *Encyclical Letter Caritas in Veritate* (29 June 2009), no. 9. The Church does

not have technical or technocratic solutions, because "Christ does not propose a revolution of a social or political kind, but a revolution of love, brought about by his complete self-giving through his death on the Cross and his resurrection." *Africae Munus*, no. 26.

49 Emmanuel Mounier, *Feu la Chrétienté*, in *Œuvres complètes*, tome III (Paris : Seuil, 1962), p. 702.

50 For Emmanuel Mounier, *Feu la Chrétienté*, p. 707–08, "The Church is now withdrawing from many of the quarrels where she had been a pleading party since the Middle Ages. She does not renounce her presence in the world, she collects herself in the most essential way, and ultimately also the most effective of her presence, which is not spreading, which is not imperialism, but a burning discretion, like the very presence of God."

51 Vincent Cosmao, *Changer le monde : une tâche pour l'Église* (Paris: Cerf, 1979), 175.

52 *Lineamenta of the Second Synod for Africa*, no. 10, in *Catholic Documentation*, nos. 2365, 2006, p. 830–61.

53 Benedict XVI, *Africae Munus*, no. 22.

54 *Lineamenta of the Second Synod for Africa*, no. 15.

55 Bernard P. Prusak, *The Church Unfinished. Ecclesiology Through the Centuries* (New York / Mahwah, Paulist Press: 2004), 7.

The Task of the Church in the Process of Peace and Reconciliation: Perspectives from *Africae Munus*

1 Benedict XVI, *Africae Munus*, no. 23.

2 J. van Oort, *Jerusalem and Babylon: a Study into Augustine's City of God and the Sources of His Doctrine of the Two Cities* (Leiden / New York: E.J. Brill, 1991), 93–163; 118–23.

3 Samuel Enoch Stumpf and James Fieser. *Philosophy: History and Problems*, 6th ed. (Boston: McGraw-Hill, 2003).

4 Samuel Enoch Stumpf and James Fieser. *Philosophy: History and Problems*.

5 Barr, Robert R. "The Two Cities in Saint Augustine." *Laval Théologique et Philosophique* 18, no. 2 (1962), 219–29. https://doi.org/10.7202/1020026ar.

6 Thomas Aquinas, edited by Thomas Gilby, *Summa Theologiae* (Garden City, N.Y.: Image Books, 1969), I-IIa. q19, a4.

7 Id., Ia-IIa. q100 , a5, ad.1.

8 Id., Ia-IIa. q100, a5, ad.1.

9 Paul A. Nde, "The Church and the State; A critical reading of John

Locke's Theologico-Polical Thought," in *International Journal of Trend in Scientific Research and Development* (IJTSRD) 5, no. 1 (December, 2020), 1588–92. https://www.ijtsrd.com/humanities-and-the-arts/philosophy/38332/the-church-and-the-state-a-critical-reading-of-john-locke%E2%80%99s-theologicopolitical-thought/nde-paul-ade

10   Benedict XVI, *Africae Munus*, no. 37.

11   J. van Oort, *Jerusalem and Babylon: A Study into Augustine's City of God and the Sources of His Doctrine of the Two Cities.*

12   Plato. *The Republic of Plato*. Translated by Allan Bloom. New York: Basic Books, 1968.

13   Jacques Maritain, *Man and the State* (Chicago: University of Chicago Press, 1951).

14   Karl H. Peschke, *Christian Ethics: Moral theology in the light of Vatican II* (Bangalore, Theological Publishing, 2010), 630–32.

15   Bruce A. Ackerman, *Social Justice in the Liberal State* (New Haven: Yale Univ. Press, 1980), 113–20.

16   John Rawls, "*Distributive Justice*" in *Economic Justice: Selected Readings,* edited by Edmund S. Phelps, 338. (Harmondsworth, UK: Penguin Education, 1973).

17   Ronald Dworkin, (1981): 283–345.

18   Bruce A. Ackerman, *Social Justice in the Liberal State*, 132–33.

19   Benedict XVI, *Africae Munus*, no. 41.

20   Vatican II Council, The Pastoral Constitution *Gaudium et Spes*, On the Church in the Modern World, 76, in *Vatican II Council: The Conciliar and Post Conciliar Documents Volume 1,* edited by Austin Flannery, O.P. (Dublin: Dominican Publications, 1975).

21   Leo XIII. Encyclical, On the conditions of working classes, *Rerum Novarum.* (May 15, 1891.) The Holy See, Dicastero per la Comunicazione - Libreria Editrice Vaticana. https://www.vatican.va/content/leo-xiii/en/encyclicals/documents/hf_l-xiii_enc_15051891_rerum-novarum.html

22   Benedict XVI, *Africae Munus*, no. 19.

23   Id., no. 25.

24   See Pius XI (1931). Encyclical, On Reconstruction of the Social Order, *Quadragesimo Anno* (May 15, 1931.) The Holy See, Dicastero per la Comunicazione - Libreria Editrice Vaticana. https://www.vatican.va/content/pius-xi/en/encyclicals/documents/hf_p-xi_enc_19310515_quadragesimo-anno.html. See also, Paul VI (19670). On the development of people, *Populorum Progressio* (March 26, 1967.) The Holy See, Dicastero per la Comunicazione - Libreria Editrice Vaticana. https://www.vatican.va/content/paul-vi/en/encyclicals/documents/hf_p-vi_enc_26031967_populorum.html. See also, John XXIII.

Christianity and Social Progress, *Mater et Magistra* (May 15, 1961.) The Holy See, Dicastero per la Comunicazione - Libreria Editrice Vaticana. https://www.vatican.va/content/john-xxiii/en/encyclicals/documents/hf_j-xxiii_enc_15051961_mater.html. See also, John Paul II. Encyclical, On Human Work, *Laborem Excercens* (September 14, 1981.) The Holy See, Dicastero per la Comunicazione - Libreria Editrice Vaticana. https://www.vatican.va/content/john-paul-ii/en/encyclicals/documents/hf_jp-ii_enc_14091981_laborem-exercens.html. And finally see, John Paul II. Encyclical, For the Twentieth Anniversary of Populorum Progressio, *Sollicitudo Rei Socialis* (December 30, 1987.) The Holy See, Dicastero per la Comunicazione - Libreria Editrice Vaticana. https://www.vatican.va/content/john-paul-ii/en/encyclicals/documents/hf_jp-ii_enc_30121987_sollicitudo-rei-socialis.html.

25 Daniel Jonah Goldhagen. *Hitler's Willing Executioners: Ordinary Germans and the Holocaust*, 1st ed. (New York: Alfred A. Knopf, 1996).

26 See Henry George and Robert Schalkenbach Foundation. *Social Problems.* (New York: Robert Schalkenbach Foundation (1883) 1966). See also, Henry George. "Thou Shalt Not Steal: An Address Before the Anti-Poverty Society, May 8, 1887," in *The Complete Works of Henry George* (New York: Doubleday, Page, and company, 1904).

27 Alex Shoumatoff. *The World Is Burning.* 1st ed. (Boston: Little, Brown, 1990).

28 Hans Küng and John Stephen Bowden, *Disputed Truth: Memoirs* (New York, N.Y.: Continuum, 2008).

29 Martin Buber, *I and Thou*, translated by Ronald Gregor Smith, First Scribner Classics edition (New York: Scribner Classics, 2000), 11.

30 Benedict XVI, *Africae Munus*, no. 42.

31 See Marion Maddox, *For God and Country: Religious Dynamics in Australian Federal Politics*. Department of the Parliamentary Library, Australia. Parliamentary Information and Research Services (Canberra: Dept. of the Parliamentary Library, 2001). See also, Nicolaus Tideman, "Peace, Justice, and Economic Reform." *The American Journal of Economics and Sociology* 60, no. 5 (2001): 167.

32 Charles F. Collier, "Rutherford: The Devil Quotes Scripture." In *Critics of Henry George: a Centenary Appraisal of Their Strictures on Progress and Poverty*, edited by Robert V. Andelson, 222–33 (Rutherford, N.J.: Fairleigh Dickinson University Press, 1979).

33 Oscar A. Romero, *Voice of the Voiceless: The Four Pastoral Letters and Other Statements* (Maryknoll, N.Y.: Orbis Books, 1985). See also, John

Paul II, "Centesimus Annus." In *Proclaiming Justice & Peace: Papal Documents from Rerum Novarum through Centesimus Annus*, edited by Michael J. Walsh and Brian Davies, 432–78. Rev. & expanded. (Mystic, Conn.: Twenty-Third Publications, 1991).

34 Benedict XVI, *Africae Munus*, no. 38.

35 Hans Küng and John Stephen Bowden, *Disputed Truth*.

36 Plato. *The Republic of Plato*.

37 John Dewey, *Democracy and Education: An Introduction to the Philosophy of Education* (New York: Free Press, 1966).

38 Paulo Freire, *Pedagogy of the Oppressed* (New York: Seabury Press, 1970).

39 Plato. *The Republic of Plato*.

40 Benedict XVI, *Africae Munus*, no. 38.

41 Id., no. 34.

42 Thomas Aquinas, *Summa Theologiae*, I-IIq.93.a3.

43 Oscar A. Romero, *Voice of the Voiceless: The Four Pastoral Letters and Other Statements*.

44 Hans Küng and John Stephen Bowden, *Disputed Truth: Memoirs*.

45 Benedict XVI, *Africae Munus*, no. 17.

46 Canon Law Society of America. *Code of Canon Law, Latin-English Edition: Translation* (Washington, D.C.: Canon Law Society of America, 1983).

47 Lucie Sarr, *"Is it Right for Priests to Hold Political or Civic Office?" La Croix International*. September 25, 2020. https://international.la-croix.com/news/religion/is-it-right-for-priests-to-hold-political-or-civic-office/13075

48 Benedict XVI, *Africae Munus*, no. 36.

49 Thomas Aquinas, *Summa Theologiae*, Ia-IIae,q.100.a5, ad.1m.

50 Joseph Bernardin, "In Agreement with Christianity," in *Yes to a Global Ethic: Voices from Religion and Politics*, edited by Hans, Küng, 140–53 (New York: Continuum, 1991). See also, Hans Küng and John Stephen Bowden, *Disputed Truth: Memoirs*. See also, Hermann Häring, *Hans Küng: Breaking Through* (New York: Continuum, 1998), 29.

51 Joseph Bernardin, "In Agreement with Christianity," See also, Hans Küng and John Stephen Bowden, *Disputed Truth: Memoirs*. See also, Hermann Häring, *Hans Küng: Breaking Through*.

52 Benedict XVI, *Africae Munus*, no. 130.

53 Block, Walter, *Defending the Undefendable: The Pimp, Prostitute, Scab, Slumlord, Libeler, Moneylender, and Other Scapegoats in the Rogue's Gallery of American Society* (New York: Fleet Press Corp, 1976).

54 Benedict XVI, *Africae Munus*, nos. 127, 129.
55 Id., no. 2.
56 Id., no. 25.

Africae Munus on Catholic Education as a Precious Resource for the Transmission of African Values: Creating the Bonds of Peace and Harmony in the Society

1 Catechism of the Catholic Church, no. 166.
2 Benedict XVI, *Africae Munus*, no. 97.
3 Id., no. 98.
4 Benedict XVI, *Africae Munus*, no. 132.
5 Id., no. 132.
6 Id., no. 134.
7 Pope Francis, *Evangelii Gaudium*, no. 53.
8 Benedict XVI, *Africae Munus*, no. 134.
9 Id., no. 134.
10 *Gravissimum Educationis*, nos. 8–9.
11 https://www.un.org/en/about-us/universal-declaration-of-human-rights, (consulted on the 3rd of February 2022).
12 https://www.unicef.org/child-rights-convention/convention-text-childrens-version (page consulted on the 3rd of February 2022).
13 A. N. Whitehead, *The Aims of Education and other Essays* (The Free Press: New York, 1967), 14.
14 J. J. Rousseau, *Emile or On Education* (Flammarion : Paris 1966), p. 38.
15 Immanuel Kant, *On Education*, trans. A. Churston (The University of Michigan Press: Ann Arbor, 1960), p. 6.
16 https://mygivingpoint.org/cause/education-equality/, (consulted on the 5th of February 2022).
17 Benedict XVI, *Africae Munus*, no. 134.
18 A. N. Whitehead, *The Aims of Education and other Essays*, 10.
19 Michael B. Adeyemi and Augustus A. Adeyinka, "Some Key Issues in African Traditional Education" in *Revue des Sciences de L'Education de McGill* 37, no. 2 (Printemps, 2002), 224.
20 Carter Good, Dictionary of Education (New York: McGraw-Hill, 1959), 191.
21 P. Snelson, Educational Development in Northern Rhodesia, 1883–1945 (Lusaka: Kenneth Kaunda Foundation, 1974), 1.
22 Michael B. Adeyemi and Augustus A. Adeyinka, "Some Key Issues in African Traditional Education" 224–25.

23   Michael B. Adeyemi and Augustus A. Adeyinka, "Some Key Issues in African Traditional Education," 227.

24   Benedict XVI, *Africae Munus*, no. 135.

25   Id., no. 134.

26   Thomas Aquinas, *De Veritate*, q. 1, q.1.

27   Alejandro Llano, *Gnoseology*, (Manila: Sinag-Tala Publishers, Inc., 2001), pp.15–16.

28   John Paul II, *"Deep Harmony which Unites the Truths of Science with the Truths of Faith,"* November 10, 1979, in L'Osservatore Romano, English weekly edition, November 26, 1979, pp. 9–10.

29   Benedict XVI, *Africae Munus*, no. 135.

30   Pope John Paul II, Address to Catholic Educators, September 12, 1984.

31   For more ethical issues consult Ian G. Barbour's *Ethics in an Age of Technology.*

32   Pope Francis, *Laudato Si*, no. 15.

33   Id., no. 90.

34   Pope Francis, *Laudato Si*, no. 95.

35   Id., no. 91.

36   d., no. 93.

37   John Paul II, *Redemptor Hominis*, no. 15.

38   Id., no. 16.

39   A. N. Whitehead, *The Aims of Education and other Essays* (New York: The Free Press, 1967), 10.

40   Id., 47.

41   Id., 10.

42   M. Roth, *Aims of Education Address* (The University of Chicago: The College, September 27, 2012), 1.

43   G. Brooks and M. G. Grennon, in *A. N. Whitehead on Learning and Education: Theory and Application*, edited by Franz G. Riffert (Cambridge Scholars Press, Newcastle 2005), 72.

44   Paul E. Johnson, *Learning Theory and Practice* (Thomas and Crowell Company, New York, 1834), 288.

45   M. Roth, *Aims of Education Address* (The University of Chicago: The College, September 27, 2012), 3.

46   A. N. Whitehead, *The Aims of Education and other Essays*, 5.

47   Barry A. Kosmin & Ariela Keysar, *Secularism & Secularity: Contemporary International Perspectives* (Hartford, CT: Institute for the Study of Secularism in Society and Culture (ISSSC), 2007).

48   Hakan M. Yavuz & John L. Esposito, *Turkish Islam and the Secular State: The Gulen Movement* (Syracuse, NY: Syracuse University, 2003), xv–xvii.

49 S. Aylward and E. Onyancha, *Secularism in Africa. A Case Study: Nairobi City*, 14.

50 L. Feuerbach, *The Essence of Religion,* translated by G. Eliot (London: Harper and Row Publishers, 1957), 31.

51 John S. Mbiti, *African Religions and Philosophy*, 2nd ed. (Heinemann, New Hampshire: 1990), 2.

52 Rabbi Moshe Reiss, *Modernity, Secularism (Democracy), Religion and Radical Islam* http://www.moshereiss.org/columns/24_modernity.htm (page consulted on the 24th May 2014)

53 John S. Mbiti, *African Religions and Philosophy* (London, Heinemann 1969), 1.

54 S. Aylward and E. Onyancha, *Secularism in Africa. A Case Study, Nairobi City*, 11.

55 S. Aylward and E. Onyancha, *Secularism in Africa. A Case Study*, 11.

56 R. Ntungwe, *Secularism in Cameroon*, unpublished Dissertation, STAMS Bambui, 1999, iv.

57 John S. Mbiti, *African Religions and Philosophy, 1969: 119*.

58 Benson O. Igboin, "Colonialism and African Cultural Values," in *African Journal of History and Culture*, Vol. 3(6), July 2011, 96.

59 Id., pp. 96–103.

60 *West Cameroon Education Policy: Investment in Education, 1963*, Published by the West Cameroon Government Press, Buea, 2.

61 *West Cameroon Education Policy: Investment in Education, 1963*, Published by the West Cameroon Government Press, Buea, 3.

62 M. Tumenta, *National Forum on Education, (Final Report)*, Yaoundé 22–27 May 1997, 17.

63 L. Rummel, "The Anti-Clerical Programme as a Disruptive Factor in the Solidarity of the Late French Republic" in *The Catholic Historical Review* 34, no. 1 (April 1948), 9.

64 W. Banboye, "Correct Perspective in Education" in *Cameroon Panorama* (January-February 1973), 18.

65 Adiele Eberechukwu Afigbo, "Culture, Education, Indigenization and Development in Africa: Some Comments," in *Towards Indigenization of Education in Africa*, edited by Theophilus Okere and Chukwudi Anthony Njoku (Owerri 2006), 13.

An Examination of *Africae Munus*
in View of the *Tria Munera* of Canon 204 §1

1 Benedict XVI, *Africae Munus*, no. 6.

2 C. 204 §1. Christifideles sunt qui, utpote per baptismum Christo

incorporati, in populum Dei sunt constituti, atque hac ratione muneris Christi sacerdotalis, prophetici et regalis suo modo participes facti, secundum propriam cuiusque condicionem, ad mission emexercendam vocantur, quam Deus Ecclesiae in mundo adimplendam concredidit *Codex Iuris Canonici auctoritate Ioanis Pauli PP. II promulgates.* Vatican City: Libreria Editrice Vaticana, 1983. English translation from the *Code of Canon Law, Latin-English Edition: New English Translation* (Washington, DC: CLSA,1998). All subsequent English translations of canons from this code will be taken from this source unless otherwise indicated.

3   Cf. Robert Kaslyn. "The Christian Faithful" *New Commentary on the Code of Canon Law,* ed. John P. Beal et al. (Bangalore: Theological Publications, 2010) 246.

4   C. 869, §2 Baptizati in communitate ecclesiali non catholica non sunt sub condicione baptizandi, nisi, inspecta materia et verborum forma in baptismo collato adhibitis necnon attenta intentione baptizati adulti et ministri baptizantis, seria ratio adsit de baptismi validitate dubitandi.

5   John Huels, *The Pastoral Companion. A Canon Law Handbook for Catholic Ministry* (Chicago: Franciscan Press, 1995) 140.

6   Robert Kaslyn, 246.

7   Id., 256.

8   Id., 258.

9   *Codex Iuris Canonici Pii X Pontifici Maximi iussu digestus Benedicti Papae XV auctoritate romulgates* (Rome: Typis Polyglottis Vaticanis, 1917).

10   A. Anandarayar, *Participation of the Laity in the Governing, Teaching and Sanctifying Office of the Church,* Canon Law society of India. https://www.canonlawsocietyofindia.org, accessed on 02/12/2022.

11   Robert Kaslyn, 258.

12   C. 208: From their rebirth in Christ, there exists among all the Christian faithful a true equality regarding dignity and action by which they all cooperate in the building up of the Body of Christ according to each one's own condition and function.

13   Benedict XVI, *Africae Munus,* nos. 100–31.

14   The question still remains as to how we understand the usage of the word Church in this context. For the word Church is reserved to those communities with a valid ordination and the eucharist, with a visible structure and a communion with the Pope. But the church of Christ does not take into consideration the juridical and ecclesiological reality of the word Church, but a personal reality of the word as incorporation into the person of Christ through baptism.

15 See, Ladislas Orsy, "Intepretation in View of Action: A Quest for Clarity and Simplicity (Canon 96)," *Jurist* 52 (1992) 587–97.

16 John Paul II, apostolic constitution, *Sacrae disciplinae leges,* January 25, 1983.

17 c. 222 §2: *Obligatione* quoque *tenentur* iustitiam socialem promovendi necnon, praecepti Domini memores, ex propriis reditibus pauperibus subveniendi.

18 Denis Tameh, *Justice, Africae Munus's clarion call: a Canon Law Perspective* (Unpublished, November 2021).

19 James Coriden, "A Challenge: Making the Rights Real," *Jurist* 45 (1985) 7: *Communicationes* I (1969) 83.

20 Id., 83.

21 Denis Tameh, *Justice, Africae Munus's clarion call: a Canon Law Perspective.*

22 C. 1341: The Ordinary must start a judicial or an administrative procedure for the imposition or the declaration of penalties when he perceives that neither by the methods of pastoral care, especially fraternal correction, nor by a warning or correction, can justice be sufficiently restored, the offender reformed, and the scandal repaired.

23 Sarath Chandra, *Explicit and Implicit Rights Common to all the Faithful in the Code of Canon Law,* Dissertation (Ottawa: St Paul University 2018).

24 Id., 90.

Ratzingerian Hermeneutics of Scripture and Eucharist Considering *Africae Munus* 39 – 41

1 Benedict XVI, *Africae Munus,* no. 40.

2 Joseph Ratzinger, *Principles of Catholic Theology. Building Stones for a Fundamental Theology,* trans. Sister Mary Frances McCarthy, S.N.D. (San Francisco: Ignatius Press, 1987), 134.

3 Ratzinger, *Principles,* 134.

4 Augustine, *The Confessions,* VIII, xii, 29.

5 Joseph Ratzinger, *Behold the Pierced One, An Approach to Spiritual Christology,* trans. Graham Harrison (San Francisco: Ignatius Press, 1986), 43.

6 Joseph Ratzinger, *Salt of the Earth. The Church at the End of the Millennium. An Interview with Peter Seewald,* trans. Adrian Walker (San Francisco: Ignatius Press, 1997), 66.

7 Benedict XVI, Post Synodal Apostolic Exhortation *Sacramentum Caritatis,* On the Eucharist as the Source and Summit of the Church's Life and Mission (Vatican City: Libreria Editrice Vaticana, 2007).

8   Benedict XVI, Encyclical Letter *Deus Caritas Est* On Christian Love (2005), 14

9   Benedict XVI, *Africae Munus*, no. 39.

10 Id., no. 40.

11 Id., no. 41.

12 Augustine, *The Confessions*, VII, x, 16.

13 Ratzinger, *Behold the Pierced One*, 89.

14 Joseph Ratzinger, *On the Way to Jesus Christ*, trans. Michael J. Miller (San Francisco: Ignatius Press, 2005), 117–18.

15 Ratzinger, *Behold the Pierced One*, 89.

16 Ratzinger, *On the Way to Jesus Christ*, 38.

17 Joseph Ratzinger, *Collected Works: Theology of the Liturgy* (San Francisco: Ignatius Press, 2014), 81.

18 Joseph Ratzinger, *Behold the Pierced One, An Approach to a Spiritual Christology*, trans. Graham Harrison (San Francisco: Ignatius Press, 1986), 51–52.

19 Id., 54.

20 Ratzinger, *Behold the Pierced One*, 107–08.

21 Augustine, *The Confessions*, X, xxvii, 38.

22 Ratzinger, *On the Way to Jesus Christ*, 39.

23 Benedict XVI, *Sacramentum Caritatis*, 23.

24 Joseph Ratzinger, *God is Near Us. The Eucharist, the Heart of Life*, edited by Stephan Otto Horn and Vinzenz Pfnür, translated by Henry Taylor (San Francisco: Ignatius Press, 2003), 53.

25 Ratzinger, *God is Near Us*, 39.

26 Ibid.

27 Ratzinger, *On the Way to Jesus Christ*, 118.

28 Joseph Ratzinger, *On the Way to Jesus Christ* (San Francisco: Ignatius Press, 2004), 125–28.

29 Id., 112.

30 Joseph Ratzinger, *God's Word, Scripture – Tradition – Office*, ed. Peter Hünermann and Thomas Söding, trans. Henry Taylor (San Francisco: Ignatius Press, 2008), 51.

31 Id., 51.

32 Id., 52.

33 Ratzinger, *God's Word*, 52.

34 Bonaventure, *Breviloquium, Prol.*: Opera Omnia, V, Quaracchi 1891, pp. 201–02.

35 Aquinas, *Summa Theologiae*, Ia-IIae, q. 106, art. 2.

36 Benedict XVI, Post-Synodal Apostolic Exhortation *Verbum Domini* On the Word of God in the Life and Mission of the Church (Libreria Editrice Vaticana: 2010), 29.

37 Ibid.
38 Pontifical Biblical Commission, *The Interpretation of the Bible in the Church* (April 15, 1993), III, A, 3: *Enchiridion Vaticanum* 13, no. 3035.
39 Augustine of Hippo, *Contra epistulam Manichaei quam vocant fundamenti*, V, 6: PL 42, 176.

Preaching Reconciliation in a Divided Zone Mindful of *Africae Munus*

1   John L. Allen Jr., "Benedict in Cameroon: a tale of two trips," in *National Catholic Reporter Online* (March 20, 2009) https://www.ncronline.org/blogs/all-things-catholic/benedict-cameroon-tale-two-trips.
2   Welcome Address of the Holy Father Benedict XVI at Nsimalen International Airport of Yaoundé. Tuesday, March 17, 2009, during the Apostolic Journey to Cameroon and Angola, March 17–23, 2009. https://www.vatican.va/content/benedict-xvi/en/speeches/2009/march/documents/hf_ben-xvi_spe_20090317_welcome-yaounde.html
3   Jean-Marc Ela, *African Cry*, translated by Robert J. Barr (Eugene: Wipf and Stock Publishers), 2005, 81.
4   R. Maxwell Bone, "We Had No Choice" - the Emergence of Secessionist Violence in Anglophone Cameroon," *Dissertation submitted for the degree of Master of Philosophy in African Studies at the University of Cambridge*, 2021, 12.
5   Emmanuel Katongole and Rice Chris, *Reconciling All Things: A Christian Vision for Justice, Peace, and Healing* (Downers Grove: InterVarsity Press. Kindle Edition. 2009). 109.
6   J. M. Vorster, "The Doctrine of Reconciliation: Its Meaning and Implications for Social Life" (November 05 2018), https://indieskriflig.org.za/index.php/skriflig/article/view/2367/5333
7   Emmanuel Katongole, *The Journey of Reconciliation. Groaning for A New Creation in Africa* (Maryknoll, Orbis Books, 2017) 5.
8   Cf. Robert J. Schreiter, *The Ministry of Reconciliation: Spirituality & Strategies* (Maryknoll: Orbis Books, 1998) 14.
9   Schreiter, *The Ministry of Reconciliation*, 14.
10 Katongole, *The Journey of Reconciliation*, 3.
11 Id., 8.
12 Benedict XVI, *Africae Munus*, no. 3.
13 Id., no. 4.
14 Id., nos. 15–16.

15 Id., nos. 17–30.

16 Id., no. 9.

17 Cf. Thomas Bienvenu Tchoungui, "A view of the family in the light of *Ecclesia in Africa* and *Africae Munus*" in *Annals of St. Cyprian School of Theology - Ngoya* (Yaounde, 2016) 198, translated by us.

18 Part II of *Africae Munus* spells out and elaborates the roles of each of these groups of people.

19 Benedict XVI, *Africae Munus*, no. 17.

20 Emmanuel Katongole, "Identity, Community and the Gospel of Reconciliation: Christian Resources in the Face of Tribalism," *The Great Lake Initiatives,* Duke Center for Reconciliation, 7. https://divinity.duke.edu/sites/divinity.duke.edu/files/documents/cfr/identity-and-reconciliation.pdf

21 Katongole, *Journey of Reconciliation*, 71.

22 Id., 72.

23 Katongole, *Journey of Reconciliation*, 73.

24 Ibid. Katongole observes that God is determined to form a new people in the world. Christian identity seeks to create, realize, and reflect "Ephesian moments" of this movement in the world.

25 Id., 78.

Challenge to Women as Peace Agents: *Africae Munus* in a Feminine Key

1 Pablo Castillo Diaz and Simon Tordjman. *Women's participation in peace negotiations: Connections between presence and influence,* 2nd ed. New York: United Nations Entity for Gender Equality and the Empowerment of Women. http://www.unwomen.org/~/media/headquarters/attachments/sections/library/publications/2012/10/wpssourcebook-03a-womenpeacenegotiations-en.pdf.

2 Lindenmayer, Elizabeth, and Josie Lianna Kaye. *A choice for peace? Forty-one days of mediation in Kenya.* New York: International Peace Institute, 2009.

3 UN Women Annual Report 2018–2019. https://annualreport.un-women.org/en/2019

4 Benedict XVI, *Africae Munus*, no. 56.

5 Id., no. 58.

6 Id., no. 57.

7 Benedict XVI, *Africae Munus*, no. 56

8 Id., no. 57.

9 Id., no. 57.

10 Id., no. 59.

11 Id., no. 56.

12 Id., no. 58.

13 Edith Stein, *Essays on Woman,* edited by Lucy Gelber and Romaeus Leuven. Second edition, revised. The Collected Works of Edith Stein vol. 2 (Washington, DC: ICS Publications, 1996).

14 Benedict XVI, *Africae Munus,* no. 57.

15 Id., no. 59.

16 John Paul II. Encyclical, *Evangelium Vitae: On the Value and Inviolability of Human Life* (March 25, 1995), no. 99. The Holy See, Dicastero per la Comunicazione - Libreria Editrice Vaticana. https:// www.vatican.va/content/john-paul-ii/en/encyclicals/ documents/hf_jp-ii_enc_25031995_evangelium-vitae.html.

17 Benedict XVI, *Africae Munus,* no. 58.

18 Id., no. 22.

19 Agbonkhianmeghe E. Orobator, *Reconciliation, Justice, and Peace: The Second African Synod* (Maryknoll, NY.: Orbis Books, 2011), 144.

20 Benedict XVI, *Africae Munus,* no. 76.

21 Benedict XVI, *Africae Munus,* no. 58.

22 Benedict XVI, *Africae Munus,* no. 57.

23 Loreen Maseno, "Gendering enculturation in Africa: a discussion of three African women theologians' entry into the enculturation scene," *Norsk Tidsskrift for Misjon* 4 (2004), 226.

24 Benedict XVI, *Africae Munus,* no. 2.

25 Id., no. 23.

26 Benedict XVI, *Africae Munus,* nos. 81–82.

27 John Paul II. Encyclical Letter, *Centesimus Annus* (May 1, 1991), no. 38. The Holy See, Dicastero per la Comunicazione - Libreria Editrice. https://www.vatican.va/content/john-paul-ii/en/encyclicals/ documents/hf_jp-ii_enc_01051991_centesimus-annus.html

28 Benedict XVI. Message, World Day of Peace, *The Human Person, the Heart of Peace* (January 1, 2007), 8 & 10. The Holy See, Dicastero per la Comunicazione - Libreria Editrice Vaticana. https://www.vatican.va/content/benedict-xvi/en/messages/peace/documents/hf _ben-xvi_mes_20061208_xl-world-day-peace.html.

29 Benedict XVI. Message, World Day of Peace, *The Human Person, the Heart of Peace,* (2007), 7.

30 Benedict XVI, *Africae Munus,* no. 59.

31 Jill Radford and Diana E. H. Russell, *Femicide: The Politics of Woman Killing* (New York: Twayne Publishers, 1992), xi.

32 Benedict XVI, *Africae Munus,* no. 7.

Health Care in the Light of *Africae Munus*:
From a merely Biomedical to a Holistic Paradigm of Health Care

1   Benedict XVI, Messages, *Eighteenth World Day of the Sick 2010* (WDS) (November 22, 2009) The Holy See, Dicastero per la Comunicazione - Libreria Editrice Vaticana. https://www.vatican.va/content/benedict-xvi/en/messages/sick/documents/hf_ben-xvi_mes_20091122_world-day-of-the-sick-2010.html

2   Bishop Michael E. Putney, 2002. "Health Care and the Churches Mission" (adapted from an Address to a workshop at St. John of God Health Care System in Perth, Australia, spring 2002), *Health Progress* (January-February, 2004). Catholic Health Association of the United States (CHA). https://www.chausa.org/publications/health-progress/archive/article/january-february-2004/health-care-and-the-church's-mission

3   Bishop Michael E. Putney, 2002, "Health Care and the Church's Mission."

4   Pope Francis, Messages, *Twenty-Fifth World Day of the Sick 2017* (WDS), (December 8, 2016). The Holy See, Dicastero per la Comunicazione - Libreria Editrice Vaticana. https://www.vatican.va/content/francesco/en/messages/sick/documents/papa-francesco_20161208_giornata-malato.html

5   Pope Francis, Messages, *Twenty-Sixth World Day of the Sick 2018* (WDS), (November 26, 2017). The Holy See, Dicastero per la Comunicazione - Libreria Editrice Vaticana. https://www.vatican.va/content/francesco/en/messages/sick/documents/papa-francesco_20171126_giornata-malato.html

6   John Paul II, Post-Synodal Apostolic Exhortation *"Ecclesia in Oceania"* (November 22, 2011). The Holy See, Dicastero per la Comunicazione - Libreria Editrice Vaticana, 34. https://www.vatican.va/content/john-paul-ii/en/apost_exhortations/documents/hf_jp-ii_exh_20011122_ecclesia-in-oceania.html

7   Benedict XVI, *Africae Munus*, no. 140.

8   Barbara Kozier, *Fundamentals of Nursing: Concepts, Process and Practice*, 7th ed. (Upper Saddle River, New Jersey: Pearson Prentice Hall, 2004).

9   Benedict XVI, *Africae Munus*, no. 140.

10 Christine M. Puchalski, "The role of spirituality in health care." *Baylor University Medical Center Proceedings* 14, no. 4, (2001): 352–57.

11 Norman K. Denzin and Yvonna Lincoln, 2011. *Handbook of Qualitative*

Research (Thousand Oaks, Calif.: Sage Publications, 2000), 509–35. See also, Michelle Byrne, "Ethnography as a Qualitative Research Methodology." *AORN Journal* 74, no. 1 (2001) 82.

12 Virginia Braun and Victoria Clark, "Using Thematic Analysis in Psychology." *Qualitative Research in Psychology* 3, no. 2 (2006), 77–101.

13 Michael Winkelman. *Culture and Health: Applying Medical Anthropology*, 1st ed. (San Francisco: Jossey-Bass, 2009), 36.

14 World Health Organisation. *Global status report on noncommunicable disease*, 2002. See also, Ellen Nolte and Martin McKee, "Integration and Chronic Care: A Review," in *Caring for People with Chronic Conditions*, ed. Ellen Nolte and Martin Mckee (New York: McGraw Hill, 2008), 64–91. Michael P. Coleman, Delia-Marina Alexe, Tit Albrecht, and Martin McKee. *Responding to the Challenge of Cancer in Europe*. Ljubljiana: Institute of Public Health of the Republic of Slovenia and European Observatory on Health System and Policies, 2008.

15 T. Plochg and Niek S. Klazinga, "Community-Based Integrated Care: Myth or Must?" *International Journal for Quality in Health Care* 14, no. 2 (April 1, 2002): 91–101. https://doi.org/10.1093/oxfordjournals.intqhc.a002606.

16 Richard Horton, "The Neglected Epidemic of Chronic Disease," *The Lancet* 366, no. 9496 (Oct., 2005), 1514. doi:https://doi.org/10.1016/S0140-6736(05)67454-5. https://go.openathens.net/redirector/bc.edu?url=https://www.proquest.com/scholarly-journals/neglected-epidemic-chronic-disease/docview/199037136/se-2.

17 World Health Organisation, *Global status report on noncommunicable disease*, 2005.

18 World Health Organisation, *Global status report on noncommunicable disease*, 2011a.

19 World Health Organisation, *Global status report on noncommunicable disease*, 2011b.

20 World Health Organisation, *Global status report on noncommunicable disease*, 2015.

21 Ministry of Public Health. *Health Sector Strategy 2016–2027*. Republic of Cameroon, 2016), 57. https://www.minsante.cm/site/?q=en/content/health-sector-strategy-2016-2027-0

22 Ministry of Public Health. *Health Sector Strategy 2016–2027*, 58.

23 Ministry of Public Health. *Health Sector Strategy 2016–2027*, 59–60.

24 Samuel Kingue, et al., "Prevalence and Risk Factors of Hypertension in Urban Areas of Cameroon: A Nationwide Population-Based Cross-Sectional Study," *The Journal of Clinical Hypertension* 17, no. 10 (October 2015): 819–24.

25 Pope Francis. Encyclical letter, *Fratelli Tutti: On Fraternity and Social*

Friendship (October 3, 2020) no. 18. The Holy See, Dicastero per la Comunicazione - Libreria Editrice Vaticana. https://www.vatican.va/content/francesco/en/encyclicals/documents/papa-francesco_20201003_enciclica-fratelli-tutti.html

26 Arthur Kleinman, *Patients and Healers in the Context of Culture: An Exploration of the Borderland Between Anthropology, Medicine, and Psychiatry.* (Berkeley: University of California Press, 1980). See also Arthur Kleinman, *Rethinking Psychiatry: From Cultural Category to Personal Experience* (New York: Free Press, 1988). See also, Arthur Kleinman, *The Illness Narratives: Suffering, Healing, and the Human Condition* (New York: Basic Books, 1988).

27 Emil Berkanovic, "Lay Conceptions of the Sick Role," *Social Forces* 51, no. 1 (1972), 53–64. See also, Elihu M. Gerson, "The social character of illness: Deviance or politics?" *Social Science and Medicine* 10, no. 5 (May 1976), 219–24. Also, Uta Gerhardt, "The Parsonian paradigm and the identity of medical sociology," *Sociological Review* 27, no. 2 (May 1979), 229–51.

28 Anselm Strauss, *Chronic Illness and the Quality of Life.* (Saint Louis: Mosby, 1975). See also, Peter Conrad, "The experience of illness: recent and new directions," in *Research in the Sociology of Health Care: The Experience and Management of Chronic Illness*, edited by Julius A. Roth and Peter Conrad, vol. 6, 1–32. (Greenwich, CT: JAI Press, 1987). Also, Robert Anderson and Michael Bury, *Living with Chronic Illness: The Experience of Patients and Their Families* (London: Unwin Hyman, 1988). Also, Michael Bury, "The sociology of chronic illness: a review of research and prospects," *Sociology of Health & Illness* 13, no. 4 (1991), 451–68.

29 Janine Pierret, "The illness experience: State of knowledge and perspectives for research," *Sociology of Health & Illness* 25, no. 3 (2003): 4–22.

30 Toomb, 2006: 121–22.

31 Statement of a 39-year-old female, interviewed on June 24, 2021.

32 Heather L. Barnett, Pamela K. Keel, and Lauren M. Conoscenti, "Body Type Preferences in Asian and Caucasian College Students," *Sex Roles* 45, no. 11/12 (2001), 867–78. See also, Jennifer S. Mills, Rachel Jadd, and Brenda L. Key, "Wanting a Body That's Better Than Average: The Effect of Manipulated Body Norms on Ideal Body Size Perception," *Body Image* 9, no. 3 (2012), 365–72.

33 Thomas J. Csordas, "Somatic modes of attention," *Cultural Anthropology* 8, (1993): 135–56. See also, Thomas J. Csordas, "Introduction: The body as representation and being-in-the-world," in *Embodiment and experience: The existential ground of culture and self*, edited by

Thomas J. Csordas, 1–26 (Cambridge, UK: Cambridge University Press, 1994). See also, Gaylene Becker, *Disrupted lives: How people create meaning in a chaotic world* (Berkeley: University of California Press, 1997). See also, Terrence S. Turner, "The Social Skin." *HAU Journal of Ethnographic Theory* 2, no. 2 (2012), 486–504. And, Chris Shilling and Nottingham Trent University. TCS Centre. *The Body in Culture, Technology and Society* (Thousand Oaks, Calif.: Sage, 2005). Also, Maxine L. Craig, "Race, beauty, and the tangled knot of a guilty pleasure," *Feminist Theory* 7, no. 2 (2006), 159–77.

34   Thomas F. Cash and Linda Smolak, *Body Image: a Handbook of Science, Practice, and Prevention*, 2nd ed. (New York: Guilford Press, 2011).

35   Katherine Presnell, Sarah Kate Bearman, and Eric Stice, "Risk Factors for Body Dissatisfaction in Adolescent Boys and Girls: A Prospective Study." *The International Journal of Eating Disorders* 36, no. 4 (2004): 389–401. See also, Jennifer W. Bradford and Trent A. Petrie, "Sociocultural Factors and the Development of Disordered Eating: A longitudinal analysis of competing hypotheses." *Journal of Counseling Psychology* 55, no. 2 (2008), 246–62.

36   Statement of a 53-year-old, interviewed on 25 May 2020.

37   Kathy Charmaz, *Good Days, Bad Days: The Self in Chronic Illness and Time* (New Brunswick, N.J.: Rutgers University Press, 1991).

38   Statement of a 70-year-old female, interviewed on November 12, 2020.

39   Statement of a 45-year-old, interviewed on June 16, 2020.

40   Kathy Charmaz, "Loss of Self: A Fundamental Form of Suffering in the Chronically Ill," *Sociology of Health & Illness* 5, no. 2 (1983):168–95. See also, Kathy Charmaz, "Struggling for a Self: Identity Levels of the Chronically Ill." *Research in the Sociology of Health Care* 6, (1987): 283–321. And, Kathy Charmaz, "The Body, Identity, and Self: Adapting to Impairment." *Sociological Quarterly* 36, no. 4 (1995): 657–80.

41   Michael Bury, "Chronic Illness as Biographical Disruption," *Sociology of Health & Illness* 4, no. 2 (1982), 167–82.

42   Brännström, Margareta, Inger Ekman, Astrid Norberg, Kurt Boman, and Gunilla Strandberg. "Living with Severe Chronic Heart Failure in Palliative Advanced Home Care." *European Journal of Cardiovascular Nursing* 5 (2006): 295–302.

43   Joel M. Charon, *Ten Questions: A Sociological Perspective* (Belmont, Calif.: Wadsworth Pub. Co., 1992), 37–38. See also, Joel M. Charon and Spencer Cahill, *Symbolic Interactionism: an Introduction, an Interpretation, an Integration*. 4th ed. (Englewood Cliffs, N.J.: Prentice Hall, 1992), 37–38.

44   Susan Sontag, *Illness as Metaphor; and, AIDS and Its Metaphors* (London: Penguin Books, 1991).

45 Steven Dansky, *Now Dare Everything: Tales of HIV-Related Psychotherapy* (New York: Haworth Press, 1994).

46 Lucy Gilson, "Trust and the Development of Health Care as a Social Institution," *Social Science & Medicine* (1982) 56, no. 7 (April 2003): 1453–68.

47 Jeffrey T. Huber and Mary L Gillaspy. *Hiv/Aids and Hiv/Aids-Related Terminology: A Means of Organizing the Body of Knowledge* (New York: Haworth Press, 1996).

48 Stephen Crystal and Marguerite Jackson, "Healthcare and the Social Construction of AIDS: the Impact of Disease Definitions," in *The Social Context of AIDS*, eds. by Joan Huber and Beth Schneider (Newbury Park, Calif.: Sage Publications, 1992). See also, Alexandra Tegius and Paul I. Ahmed, "Living with AIDS: An Overview," in *Living and Dying with AIDS*, ed. Paul I. Ahmed (New York: Plenum Press, 1992) 3–18.

49 Susan Sontag, *Illness as Metaphor; and, AIDS and Its Metaphors.* See also, Deborah Lupton, "Femininity, responsibility and the technological imperative: Discourses on breast cancer in the Australian Press" *International Journal of Health Sciences* 24, no. 1 (1994): 73–89. See also, Phil Brown, "Naming and Framing: The Social Construction of Diagnosis and Illness." *Journal of Health and Social Behavior* Special Issue, (1995): 34–52.

50 Anne Karpf, *Doctoring the Media: The Reporting of Health and Medicine* (London: Routledge, 1988).

51 Ama de-Graft Aikins, "Healer Shopping in Africa: New Evidence from Rural-Urban Qualitative Study of Ghanaian Diabetes Experiences," *BMJ* 331, no. 7519 (2005): 737–42. See also, Green, Robin J., Michael M. Greenblatt, Michael Plit, Sylvia Jones, and Bruno Adam, "Asthma Management and Perceptions in Rural South Africa," *Annals of Allergy, Asthma, and Immunology* 86, no. 3 (March 2001): 343–47. See also, Jude U. Ohaeri, Oladapo B. Campbell, Abiodun O. Ilesanmil, and Beatrice M. Ohaeri, "Psychosocial Concerns of Nigerian Women with Breast and Cervical Cancer," *Psycho-Oncology* (Chichester, England 7, no. 6, 1998), 494–501.

52 Jude U. Ohaeri, Wuraola A. Shokunbi, Kehinde S. Akinlade, and Lola O. Dare, "The Psychosocial Problems of Sickle Cell Disease Sufferers and Their Methods of Coping," *Social Science & Medicine* (1982) 40, no. 7 (1995): 955–60.

53 Peter O. Ebigbo and J. M. Oli, "Stress in the life of Nigerian diabetics," *Zeitschrift für Psychosomatische Medizin und Psychoanalyse* 31, no. 3 (1985), 267–83.

54 Ohaeri et al., *The Psychosocial Problems of Sickle Cell Disease Sufferers and Their Methods of Coping*, 955–60.

55 Pope Francis, Messages, *Twenty-Ninth World Day of the Sick 2021* (WDS) (December 20, 2020). The Holy See, Dicastero per la Comunicazione - Libreria Editrice Vaticana. https://www.vatican.va/content/francesco/en/messages/sick/documents/papa-francesco_20 201220_giornata-malato.html

56 Benedict XVI, *Africae Munus*, no. 140.

57 Paul Gilbert, *The Compassionate Mind: A New Approach to Life's Challenges* (London: Constable and Robinson, 2010).

58 Paul Gilbert, *The Compassionate Mind: A New Approach to Life's Challenges*. See also, Clara Strauss, Billie Lever Taylor, Jenny Gu, Willem Kuyken, Ruth Baer, Fergal Jones, and Kate Cavanagh. "What Is Compassion and How Can We Measure It? A Review of Definitions and Measures." *Clinical Psychology Review* 47 (2016): 15–27.

59 Statement of a 58-year-old, interviewed on 15 February 2021.

60 Jonathan Matusitz and Jennifer Spear, "Effective Doctor-Patient Communication: An Updated Examination." *Social Work in Public Health* 29, no. 3 (2014): 252–66. See also, Gwen van Servellen, *Communication Skills for the Health Care Professional: Concepts, Practice, and Evidence*, 2nd ed. (Sudbury, Mass.: Jones and Bartlett Publishers, 2009). See also, Edwin D. Boudreaux, Cris V. Mandry, and Karen Wood, "Patient Satisfaction Data as a Quality Indicator: A Tale of Two Emergency Departments," *Academic Emergency Medicine* 10, no. 3 (2003), 261–68. See also, Bérengère de Negri, Lori DiPrete Brown, Orlando Hernández Julia Rosenbaum, and Debra Roter, *Improving interpersonal communication between health care providers and clients* (Bethesda, MD: USAID Quality Assurance Project, 1997). 3–59.

61 Shelley E. Taylor, "Social support: A Review." In *The Handbook of Health Psychology*, ed. Howard S. Friedman, 189–214. (New York, NY: Oxford University Press, 2011).

62 Catherine A. Heaney and Barbara A. Israel, "Social Networks and Social Support," in *Health Behavior and Health Education: Theory, Research, and Practice*, eds. Karen Glanz, Barbara K. Rimer, K. Viswanath, and C. Tracy Orleans, 4th ed., 189–210. (San Francisco, CA: Jossey-Bass, 2008).

63 T. A. Wills, "Social Support and Interpersonal relationships," in *Prosocial Behavior*, ed. Margaret Clark, 265–89. In the series: *Review of Personality and Social Psychology* 12 (Newbury Park, CA: Sage Publications, 1991.

64 Bert N. Uchino, *Social Support and Physical Health: Understanding the Health Consequences of Relationships* (New Haven: Yale University Press, 2004).

65 Statement of a 34-year-old, interviewed on 13 October 2020.

66 Janine Pierret, "The illness experience: State of knowledge and perspectives for research," *Sociology of Health & Illness* 25, no. 3 (2003): 4–22. See also, Caroline Sanders, Jenny Donovan, and Paul Dieppe, "The Significance and Consequences of Having Painful and Disabled Joints in Older Age: Co-existing Accounts of Normal and Disrupted Biographies," *Sociology of Health & Illness* 24, no. 2 (2002): 227–53.

67 See Harold G. Koenig, Michael E. McCullough, and David B. Larson, *Handbook of Religion and Health* (New York: Oxford University Press, 2001). And, Christina M. Puchalski, Robert Vitillo, Sharon K. Hull, and Nancy Reller, "Improving the Spiritual Dimension of Whole Person Care: Reaching National and International Consensus," *Journal of Palliative Medicine* 17, no. 6 (2014): 642–56.

68 *New Charter for Health Care Workers* (2016).

69 Pope Francis, Messages, *Twenty-Ninth World Day of the Sick 2021* (WDS), (December 20, 2020).

70 Benedict XVI. Encyclical Letter, *Spe Salvi* (November 30, 2007), no. 38. The Holy See, Dicastero per la Comunicazione - Libreria Editrice Vaticana. https://www.vatican.va/content/benedict-xvi/en/encyclicals/documents/hf_ben-xvi_enc_20071130_spe-salvi.htm

71 Pope Francis, Messages, *Twenty-Eighth World Day of the Sick 2020* (WDS), (January 3, 2020). The Holy See, Dicastero per la Comunicazione - Libreria Editrice Vaticana. https://www.vatican.va/content/francesco/en/messages/sick/documents/papa-francesco_20200103_giornata-malato.html

The African Concept of Person:
A Source of Renewal in *Africae Munus*

1 Sr. Katherine Feely, SND. "The Principle of Human Dignity: The Ten." *Human Dignity.* Charitas.org. Education for Justice. (2021): 1. https://www.caritas.org.au/media/kjokhdon/education-for-justice-dignity.pdf?sfvrsn=dd1f90aa_0

2 Benedict XVI, *Africae Munus*, no. 113.

3 Id., nos. 95–96.

4 José Luis Gutiérrez Aranda, African Europe Faith and Justice Network (AEFJN). 2017: 2.

5 Léopold Sédar Senghor, *Liberté I, Négritude et Humanisme* (Paris: Editions du Seuil, 1964), 9.

6 https://www.thegardian.com>sep. Sep. 28th, 2006. Retrieved 13–02–22.

7   Hlumelo Siphe Williams, "What Is the Spirit of Ubuntu? How Can We Have It in Our Lives?" in *Global Citizen*, (October 19, 2018). https://www.globalcitizen.org/en/content/ubuntu-south-africa-together-nelson-mandela/

8   Cf. Top 25 Quotes by Desmond Tutu (521), 2017, Retrieved 04/03/22.

9   Molefi Kete Asante, Yoshitaka Miike, and Jing Yin, eds., *The Global Intercultural Communication Reader* (New York, NY: Routledge, 2008), 114.

10   Ibid.

11   Bernard Fonlon, *The Idea of Culture*, ABBIA, vol. 1 (Yaoundé, Cameroon: Ministre de l'education nationale, 1964), 16.

12   Johann Broodryk, *Ubuntu: Life Lessons from Africa* (Pretoria: Ubuntu School of Philosophy, 2002), 26.

13   Molefi Kete Asante, *The Global Intercultural Communication Reader*, 114.

14   Dirk J. Louw, "Ubuntu: An African Assessment of the Religious Other" in Paper presented at the Twentieth World Congress of Philosophy. Paideia Project On-Line._Boston University. Twentieth World Congress of Philosophy, Boston, Massachusetts U.S.A., 10–15 August 1998. Accessed January 11, 2022. http://www.bu.edu/wcp/papers/Afri/AfriLouw.htm

15   Paul Mzeka, *The Core Culture of Nso* (Agawam M.A. USA: J. Radin, 1980): 22.

16   Id., 22; see also Bénézet Bujo, *African Theology in its Social Context* (Eugene, Oregon: Wipf & Stock, 2006): 2.

17   Id., 2.

18   Id., 3.

19   Christian Mofor, *Plotinus and African Concepts of Evil: Perspectives in Multi-Cultural Philosophy* (Bern; New York: P. Lang, 2008), 184–85.

20   Leonard Tumaini Chuwa, *African Indigenous Ethics in Global Bioethics: Interpreting Ubuntu. Advancing Global Bioethics*, vol.1 (New York: Springer, 2014): 10.

21   Dona Richards, "European Mythology: The Ideology of 'Progress,'" in *Contemporary Black Thought: Alternative Analyses in Social and Behavioral Science*, eds. Molefi K. Asante and Abdulai S. Vandi (Beverly Hills: Sage, 1980), 76–77.

22   Dona Richards, "European Mythology: The Ideology of 'Progress,'" 76–77.

23   Leonard Tumaini Chuwa, "Interpreting the Culture of Ubuntu: The Contribution of a Representative Indigenous African Ethics to Global Bioethics." (PhD diss., Duquesne University, 2012). Retrieved from https://dsc.duq.edu/etd/408.

24 Senyuy Chemson, *The Nso Area Co-operative Union and the Integration of Youths*, unpublished dissertation, University of Yaoundé (1978), Second edition, (2022), 7.

25 Senyuy Chemson, *The Nso Area Co-operative Union and the Integration of Youths* (2022), 7.

26 Nsaikimo K. Fai, *Two hundred and Fifty-five Original Nso Proverbs* (Kimbo, Cameroon: Abong Lens Designers, 2015), no. 10: 3

27 Benedict XVI, Encyclical letter, *Caritas in Veritate*. The Holy See, Rome: Dicastero per la Comunicazione - Libreria Editrice Vaticana. June 29, 2009), no. 4.

28 Id., no. 5.

29 Id., no. 9.

30 Id., no. 27.

31 Id., no. 34.

32 Id., nos. 62–64.

33 Benedict XVI, *Africae Munus*, no. 91.

34 Benedict XVI, *Caritas in Veritate*, nos. 74–77.

35 Pontifical Council for Justice and Peace (2004). *Compendium of the Social Doctrine of the Church*, accessed Oct 25, 2022 (Rome: The Holy See, Dicastero per la Comunicazione - Libreria Editrice Vaticana, 2004), no. 561. https://www.vatican.va/roman_curia/pontifical_councils/justpeace/documents/rc_pc_justpeace_doc_20060526_compendio-dott-soc_en.html

36 Pontifical Council for Justice and Peace (2004). *Compendium of the Social Doctrine of the Church*, no. 567.

37 Malidona Patrice Somé, *The Healing Wisdom of Africa: Finding Life Purpose Through Nature, Ritual, and Community* (New York: Penguin Putnam Inc., 1998), 38.

38 Johann Broodryk, *Ubuntu Management and Motivation* (Johannesburg: Gauteng Department of Welfare/Pretoria: Ubuntu School of Philosophy, 1997a), 26.

39 Godfrey Tangwa, *Elements of African Bioethics in a Western Frame* (Bamenda, Cameroon: Langaa Publishers, 2010).

40 Nsaikimo K. Fai, *Two hundred and Fifty-five Original Nso Proverbs*, no. 88: 22.

41 Bernard Fonlon, *The Idea of Culture*, 8.

42 Ibid.

43 John S. Mbiti, *African Traditions and Religions* (New Hampshire, UK.: Heinemann Educational Books, 1990), 141.

44 Kwame Gyekye, "Person and Community: In Defense of Moderate Communitarianism," in *I Am Because We Are: Readings in Africana Philosophy*, eds. Fred Lee Hord, Mzee Lasana Okpara, and Jonathan

Scott Lee, revised edition (Amherst: University of Massachusetts Press, 2016), 143.

45 John S. Mbiti, *African Religions and Philosophy*, 106.
46 Leonard Tumaini Chuwa, *African Indigenous*, 2.
47 Peter Kasanene, "Ethics in African Theology," in *Doing Ethics in Context: South African Perspectives*, eds. Charles Villa-Vicencio and John W. De Gruchy (Maryknoll, N.Y. : Cape Town, South Africa: Orbis Books; David Philip, 1994), 140.
48 John S. Mbiti, *African Religions and Philosophy*, 1–2.
49 Ibid.
50 Bénézet Bujo, *Foundations of an African Ethic: Beyond the Universal Claims of Western Morality* (New York: The Crossroad Publishing Company, 2001), 26.
51 Ifeanyi A. Menkiti, "Person and Community in African Traditional Thought," in *African Philosophy: an Introduction*, ed. Richard A.Wright, 3rd ed. (Lanham: University Press of America, 1984), 170–72.
52 Bénézet Bujo, *Foundations*, 89.
53 Fai, *Two hundred and Fifty-five Original Nso Proverbs*, nos. 88: 22.
54 Bénézet Bujo, *African Theology in Its Social Context* (Maryknoll, N.Y.: Orbis Books, 1992), 21–22.
55 Seyla Benhabib, *Situating the Self: Gender, Community, and Postmodernism in Contemporary Ethics* (New York: Routledge, 1992), 111.

The African Concept of Person: A Source of Renewal in *Africae Munus:* A Critical Response

1 Nsaikimo K. Fai, *Two hundred and Fifty-five Original Nso Proverbs* (Kimbo, Cameroon: Abong Lens Designers, 2015), nos. 73: 20.

The Task of the Church in the Process of Peace and Reconciliation: Perspectives from *Africae Munus*: A Critical Response

1 Benedict XVI, *Africae Munus*, no. 23.
2 William Talla, *An Open Letter to The Bishops of Cameroon* (2012), 3
3 Paul Verdzekov, Archbishop, "Meddling in Politics, Church and Party Politics," in *Cameroon Panorama*, editorial September 1969.
4 Paul Verdzekov, *Meddling in Politics*.

5   *Code of Canon Law, Latin-English Edition: New English Translation* (Washington, DC: Canon Law Society of America, 1999), Canon 375 no. 1.
6   *Code of Canon Law, Latin-English Edition: New English Translation,* Canon 152.
7   Talla, *Open Letter to the Bishops of Cameroon.*
8   Talla, *Open Letter to the Bishops of Cameroon,* conclusion.
9   Talla, *Open Letter to the Bishops of Cameroon,* 5.

Ratzingerian Hermeneutics of Scripture and Eucharist Considering *Africae Munus* 39 – 41: A Critical Response

1   Benedict XVI, *Africae Munus,* nos. 39–41.
2   Id., no. 39.
3   Robert Sarah, *The Power of Silence: Against the Dictatorship of Noise,* trans. J. M. Miller (San Francisco: Ignatius Press, 2017), 310.
4   Benedict XVI, *Sacramentum Caritatis,* no. 51.
5   Vatican II, *Lumen Gentium,* no. 11.

Preaching Reconciliation in a Divided Zone Mindful of *Africae Munus*: A Critical Response

1   Katongole, *Journey of Reconciliation,* 78.
2   Benedict XVI, *Africae Munus,* no. 10.
3   Stan Chu Illo, "Africae Munus and the Challenges of a Transformative Missional Theological Praxis," in *Africa's Social Context, Transformation: An International Journal of Holistic Mission Studies,* 2014, 31: 116.
4   Marcel Uwineza, S.J., "Reconciliation: an agenda for the church in Africa," *Thinking Faith: The online journal of the British Jesuits,* 14 October 2009 at https://www.thinkingfaith.org/articles/20091014_1.htm
5   Benedict XVI, *Africae Munus,* nos. 88–94.
6   Id., no. 11.
7   Id., no. 10.
8   Id., no. 157.
9   Katongole, *Journey of Reconciliation,* 78.
10 Benedict XVI, *Africae Munus,* no. 19.
11 Frantz Fanon, *Toward the African Revolution*: Political Essays. Trans. Haakon Chevalier (New York: Grove Press,1964), 102.

12 Catholic News Service of Nigeria (CNSN), Africae Munus: A Motivating Impetus for Church in Africa – Cardinal Pengo, November 25, 2011. Symposium of Episcopal Conferences of Africa and Madagascar (**SECAM**).

Challenge to Women as Peace Agents:
Africae Munus in a Feminine Key:
A Critical Response

1 Marguerite A. Peeters, *The New Global Ethic: Challenges for the Church* (Bruxelles: Institute for Intercultural Dialogue Dynamics, 2007), 74.

Health Care in the Light of *Africae Munus*:
From a Merely Biomedical to a Holistic
Paradigm of Health Care:
A Critical Response

1 Benedict XVI, *Light of the World, A Conversation with Peter Seewald* (Ignatius Press, San Francisco, 2010), 193–94.
2 Clement of Alexandria, *Quis Dives Salvetur, 29* in *Patrologia Graeca 9*, 633 in Benedict XVI, *Africae Munus*, no. 9.